ALCOHOL, SOCIAL WORK AND COMMUNITY CARE

Stewart Collins and Jan Keene

VENTURE PRESS

BASW website: http://www.basw.co.uk

Published by
VENTURE PRESS
16 Kent Street
Birmingham
B5 6RD

British Library Cataloguing-in-Publication Data
A catalogue record for this book is available from the British Library

ISBN   1 873878 52 4 (paperback)

Cover design by:
Western Arts
194 Goswell Road
London
EC1V 7DT

Printed in Great Britain

Contents

Chapter 1
Introduction

Alcohol has a powerful presence in our lives: it is easily purchased, legally available for adults, and is cheap. For instance, on average, it took 23 minutes work to earn the cost of a pint of beer in the 1950s. By the 1980s it required only 11 minutes' work to earn enough money for a pint of beer (Royal College of Psychiatrists 1986, Alcohol Concern 1988). The popular media are saturated with advertisements for alcohol. For instance, it plays a large part in television advertising. Even more prevalent is the display of drinking occasions on television which "takes up thirteen hours per week and . . . during peak viewing hours alcohol is displayed at the rate of three scenes per hour" (Royal College of Psychiatrists 1986: 23). Popular sports, such as football, also actively promote the use of alcohol with drink labels used in sponsorship on the shirts of famous teams. Drink becomes associated with achievement, prominent personalities, fun, relaxation, good times, and celebrations. The club, pub, or wine bar is seen as a venue for conviviality and free-flowing discussion; an opportunity for winding down from the difficult day or week; a setting for forgetting the demands and stresses of life; a chance to express pent up feelings and opinions and share them with others. So, alcohol can bring many rewards; people feel less inhibited, and pleasurable effects are experienced very quickly.

There is a downside to all of this. The relaxation, the unwinding, the celebrations, can spill over into uninhibited horseplay, arguments and, at extremes, violence, drunk driving and other offences. Equally, drink can be used as a prop to sustain lonely, pressurised lives, a temporary way out from the harsh realities of everyday demands, which still remain very similar and return "the morning after".

Considerable evidence exists which indicates that alcohol-related harm is associated with accidents, relationship problems, problems at work, physical and mental ill health, and crime. For example, it has been estimated that between 8 million and 14 million working days are lost because of alcohol misuse and the cost of such absences in England and Wales is estimated at over £1.5 million and close to £2 million per year (McDonnell & Maynard 1985, Maynard 1989). Also in England and Wales 8.5 million people, that is 6 million men and 2.5 million women, drink above the medically recommended levels of 21 units per week for men and 14 units per week for women and nearly 3 million people are alcohol dependent (HMSO 1996).

NHS responses to alcohol-related problems cost an estimated £150 million per year, while the deaths of 28,000 every year are drink related and one in four male hospital admissions is related to alcohol. In addition up to 65% of suicide attempts are linked with heavy drinking and 40% of incidents of domestic violence (Walker *et al*. 1996).

General Policy Developments from the 1950s to the Present
It is interesting to locate the present response to alcohol-related problems in the UK outlined above within a context of developments during the immediate-post-war period. In the early 1950s the WHO (World Health Organisation) established an alcoholism sub-committee of the Expert Committee on Mental Health. The Committee focused upon the lack of interest in alcohol depen-dence, arguing for in-patient care for the most serious cases alongside a range of out-patient treatment for the majority of those experiencing drink problems (WHO 1951, Robinson & Ettorre 1980). However, "the emphasis was on treatment over prevention, and on a medical rather than a social response, [it] supported those in the U.K. calling for the introduction of specialised services within the N.H.S." (Harrison *et al*. 1996 : 242). Clinical practice, senior hospital doctors, and precedent tended to predominate over rational analysis of policy objectives, while "professionally led institutionalisation [based on hospitals] was still the dominant form of service provision across client groups" (Harrison *et al*. 1996 : 242). Thus, from the early 1950s, up to the mid-1970s in Great Britain there was rapid development in the establishment of a network of in-patient treatment units for "alcoholics" – the Alcoholism Treatment Units within psychiatric settings. This led to better provision of help for those with alcohol dependency problems, a more benign and tolerant attitude developed amongst medical practitioners and considerable research endeavours explored various aspects of "alcoholism". Also more sympathetic responses may have been produced amongst family members, friends and employers (Glatt 1974, Robinson & Ettorre 1980, Room 1984).

In 1968 the memorandum *Treatment of Alcoholism* mentioned the term "community" for the first time (Ministry of Health 1968). There was greater emphasis in this document on the importance of out-patient services, but community provision was not perceived as an alternative to hospital treatment. At this point, community-based services were seen as synonymous with "after care". In-patient services were still seen as essential, with community-based services as "back up" to reduce the length of hospitalisation (Glatt 1974).

It became clear, however, that such an approach focused upon dependent drinkers, exhibiting the most dramatic features of problem drinking, the most serious physical and social consequences, at the expense of heavy drinkers and those who experienced difficulties as a result of occasional intoxication. Therefore, help was less readily available for those in the community with drink problems before serious personal and social damage occurred (Collins *et al.* 1990). By the mid-1970s an awareness had developed that long term, short term and self-help procedures could be located in community settings involving a number of front-line workers, such as GPs, health visitors, nurses, social workers, probation officers, and volunteers. Several policy documents and research studies in the early and mid-1970s encouraged new developments leading to a greater emphasis on community-based services. These included DHSS circulars, Home Office initiatives and the Maudsley Alcohol Pilot Project (DHSS 1973, 1975, Home Office 1971, Cartwright *et al.* 1975, Shaw *et al.* 1978). The title of the third circular from the newly created DHSS, *Community Services for Alcoholics*, revealed the start of a policy change (DHSS 1973). While several new alcoholism treatment units were to be established, with plans to make such units available to every major population centre, there was also an acknowledgement of the need for the "complementary development of a range of community based services" (Harrison *et al.* 1996 : 244). Also government was becoming concerned, at a time of increasing financial restraint, that highly selective, in-patient, hospital located provision, largely based on long term group work with long waiting lists, could not cope with the wide scale of alcohol-related and alcohol-dependency problems – the latter estimated at 400,000 in England and Wales (DHSS 1975). The Maudsley Alcohol Pilot Project (Cartwright *et al.* 1975) was particularly significant in emphasising the importance of primary level community agents. It has been highly influential in informing developments up to the present – the late 1990s – not just because of its focus on the importance of community helpers, but also for its analysis of the need for improved education and training, the need for increased confidence by workers in intervening with those experiencing alcohol problems, and in its advocacy of the development of a system of supportive specialists through community alcohol teams.

Around the same time the White Paper *Better Services for the Mentally Ill* (DHSS 1975) had encouraged a future emphasis on locally based treatment services, along with a reconsideration of the role and location of specialised alcoholism treatment units. The paper "reviewed the development of community services and concluded that it had been uneven and ill co-ordinated, with local authorities often regarding provision for problem drinkers as lying outside the mainstream of residential care" (Harrison *et al.* 1996 : 245). The Government also encouraged the development of hostels and rehabilitation units for those with drink problems, which, in fact, produced only limited response from local authorities (DHSS 1975). A greater emphasis was placed on prevention and better training for primary-level staff along with a wider range of services for problem drinkers (DHSS & Welsh Office 1977, 1978, 1979). The language of the disease concept of "alcoholism" was abandoned. Alcoholism treatment units were now to act as a resource for local communities. It was intended that no more regional hospital units should be established (DHSS & Welsh Office 1978). Hence, ATUs were no longer seen as the core of alcohol service provision, with multidisciplinary, primary-level staff making more significant contributions, with the support of community-based rather than hospital-based specialists. In addition, policy debates were probably influenced by research which suggested that intensive hospital treatment was no more effective than brief intervention (Orford & Edwards 1977).

It should be noted that the movement towards a community-based response in the alcohol field was only part of a number of more general movements in that direction, including the move towards "community care" and "community mental health", which placed prevention of institutionalisation high on the agenda, emphasising the use of local resources in addition to multidisciplinary professional help.

The Present Range of Community Provision
At the present time the range of community-based provision includes some community alcohol teams, residential care, and local advisory and counselling services. Only about 14 CATs were established by the mid-1980s (Clement 1987) and many seem to have been pressed into direct client/user provision, away from the original model which emphasised consultancy, teaching, support and training roles for the primary care worker. Lack of agency line management support to workers has hindered the development of consultancy services, while some groups, such as GPs, have proved difficult to engage in the education and training process required in order to intervene more effectively with those experiencing alcohol-related problems.

Councils on alcohol, or alcohol advisory services, as many are called, and Alcoholics Anonymous (AA) remain the main agencies which provide community-based services for problem drinkers outside probation, social services and social work departments. There are over 90 regional and local councils in England, Scotland and Wales, with Alcohol Concern in London and the Scottish Council on Alcohol in Glasgow acting as national co-ordinating bodies. The councils, or alcohol advisory services, vary greatly in size, ranging from almost 50 staff in one case to other situations where very small numbers of staff are involved. Many alcohol advisory services depend heavily on volunteers. They have been through nationally administered training schemes, covering approximately six residential week-ends or their equivalent, and give three to four hours' work with clients per week on a regular basis, supported by regular supervision (Scottish Council on Alcohol and Wilson 1986).

It is unusual to find the disease concept regarded as a basis for drinking problems or abstinence as the only answer. There tends to be an emphasis on individual and couple work rather than group counselling.

AA is perhaps the most-well-known source of help for problem drinkers, with around 2,000 groups in England and Wales, which are self-financed and primarily use group-based approaches, sometimes linked with one-to-one support from a "sponsor". The emphasis is upon seeing the "alcoholic" as having an incurable disease, with a spiritual component in the recovery process. For more-detailed discussion of AA approaches see Chapter 2. Therefore, at the present time, there is a range of community-based provision for problem drinkers made available by a variety of agencies including, in 1992, before the introduction of Community Care, about 160 organisations which provided residential care for people with substance problems who were on income support (MacGregor *et al.* 1993). Financial support for residential provision, of course, has since been transferred from the Department of Social Security to local authorities. Residential provision includes units specialising in crisis work, detoxification, nursing care, residential rehabilitation and therapeutic communities. In addition, there are about 15 to 25 private clinics, not publicly funded, and not directly linked with community care legislation (Alcohol Concern 1987).

Thorley's Model of Problem Drug Use
Traditionally, there has been a tendency to focus on those at the "heavy" end of the continuum of drink problems, i.e. dependent drinkers who have been labelled "alcoholic", who have required residential treatment and detoxification. But this presents only a small part of the picture. In this book, while recognising the importance of "disease" and "medical" models, we focus upon various parts of the continuum based upon Thorley's (1982 & 1985) model of problem drug use:-

Diagram 1:
Thorley's model of
problem drug use

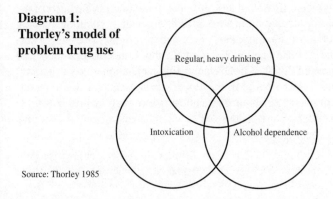

Regular, heavy drinking

Intoxication

Alcohol dependence

Source: Thorley 1985

This model is not without its problems, but it does enable us to avoid making rigid distinctions between "normal" and "abnormal" drinking and to be aware that individuals can move around a continuum. Thus, in considering young people (i.e. 12 to 18 years old) with drink problems it is much more likely that they will encounter occasional intoxication, with a few regular heavy drinkers and virtually none who could be considered alcohol dependent (see also Chapter 5 for more detail).

Intoxication
Intoxication is occasionally experienced by most of those who enjoy social drinking at one time or another. Often the negative after effects of single session excessive use are short term, such as a hangover and a headache. It is intoxication at the wrong time and in the wrong place that can have serious implications. Such as driving a car when over the legal limit for driving, after consuming 2.5 pints of beer (80mg/100ml or 80 milligrammes of alcohol in 100 millilitres of blood) and one's ability to drive will be *already* impaired before that limit is reached. Alternatively, getting intoxicated in a town or city centre pub having a reputation for "trouble" on a Saturday night may well lead to incidents of violence after closing time.

Statistics indicate that intoxication is a serious problem in England, linked with criminal charges such as assault, breach of the peace, criminal damage, and burglary (Jeffs & Saunders 1983, Royal College of Psychiatrists 1986). In Scotland, research by the Scottish Health Education Co-ordinating Committee has indicated that intoxication "is strongly associated with parasuicides, fire fatalities, homicides, hospital admissions with head injuries and fatal road traffic accidents" (SHECC 1985 : XV).

Regular Heavy Drinking
Regular heavy, often daily or near-daily, use of alcohol over a prolonged period of time also can be associated with social and legal difficulties; it has a cumulative effect and it is primarily linked with physical illness such as cirrhosis of the liver. Regular, heavy alcohol users have a fortyfold greater risk of developing some cancers such as of the upper digestive tract, becoming increasingly susceptible to diseases of the circulatory system, other digestive disorders and respiratory infections (Taylor 1981). One in five male admissions to general medical wards are related to patient's use of alcohol (Quinn & Johnstone 1976), while regular heavy drinking by pregnant women may be problematic in relation to their unborn children (Plant 1985).

The Dependence Syndrome
Physically and psychologically dependent drinkers have been categorised traditionally as "alcoholics". Physical dependence can cause serious health

problems and those who are physically dependent, when ceasing use of alcohol, can experience withdrawal symptoms. Medical, social, and legal problems can be associated with dependence, including mental health, family and work difficulties, financial worries and involvement with offences. Dependence has a relapsing, often repetitive, nature including the risk, or actual experience of harm.

The key indicators of dependence seen over a period of one to 12 months include:–

1. Narrowing of the drinking repertoire. Difficulty in controlling, in setting limits to the amount of drink and in stopping drinking in certain situations, in order to achieve the required blood alcohol level.

2. A preoccupation with drinking and its effects, to the extent that other activities and relationships are neglected and given lower priority than drinking.

3. Increased tolerance to alcohol which requires a person to need a higher intake of alcohol to achieve the same effects originally produced by lower doses.

4. Repeatedly experiencing physical and psychological withdrawal symptoms, such as tremor, nausea, sweating, and mood change.

5. Drinking regularly to relieve or avoid experiencing withdrawal symptoms.

6. Reinstatement (or relapse) after abstinence to a similar pattern of drinking as beforehand. Continuing use despite knowledge of problems and harmful consequences.

7. Subjective awareness of a sense of compulsion to drink.

    (Edwards & Gross 1976, Social Work Services Group 1987, Chick & Cantwell 1994.)

For more details about intoxication, regular use, and dependence see Chapters 2 and 8.

Drinking Units and Levels of Drinking

The topic of what constitutes "safe levels" of consumption has been the subject of continuing debate. A great deal depends on the setting, the companions for drinking, the expectations of drink, how quickly it is taken, whether food has been available, and the size or weight of the person concerned. In other words, the interaction between drink, the person and the environment is important.

However, the Health Education Council (1985), the Royal Colleges of Physicians (1987) and Psychiatrists (1986) have laid down generally agreed guidelines for safe, hazardous and harmful levels of drinking, based upon drinking units and drinking levels for each week.

Drinking Units
Standard measures of drinks served in most clubs, pubs and wine bars do contain roughly the same amount of alcohol. A half-pint of bitter, heavy lager or cider; a glass of wine, sherry or port, a single measure of spirits, all contain about 8 - 10 grammes of alcohol.

Half-pint of beer = one glass of wine = one measure of spirits = one standard unit of alcohol. Obviously the strengths of some drinks vary, with some "special" lagers, "real" ales, and strong ciders counting for more units. So:–

	Units
1 pint of ordinary beer or lager	2
1 pint of Guinness, some real ales or strong lager	3
1 pint of strong cider (eg. Blackthorn or Strongbow)	4
1 can of ordinary beer or larger	1½
1 can of "special" lager	3
1 glass of table wine	2
1 litre bottle of table wine	10
1 litre bottle of sherry or port	14
1 litre bottle of spirits (whisky, gin vodka)	30

Drinking Levels
It has been estimated that approximately 6% of both the adult male and female population of Britain are non-drinkers, while around 15% of males and 32% of females are only occasional drinkers. The major medical authorities and health promotion bodies had agreed on recommended limits for "sensible" drinking. These were no more than 21 units a week for men and no more than 14 units for women. Almost one man in four drinks more than the "sensible" limits and about one woman in 12 more than hers, while approximately one man in 16 is a regular, very heavy drinker.

	MEN (units per week)	% of all adult male population	WOMEN (units per week)	% of all adult female population
Light drinking, safe for health, low risk	1-21	55	1-14	54
Moderate, hazardous drinking, increased risk	22-35	12	15-21	6
Regular, fairly heavy, hazardous drinking, increasing risk, harm to health	36-50	6	22-35	1
Regular, very heavy drinking, high risk, definitely harmful and damaging to health	51+	6	36+	1

Adapted from : Office of Population Censuses & Surveys in Davis (1989)

Debates about "safe levels" of drinking reached a climax in December 1995, when Stephen Dorrell, the then Health Secretary, announced the redefinition of "safe limits" at the lower end of the scale, with a shift to daily benchmarks rather than weekly levels. The Government report *Sensible Drinking* outlined that men should drink no more than three or four units a day and women two or three units per day. The Government stated that it wanted to move from the concept of weekly limits as they encouraged binge drinking. One critical interpretation is that new guidelines effectively increase the weekly limits to

9

28 units for men (rather than 21) and 21 units for women (rather than 14), although the Government had denied such intentions. The new guidelines – based on evidence that a small amount of alcohol protects against heart disease – are a reversal from previous policy, which was to reduce drinking levels, or at least not to encourage higher consumption. The recent report goes on to advise that there are health benefits in drinking one to two units per day for men aged over 40 and for women after the menopause, protecting against some forms of heart disease.

Structural and Political Perspectives

Many would argue that there is a heavy government investment in the production and generation of wealth by the alcohol industry. It is a major source of employment for farmers, brewers, distillers, bottle and can producers and others involved in production, distribution and retailing of drink. Significant contributions are made to the balance of trade, while government receives over 5% of its income from excise duty and VAT on drinks (Thurman 1981). Hence government's actions are often underpinned by fiscal considerations, profitability and electoral concerns (Dorn 1983).

Some authors have noted clearly that preventive approaches to alcohol problems cannot exist in isolation but should work in concert, as part of a coherent health policy from central government (Ritson 1994, Harrison *et al.* 1996). Such policy is liable to fragmentation, by broader sectoral policies of the Government, with more than 14 government departments being concerned with alcohol policies, including trade and industry, treasury, law enforcement, and health and social services. Hence policies that affect alcohol can be adopted and implemented without concern for their impact on alcohol problems and persistent pleas have insisted that a coherent government response requires much closer co-ordination (Ritson 1994, Harrison *et al.* 1996). Maynard (1985 : 238) has put it succinctly – "no one in the Whitehall village has the designated role . . . to mobilise and implement an effective alcohol policy".

One aspect of alcohol-related problems that has received attention at both national and local levels has been drink driving, where substantial funding and publicity have been supported by intensive law-enforcement campaigns. In addition, local action to enforce by-laws on drinking in the streets has had some impact, leading to a decline in public disorder offences by young people. But these are exceptions, despite work that has explored possibilities for local creative prevention programmes and opportunities (Tether & Robinson 1986,

Robinson *et al.* 1989). Therefore, "local initiatives have yet to make a significant impact on national rates of alcohol related problems . . . [and] . . . we have only just begun to tap the potential of local prevention activity and to understand how this should best be supported at a national level" (Harrison 1996 : 5).

Therefore, problem drinking clearly takes place within a political, structural and local context, where many clients and users of social work and probation are living in poor housing, facing or experiencing unemployment, startling poverty, and discrimination. Discrimination and oppression permeate society's structures, with ageism, racism, sexism, disabilism and homophobia particularly prominent. Therefore, a problem drinker can face either double discrimination and jeopardy, for instance, as an elderly problem drinker, or triple discrimination and jeopardy, for instance, as a black, female, problem drinker. If a person is disapproved of as a heavy drinker, then that disapproval is likely to be all the greater if the client/user is black, elderly, female, disabled, a gay man, or lesbian. The lack of surveys into the needs of problem drinkers who are disabled, gay or lesbian, who are older, who are members of black communities contributes further to myth and stereotyping (CCETSW 1995). Indeed, existing services, research, and models of working with problem drinkers have been, and are, dominated by white, middle class, middle aged, heterosexuals, and are based upon western culture which is inherently Eurocentric. Elizabeth Ettorre has expressed precisely "the general tendency to ignore overall social and political concerns, necessary for a full understanding of alcohol and its use in society. As a result theories in the alcohol field tend to be apolitical and to legitimate inequalities based on sex, race and class" (Ettorre 1992 : 34). Ettorre goes on to note pungently "racism, classism, ageism, heterosexism and every other system of inequality that erodes . . . power . . . courage . . . integrity and . . . self esteem serve to contribute to drinking problems, perpetuate them and intensify their painful effects" (Sandmair 1980 : 242 & Ettorre 1992 : 37). Indeed, current definitions of "alcoholism" and alcohol dependency tend to focus on individual, behavioural or physiological problems. There is more concern with "causes" or aetiological explanations and epidemiological issues than with issues of social inequality. "These concerns have served the interests of the medical profession, keep them theoretically in power and allow traditional ideas to go unchallenged" (Ettorre 1992 : 40). Explanations of alcohol problems around "alcoholism" and alcohol dependency, which developed out of a need to deal with alcohol misuse in clinical populations, have tended to prioritise treatment and rehabilitation issues, with the result that social, economic and political issues in clinical and non-clinical populations have been largely absent.

For more detail of discrimination, oppression and work with black communities and elderly people see Chapters 6 and 7. For more details of work with women who experience drink problems, see Ettorre (1992), Kent (1990), and Waterson (1996) and Thom & Green (1996). For details of work with lesbian drinkers see Hawkins (1976).

The Aims of the Book

While this book concentrates upon alcohol problems, in recent times there has been a move towards considering the similarities among addictive behaviours generally. Reasons underpinning addictive behaviour and the processes of stopping all have much in common (Orford 1985, Prochaska & DiClemente 1986). It is important to share knowledge and skills from these "commalities", [sic] across excessive appetites for food, sex, gambling, drugs and drinking (Orford 1985). Some argue for combining drug and alcohol agencies and providing joint training on account of commonalities in identification, assessment, intervention, relapse prevention approaches and overlap between agencies (Home Office 1990). Others argue against combined agencies on account of differences in helping or treatment aims, differences in the needs of the two groups, and the legal versus illicit status of drink and other drugs. Whatever these controversies, the focus here is upon those experiencing problems with drink, although much of the material will be relevant to work with drug misusers in general.

This book builds upon an earlier text, edited by Stewart Collins, *Alcohol, Social Work and Helping* (1990), which examined historical perspectives on drinking problems and services, proactive social work intervention and new developments in working with problem drinkers. Other chapters included working with women, the family and groups.

In this book, after the introduction, there is a chapter which examines different theories and models that can be used in working with problem drinkers. In turn, this is followed by a chapter on community care developments, looking at assessment and management. Then there is a general chapter on the role of social workers as providers of both social care and counselling help. These chapters were written by Jan Keene.

The introduction and four later chapters were written by Stewart Collins. The later chapters focus upon working with particular client or user groups, i.e. working with young people, with elderly people, with black communities and with offenders.

The social worker or probation officer is faced with a range of policies and psychological and sociological approaches in working with those experiencing alcohol problems. In this book we shall draw upon relevant research. We shall look at ways to develop and improve the practices of social workers, probation officers and their organisations within the context of community care. We shall examine discrimination and the incidence of alcohol problems amongst various client/user groups and the models, knowledge, skills and competences which inform work with these groups. Hence, while our approach, to some extent, will draw upon material drawn from sociology and social policy, it will focus upon "psychological" and social interventions such as social learning and cognitive behavioural approaches, as it is these approaches which may have most to offer the neophyte or experienced worker in their interactions with individuals, families or groups experiencing problems with drink. Cognitive behavioural approaches focus very much on current behaviour, with behaviour change the focus of the helping endeavour. The circumstances which influence drinking also are seen as being of particular interest – the when, where, who, why and how of drinking, as seen in Chapter 8.

However, in general, we feel that the "golden rule" in working with people experiencing drink problems should be the provision and use of whatever helping means seems appropriate for that particular individual at that particular time in their drinking life. We support the need to maintain a range of different options for different clients and users. Therefore, social workers and probation officers sometimes will need to refer on to, and work with, other helping agents who may be strongly influenced by "disease" or "medical" model thinking, such as AA, some general practitioners, psychiatrists, some residential facilities and self-help groups. Hence, knowledge and understanding of these approaches are important for social workers.

Andrew Sheppard (1995) has expressed well the tensions faced in working with drug and alcohol problems when commenting :–

> *"The post modernist challenge . . . replaces the search for truth with a celebration of many competing, more or less effective truths."*
> (Sheppard 1995 : 137.)

A Framework for Intervention

It is not always easy to put together the interrelationships between individual personalities, their use of drink, its history, and their family and social functioning. Awkward questions are posed. Such as, is problem drinking generated by personality characteristics or is excessive anxiety or depression a consequence of problem drinking? What is the role of the partner or social factors, such as unemployment or poor housing, in maintaining or changing the *status quo*? Traditionally it has been suggested that if problem drinking is reduced or stopped, then other aspects of the person's life will stabilise. However, for some problem drinkers a positive change in drinking patterns can expose several other problems. Therefore it is important to note and recall the interrelationship between drinking, social functioning and psychological states.

Diagram 2 (Adapted from Saunders 1994)

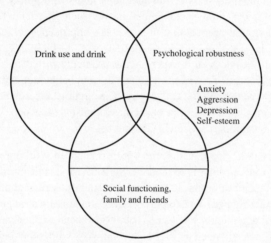

The more extreme the drink problem, the more the user's psychological state will be influenced. Pre-existing levels of anxiety and depression will be exacerbated by drinking and provide additional impetus for it. What matters is that the two interact and can accelerate drinking. Poor relationships and difficult family life will be made worse by problem drinking and problem drinking can escalate. Equally, positive interactions can be established so that reduced drinking can lead to improved self-esteem, lower levels of anxiety and depression, and better relationships with family and friends. The major point is that various aspects of a problem drinker's life may need to be worked on and just reducing or stopping drinking may not be sufficient in itself (Saunders 1994). The interface or interaction between drinking behaviour, the individual's psychological state, and social functioning all offer possibilities for effective intervention by social workers. Various pieces of research have reinforced this point. For example, Prochaska & DiClemente (1986) have shown that social factors such as healthy partnerships and family support were vital in maintaining change in moving away from problem-drinking patterns. Billings & Moos (1983) found those who had overcome drink problems had significantly higher levels of family support, job satisfaction (where possible) and fewer negative life events and better coping skills. Havassy *et al.* (1991) found that close friends, sound partner relationships and strong group affiliations were significantly associated with moving away from, and successfully avoiding, drink problems. Thus there is an obvious need to focus on social as well as psychological functioning and social workers should be ideally placed to help in such matters. Therefore, cognitive behavioural approaches should be "based on the notion of the individual acting in a *social* world" (Saunders 1994 : 170). Clearly, the social worker should be working not only with individuals but also partners, families, his/her own agency and other relevant organisations as suggested by advocates of systems-based approaches (Pincus & Minahan 1973). Barber (1995 : 26) has expressed this most succinctly:–

> *"Social work . . . must give expression to the dual focus on person and environment. . . . For social workers it is not just the (drinking) process that requires assessment and understanding, it is the totality of people's lives, including all their interactions with the broader social environment. In other words, social workers must look* outwards *to the social context of [drinking] behaviours, as well as* inwards *towards the psychology of individual users."*

Social Work and Problem Drinking
Several studies have highlighted the high proportion of problem drinkers encountered by social workers in their day-to-day child abuse work, with alcohol a factor in 74% of one social services department's child abuse cases (Oliver 1985, Mather 1988, Davidson 1992, Walker *et al.* 1996). Other studies have indicated the significant prevalence of alcohol in 20% to 40% of family cases (McGarva 1979, Osborn & Leckie 1980, Abel 1983, Barrie 1988, Isaacs & Moon 1985) while a recent survey of 3,000 probation officers revealed that 30% of their caseloads had "severe" problems with alcohol (NAPO 1994).

Yet social workers have tended negatively to stereotype problem drinkers as a result of "incidents with drunken clients [and may have experienced] threats of violence, unreasonable demanding behaviour, truculence and annoyance to office receptionists and staff [which] can lead to a social worker harbouring fear and anger about clients abusing alcohol" (Collins *et al.* 1988 : 19). Such feelings combined with resentment concerning stereotypes of "unpredictability", "deviousness" and "manipulation" may lead a worker to form a judgement about the problem drinker as someone who is "beyond help" and "less deserving" of time and effort (Smith 1988). Indeed, many problem drinkers who follow a less stereotyped pattern than the "ill alcoholic" may remain either unrecognised by social workers, or assessed in ways which avoid exploring their difficulties with drink and lead to swift referral to "medical" help or AA (Lawson 1994).

In fact, many workers may feel that they do not have a right to question clients or users about their drinking patterns. While some traditional social work values – such as acceptance and self-determination – are very important they can get in the way of a worker's ability to identify and assess drinking patterns and thus facilitate appropriate intervention. Also such feelings of reluctance to intervene may arise from the worker's *own* attitudes and ambivalence about drinking, and the liking for it, alongside a reluctance to "label" the client/user, with an anticipation of hostility and rejection if questions are raised by the worker about drinking. Sometimes drink problems are "played down"; they are seen "sympathetically" and perceived as an understandable response to poverty, stigma and discrimination rather than problems that can be worked with and resolved.

It is also clear that many clients and users of social work receiving help from social services departments will not directly present with drinking problems at all, but rather with child care, housing and family relationship difficulties, offending, financial crises, and domestic violence. Therefore, there is a need for social workers to be alert, in order to identify difficulties with drink that may lie behind the original "presenting problem".

In the recent past some writers have highlighted the deficiencies in pre-qualifying social work education and training in preparing workers to identify, assess and intervene effectively with problem drinkers (Isaacs & Moon 1985, Collins *et al.* 1988, Harrison 1992). Others have noted the lack of appropriate informed supervision after qualification (Shaw *et al.* 1978). Thus the well-known negative or "vicious" cycle in working with problem drinkers must be broken (Leckie 1990). There is a need for adequate education and training, the development of appropriate competences and good levels of knowledge and skill to enable sound levels of recognition of problem drinking, accompanied by a commitment to effective intervention, backed up by appropriate support, supervision and policies from agencies (Leckie 1990, Lawson 1994). This has been expressed in another way by Shaw (1978) as the need for social workers to develop confidence, therapeutic optimism, commitment, role adequacy, role legitimacy and, especially, to have support in their work with problem drinkers.

In pre-Community Care days some statutory social work agencies already had highlighted the need for informed supervision and the high prioritisation of work with problem drinkers. As seen, for example, in social services departments in Avon, Bradford, Hereford, and Rotherham and in the former Central and

Strathclyde Region social work departments in Scotland. These departments produced policy documents, instigated research, and developed support and training resources for problem drinkers. Some departments appointed specialist addiction workers. In particular, high level appointments such as at Principal Officer level in the former Strathclyde Region were particularly valuable, with the person holding responsibility for developing policies, arranging consultancy work and training events, and liaising with relevant agencies. There have been other positive developments in some areas. For example, the need for social workers to receive effective support from line managers led to the establishment of a four-day training course for social work managers in Scotland at Paisley University (Duffy 1993). This course increased line managers' awareness of alcohol-related problems. It facilitated the provision of informed and skilled support for social workers who were not feeling confident in their interventions with clients/users experiencing alcohol-related problems. In addition, the Welsh Office Social Services Inspectorate commissioned Alcohol Concern Wales to develop a training initiative on alcohol use and child mistreatment. This led to recommendations for relevant training courses for senior managers in social services, to enable them to develop environments which gave greater legitimacy to work with alcohol-related problems (CCETSW 1995).

The Government Advisory Council on the Misuse of Drugs had recommended that those responsible for initial professional education and training should "give priority to determining the basic levels of drug related knowledge, skills and understanding appropriate to their profession" (Home Office 1990, para. 5.29). Therefore, the Central Council for Education and Training in Social Work has provided guidelines to social work courses for developing competences in effective identification, assessment and intervention in work with substance misuse problems at both pre-qualifying and post-qualifying levels (CCETSW 1992, CCETSW 1995). Thus, as a result of the pre-qualifying guidelines, social work has become "the first profession in the U.K. to determine the minimum knowledge and skills that practitioners need in relation to substance problems" (Alaszewski & Harrison 1992 : 336). Similarly, attention has been given to helping social work educators develop their confidence, knowledge and skills. There has been a significant growth in the growing availability of learning resources and teaching packs on work with problem drinkers (Harrison 1993, Scottish Council on Alcohol 1990).

Furthermore, the professional association BASW also produced policy and practice guidelines (BASW 1989), while the Department of Health's Health of the Nation Report (1993) placed more emphasis on the need for social workers and other primary care agents to respond to drinking problems before they became more severe. This approach was endorsed in the NHS and Community Care Act (1990).

Social Work, Problem Drinking and Community Care

The Local Authority Circular, number two, (1993) points out the responsibility of local authority social workers to assess misusers of alcohol and drugs and to arrange relevant care "packages". While some authorities are using non-statutory agencies to perform these tasks, others are using a small number of their own specialised staff and yet others are choosing to incorporate the needs of people with substance misuse problems into mainstream assessment and care management structures. These matters are explored further in Chapter 3.

As regards alcohol services generally, between 1990 and 1995 £6.2 million was distributed to 12 new projects and 45 existing ones. Also in 1995 the Department of Health allocated £2.5 million to establish new support agencies, alongside another £2.5 million allocated through the Drug and Alcohol Specific Grant (Alcohol Concern 1996).

The movement of public funding of residential care for problem drinkers to local authorities has caused fears that some residential facilities may have to close. Up to 1993 that had been the case in a few instances (MacGregor *et al.* 1993). Furthermore, the number of people with substance problems occupying registered beds had declined by 23% from over 2,000 to around 1,500 (MacGregor *et al.* 1993). The requirement to assess the needs of people with alcohol problems has presented local authorities with a significant task. In the past, this had been no more than a peripheral concern, compared to the more familiar role of assessing the needs of elderly people, people with disabilities and those experiencing mental health problems (Harrison *et al.* 1996).

Now,

> *"With the shift of priority brought about by the new community care arrangements, managers and generic social work practitioners [are] obliged to face [an] acknowledged lack of experience [in] the alcohol and drugs field."* (Harrison *et al.* 1996 : 255.)

Thus the need to develop additional experience, knowledge and skills in assessing those with alcohol-related problems could encourage many social work agencies to reassess priorities and therefore "help to end the marginali-sation of this client group within social services" and provide other innovative community projects (Harrison *et al.* 1996 : 258). In turn, alcohol agencies running residential establishments could be encouraged to enter into more intensive and extensive dialogue with social services and social work departments, thus further increasing awareness of the needs of problem drinkers. Therefore, there are a number of developments which are encouraging the promotion of more-effective interventions by social workers in work with alcohol problems. Yet the incentives to develop take place within a climate of very rapid change, pressure, stress, cuts and multiple, competing demands that are made upon social work education and social workers and their organisations.

In pre-qualifying social work education CCETSW's (1992) document on substance misuse problems – number 14 in a series – is but one of a cluster of similar papers which suggest and urge, but do not prescribe – do not actually require – social work programmes to give more time and attention to particular topics for particular client/user groups. The paper linked with alcohol problems will compete for attention by social work educators along with the other papers. Will the substance misuse paper get hidden amongst a mass of similar guidelines? Will the courses have sufficient access to appropriate fieldwork placements, along with practice teachers who are sufficiently knowledgeable, skillful and competent to help social work students develop the required competences in work with problem drinkers?

Furthermore, the guidance document *Alcohol and Drugs Services and Community Care* (Department of Health 1993) was made available to social work agencies only three weeks before the Community Care Act became operative. This short notice, allied to the lack of previous local authority experience in this field, left most local authorities "ill prepared for their new task" (Harrison *et al.* 1996 : 249). There have been several indications that much more work needs to be done in social work agencies. For example, a Social Services Inspectorate Report (SSI 1995) of five local authorities was very critical, noting that there were :–

- No specific alcohol or drug policies
- No purchasing strategies
- No user and carer involvement in planning
- Resource led rather than needs led assessments
- Lack of clarity about the role of care managers
- Largely inaccessible services and "in most cases . . . service users . . . often had to jump through hoops and to express high levels of motivation before gaining access to a service at all"
  (SSI 1995 in Cohen 1995 : 16.)

Alcohol misuse strategies were found to be well down the departments list of priorities. Although some were close to preparing action plans and implementing service requirements or joint purchasing strategies, as one departmental representative said:–

> *"Services to tackle alcohol and drug misuse do come lower down the priority list – they consume about £200,000 while the budget for mental health is £1.4 million and for learning disabilities £2.3 million."*
> (Morris in Cohen 1995 : 16.)

Therefore, as the President of the Association of Directors of Social Services tersely put it : "There is clearly some way to go to move addictive services to the centre of policy and financial priorities" (SeQueira in Cohen 1995 : 17). Furthermore, as the Director of Alcohol Concern has highlighted, there is also a danger that drugs work could be given priority by central government over work with alcohol problems. A survey conducted by Alcohol Concern which questioned key personnel working for over 200 health authorities, social services departments and probation services indicated that 6 out of 10 still did not have a system for identifying and recording clients who have drinking problems while fewer than half had made a study of the level of problem drinking in their area (Alcohol Concern 1996).

Pessimism or Cautious Optimism?
In conclusion, amongst some pessimism and cautious optimism, it is clear that individual social workers alone cannot solve the whole range of difficulties presented by problem drinkers. They can intervene effectively with sound knowledge skills, confidence and appropriate competences, given appropriate pre-qualifying and post-qualifying learning opportunities. This needs to be accompanied by informed and positive supervision from line managers who, in turn, are members of agencies with clearly defined policies and priorities in relation to work with problem drinkers. Yet, as always, the provision of effective, appropriate national policies and adequate resources is required from central government, so that good-quality services are available to meet the needs of the full range of problem drinkers in any local community. Only then can we be more certain that such needs will be met.

Chapter 2
Theories and Models of
Alcohol Treatment

Introduction
This chapter examines different theories or models of alcohol misuse and treatment. It considers, first, the cognitive behavioural model. Community alcohol teams and generic social care professionals in Britain usually adhere to this approach, aiming to help clients to control their drinking behaviour. The second model is the medical one, which focuses on the physiological effects of alcohol dependency. The third examines the "dependence syndrome" and the biopsychosocial approach, both also popular in alcohol treatment agencies and within the medical profession. Finally, the "disease" model of Alcoholics Anonymous and the Minnesota Method is considered.

Models of Dependence and Treatment
Outcome research in the alcohol field has been unable to distinguish between one treatment model and another in terms of effectiveness. All models seem to be equally effective in reducing severity of dependence and/or drinking behaviour (Lindstrom 1992). Any one model results in a successful treatment outcome for between a third and a half of cases. In the light of this information researchers have tried to identify individual differences or characteristics which predispose some people to do better with particular treatments. They have failed to identify significant individual or personality differences (Keene 1994).

Useful Methods
It is interesting that, whilst models of alcohol dependency and treatment are radically different, in practical terms they tend to use similar methods. Recent reviews of outcome studies suggest that some methods may be more successful than others. Lindstrom (1992) and Hodgson (1994) identify aspects of treatment that appear to be more useful than others, particularly social factors and improved social functioning, which prove significant in terms of pre-treatment characteristics and treatment outcome.

Importance of Aftercare
Although researchers are beginning to identify methods that lead to a success-ful treatment outcome this success is often not maintained after treatment. The majority of those who complete treatment successfully will relapse within one or two years. Relapse within the two years following treatment has been shown to be correlated with social and emotional factors. When the reasons for loss of

treatment gains are examined (Marlatt 1985 and Wilson 1992) the main precursors of relapse are identified as negative emotional state, interpersonal conflict, and social pressure. This raises the possibility that maintenance of treatment gains may be correlated with psychological and social factors rather than treatment variables themselves (Moos *et al.* 1990, Lindstrom 1992). Marlatt (1985) proposes that relapse prevention after any treatment intervention will improve the effectiveness of the treatment.

The Importance of Motivation and the Change Process
The importance of process in treatment has been highlighted by Prochaska and DiClemente (1986), who argue that sequences or stages in the process of individual change over time may be significant in determining effectiveness of interventions. Attempts have been made to monitor the stages of this process (Rollnick *et al.* 1992). Prochaska and DiClemente propose that an assessment of motivation prior to any treatment intervention will improve the effectiveness of that treatment.

Cognitive Behavioural Models
The cognitive behavioural approach to alcohol problems applies a range of tried and tested psychological theory and methods to alcohol problems. There is much research concerned with the effectiveness of cognitive and behavioural techniques in dealing with behavioural disorders.

Psychologists explain the psychological approach to addiction as a "common set of principles [used] to relate the abnormal, harmful use of alcohol to its normal harm-free use". Drinking and drinking problems are seen as "lying on a continuum, rather than being divided into unhelpful either/or categories". The position of cognitive behavioural psychologists is: "It is a great mistake to regard excessive drinking as a purely medical problem. . . . Problem drinking obviously has many medical aspects but, in the attempt to change harmful drinking behaviour, the disease theory of alcoholism has been found to be unhelpful and a hindrance to progress in the field." (British Psychological Society 1987 : 3.)

However, the critics of this approach would suggest that while psychological social learning theories and methods of treatment are useful in dealing with psychological dependencies, they have not yet been shown to be effective in serious cases of combined physiological and psychological dependency.

Social learning theory is a general one offering an explanation of behaviour formation and maintenance. It assumes that behaviour can be either positively or negatively reinforced and that the sooner the reinforcement occurs the more effective it will be. Therefore short term positive reinforcement could be seen to outweigh long term negative reinforcements. The development of behavioural habits can also be influenced by "modelling" and other social factors such as the need to conform. (Bandura 1977; Bergin & Garfield 1978; Bolles 1979; Catania & Harnad 1988.) Most contemporary behavioural psychologists also include a cognitive element in both their theory and practice. The way persons define or interpret their experience is considered to have a strong influence on their behaviour. (Beck 1989; Ellis 1962, 1987; Kelly 1955; Orford 1977.)

The cognitive and behavioural change methods derived from social learning theory and cognitive psychology can be effective for certain conditions ranging from depression to phobias and more significantly for obsessive/compulsive behaviours. (Bandura 1977; Beck 1989; Brown & Lewinson 1984; Ellis 1987;) These methods have also been demonstrated to be effective in helping people control their drinking and in reducing drink-related harm. Though it should be stressed that, while observable behaviour can be measured scientifically, cognitions cannot. (Heather & Robertson 1981; Babor *et al.* 1986; Chick *et al.* 1985; Hodgson 1976; Hester *et al.* 1989.)

Cognitive processes are now considered influential in both loss of control and relapse (Brown *et al.* 1985). Cognitive findings are also reviewed by Marlatt (1978) who illustrates the influence of expectation and social cues in loss of control and relapse. The influence of cognitive psychology is also demonstrated in the work of Orford, Heather, Stockwell, Hodgson, and Robertson. Their work on the psychological interpretation of alcohol problems and dependence has to a greater or lesser extent adapted psychology to the particular problems of alcohol. These theories, while developed from rather generalised ones of behaviour, have integrated them with a cognitive approach to encompass the phenomenon of "addiction" as a subject in its own right (e.g. Marlatt & Gordon 1985, Heather & Robertson 1989, and Orford 1985).

Abstinence or controlled drinking?
Cognitive behavioural techniques can be applied whether the aim is abstinence or controlled drinking, but the theory underlying this approach would suggest that any behaviour can be unlearnt and relearnt and drinking behaviour is no exception.

There are many data to substantiate the claim that controlled drinking is possible. Critics would argue that this shows that the disease concept is untenable and the AA treatment aim of abstinence unnecessary. Studies by

Litman (1977) indicate that clinically diagnosed "alcoholics" may either return to normal drinking or show great malleability of drinking behaviour in response to experimental manipulation of cues or rewards. There has been more empirical evidence to substantiate these views (Orford 1985; Babor *et al.* 1986; Heather & Robertson 1986; Sanchez-Craig 1986; Donovan & Marlatt 1980; and Edwards 1986b and 1988). For example, Babor *et al.* show that both light and heavy drinking can be brought under individual control and drinking levels maintained or cut down. However, although research indicates that non-serious drinkers can be helped to control their drinking at an "early stage", (Edwards 1986a) the research cannot distinguish between those who will progress to a "later" stage and those whose drinking would not become harmful at all.

The question of whether controlled drinking is a practicable aim for physically dependent drinkers remains highly controversial, but it is generally accepted that this approach is the most effective for the majority of less serious drinking problems and for interventions at early stages.

Brief interventions at early stages
There is no doubt that much of the most useful recent research in the alcohol helping field has been carried out by cognitive/behavioural psychologists in the areas of "early intervention" and "brief interventions". Whilst these terms are often used interchangeably, the first usually refers to any intervention used at an "early stage" of possible dependency and the second to the short-term cognitive/behavioural interventions.

A review of early intervention strategies (Babor *et al.* 1986 : 23) suggests that "modest, but reliable effects on drinking behaviour and related problems can follow from brief interventions, especially with the less serious type of problem drinker". The types of intervention evaluated include information, advice, self-help manuals, and periodic monitoring of progress by a health worker. The authors conclude that "low intensity, brief interventions have much to recommend them as the first approach to the problem drinker in the primary care setting". This work is corroborated by Chick *et al.* (1985), who conclude that nurses can effect significant change in patients drinking behaviour, if intervention is made before the problem has become too severe. Lindstrom (1992 : 31) states: "There is ample evidence demonstrating that brief interventions may be modestly but reliably effective in helping the less serious type of problem drinker."

The research and discussion concerning the possibility of severely alcohol dependent, or "addicted", clients returning to controlled drinking, using the behavioural techniques of early intervention, are less optimistic (Lindstrom 1992). Though there is much controversy over this issue, there is little research to indicate that controlled drinking is a viable option for most severe "alcoholics" whatever the type of intervention. There is much controversy then, not concerning whether cognitive behavioural methods are useful for alcohol-related problems as a whole, but regarding how far the methods are useful when dealing with the biopsychosocial phenomenon of "addiction".

The Medical Model

What is the effect of physiological responses to alcohol and physical addiction? The medical perspective focuses on the short and long term physiological effects of alcohol. Neither social learning theory nor cognitive psychology, takes adequate account of physiology. It can, for example, be demonstrated that physiological factors influence the significance of psychological expectancy factors. Research with subjects who are physically dependent demonstrates that they respond to the alcohol content in drinks, whereas the response of less dependent subjects is determined mainly by their beliefs and expectancies about drinking. That is, the effect of an initial drink on a severely dependent subject's craving to drink further is not merely the result of cues, beliefs and rationalisation; it occurs without the drinker being aware that he has consumed alcohol. It has also been demonstrated that there is a statistically significant increase in craving three hours after a "primary dose". (Hodgson & Stockwell 1977.) This suggests that an altered physiological state is a component of craving but only for seriously dependent "alcoholics". For less serious "alcoholics" this physiological state is seen only as a component of craving when the "alcoholic" believes he or she has consumed alcohol. Marlatt *et al.* (1973) carried out a similar experiment in order to test whether people addicted to alcohol lose control of their drinking – a premise integral to the disease theory and opposed to the cognitive behavioural approach. They found no difference between "alcoholics" and social drinkers in alcohol consumption based on the actual primer of drink (physiological stimuli) but found increases based on expectation. There is therefore conflicting evidence regarding the interaction of physiological or behavioural factors and subjective expectations and cognitions.

The Dependence Syndrome and the Biopsychosocial Approach

The concept of a biopsychosocial dependence syndrome underlying this definition was initially developed by Edwards and colleagues (1976).

The dependence syndrome includes:–

a) Altered behavioural states

b) Altered subjective states

c) Altered psychobiological states.

The syndrome is defined as a "cluster" of physiological, behavioural and social phenomena. (Edwards & Grant 1977.)

The essential seven components of the dependence syndrome are as follows:-

- Narrowing of the drinking repertoire
- Salience of drink-seeking behaviour
- Increased tolerance to alcohol
- Repeated withdrawal symptoms
- Relief or avoidance of withdrawal symptoms by further drinking
- Subjective awareness of compulsion to drink
- Reinstatement of the syndrome if the client begins to drink again after a period of abstinence.

This concept of a "continuum of dependence" has been developed with the World Health Organisation and utilised for both clinical and screening purposes (Edwards 1986a). In this approach, dependence is understood as a biopsychosocial continuum along which anybody can travel under certain circumstances. The concept has been developed as a guide for clinicians and practitioners.

The syndrome includes: characteristics from physiological, behavioural and disease models; physiological characteristics such as tolerance and withdrawal; behavioural characteristics such as narrowing of the drinking repertoire, together with characteristics identified by Alcoholics Anonymous, such as the salience of drinking and reinstatement of the syndrome (which the WHO refers to as "remission"). The syndrome therefore can be seen as incorporating aspects from the AA and cognitive behavioural models, together with a physiological component. However, the terminology is largely medical and, as such, is seen by those who are not doctors as too closely related to the medical or disease models, being criticised by both AA advocates and cognitive behavioural psychologists. The former state that dependence is a disease and not a medical problem (LeFevre nd) and the latter assert that it is based on a physiological perspective and is therefore an ineffectual attempt to support the disease perspective in the face of the evidence of behavioural research (Heather & Robertson 1981). Hodgson in an article entitled "The Alcohol Dependence Syndrome a Step in the Wrong Direction" (1980) criticises the notion of a syndrome as too medical (although he does concede that the concept of a dependence state is valid), and yet if there is no sequential syndrome then the rationale for early intervention is less apparent.

Definitions of dependency are compounded by confusion between "dependence" and "disability" (Edwards 1988). He states that because these terms are confused the problem of definition becomes much worse. In previous work, Edwards and Orford *et al.* (1977) had found little difference between treatment approaches and this work is often cited as the best example of an outcome study illustrating no difference between the two options of "treatment" and "advice". The authors defined different patient types in terms of "disability" and "dependence". Orford *et al.* (1979) carried out a two year follow up of this study which confirmed the authors' initial hypothesis, finding that the long term results were different for different categories of client. Those clients considered more seriously dependent achieved better results in the treatment group and others (suffering only "disability") did better in the group receiving only advice. There was an interaction between the types of client and the goals they achieved, with the seriously addicted clients achieving better results through abstention and the others tending to achieve good results through controlled drinking.

Edwards believed that if the dependence syndrome was severe, then the chances of returning to controlled drinking were low. If the syndrome was mild, then controlled drinking would be possible. He felt it essential, but problematic, to group subjects in terms of degrees of dependence rather than in terms of "disability". Edwards concluded: "For people who are disabilitated simple strategies of social adjustment or psychotherapy (coping mechanisms) might be useful in reversing the 'dependence syndrome'. There is an important contrast here with the benefits of such general strategies for severe dependence, where similar approaches may be expected to lead to remission." (Edwards *et al.* 1988 : 149.) That is, what is good for someone not heavily addicted may be a disaster for someone who is heavily addicted, and vice versa. (See also Edwards *et al.* 1988 and 1989.)

The problem of deciding whether dependency has caused certain "disabilities" or whether certain "disabilities" have led to and aggravated dependency has not been resolved. It seems very difficult, if not impossible, to discover simple objective criteria for assessing this, for professionals and clients alike.

The Twelve Step Disease Model: Alcoholics Anonymous and Minnesota Method

a) Alcoholics Anonymous

Alcoholics Anonymous is one of five self-help groups within the "Anonymous Fellowship" based on a model of spiritual disease. The other four groups are: Alanon (for families of alcoholics); Alateen (for the teenage children of alcoholics); Narcotics Anonymous (for drug addicts); and Families Anonymous (for the families of drug addicts). Alcoholics Anonymous is, however, by far the largest and has a longer history, being founded in 1935; the other Anonymous Fellowship groups developed more recently as offshoots from the original Fellowship.

The AA approach is in direct conflict with conventional medical, psychological and sociological concepts of alcoholism in Britain and shares instead those of early-twentieth-century models of spiritual disease. Despite its opposition to British Establishment views, the Anonymous Fellowship has established a widespread network of self-help groups and residential rehabilitation centres in Britain today.

In contrast, in America the "spiritual disease" model and the Minnesota Method derived from it provide the dominant theory and method in professional circles. Although the approach is most prominent in the northern states of America and in the alcohol rather than drugs field, it is clear that professional respectability is conferred on the model there (Sanchez-Craig 1990 and Fingarette1988).

The theory underlying AA and the Minnesota Method is often poorly understood by outsiders who have not actually gone through the process of "working the programme". The publications of those who *have* been through the programme are often uncritically crusading. Therefore it is useful to give a straightforward description of the philosophy and methods of AA and Minnesota.

There is little research available evaluating AA. The work of the AA General Service Board Survey of members in the United States and Canada concludes that the service is effective (Robinson 1979). However, the work of outsiders, for example Bebbington (1976), indicates that no such conclusion can be drawn. Surveys of Alcoholics Anonymous in Great Britain have been carried out by the General Service Board of Alcoholics Anonymous (1982 and 1986). Their reports give a favourable impression, stating that in 1986 there were 2,176 groups and nearly 6,000 members in Britain. The survey work is interesting and indicates that large numbers of people have derived benefit from the help offered. Unfortunately, there is little information concerning those people who do not succeed either in remaining abstinent or in continuing to attend groups.

b) The Minnesota model

The Minnesota model is based on the steps of AA but with significant differences in approach. Minnesota services are often based within residential communities and offer a structured therapeutic approach with professional or volunteer supervision of clients. The use of the Minnesota model is widespread in treatment services in both Britain and America. Although studies carried out would seem to indicate that almost half of all clients appear to benefit from this approach, there is little research carried out independently. As with the monitoring of Alcoholics Anonymous, most of the evaluative studies are produced by adherents or clinicians working with this model. However, the Minnesota Method does lend itself to more-structured outcome studies. Spicer & Barnett (1980) have produced work for the Hazelden Foundation (the source of most Minnesota literature); and Rossi *et al.* (1963) have conducted a study of the effectiveness of the methods. These studies suggest 45% success or "effectiveness", but as Cook (1988) points out, their work has a number of methodological flaws. Similarly, Laundergarden (1982) carried out a follow-up study of discharges over a two year period. The sample of clients who responded to questionnaires was not necessarily representative of the population leaving treatment and, as with other similar studies, those clients who drop out of treatment (especially at an early stage) were not considered in any detail.

LeFevre (nd:23) sums up the essentials of the first five steps used in the Minnesota model. First, he identifies the essence of AA in Step One. "The essential process of Step One is surrender: the recognition that one is beaten, that one's own perceptions of reality are inappropriate and that one's life has become unmanageable." Step Two is seen as taking away the "false self-reliance" and leading the client to "come to believe that a power greater than ourselves could restore us to sanity". The Minnesota model does however allow flexibility with regard to the spiritual aspects of AA. "To expect a sudden conversion to spiritual belief, is to expect too much and it is fortunately completely unnecessary. The group itself is commonly adopted as the 'Higher Power'." Step Three involves a logical progression from Steps One and Two, to make "a decision to turn our will and our lives over to God as we understood him" and Step Four "a searching and fearless moral inventory of ourselves". Step Five embodies telling someone else these wrongs.

These five steps are obviously closely related to those of AA. Minnesota treatment centres will direct the client through these first five stages; the client then leaves the project and works through the final eight steps in Alcoholics Anonymous self-help groups, under the guidance of a sponsor.

The Minnesota method is usually used in closed therapeutic communities: "the challenge was to develop control over the total treatment environment in which alcoholics lived" (Anderson 1981 : 4). As a consequence, a completely structured and disciplined environment was developed "utilising a number of meaningful patient activities intended to produce positive behavioural changes." The programme is short (60 days) and intensive (Anderson 1981 : 5).

Supporters of the Minnesota model and the AA philosophy believe that intensive involvement is essential for people to work through the programme successfully. For example, AA members are often advised to attend at least two or three meetings a week, and sometimes to attend 60 meetings in 60 days.

c) The twelve step model: philosophy and method
The disease or "spiritual disease" model is encapsulated in the philosophy and methods of the Alcoholics Anonymous groups and the Minnesota method of therapy.

The theory was not developed by professionals or academics but by lay persons who had alcohol problems themselves. Academic credibility was conferred on the approach when Jellinek developed a similar theoretical approach from research findings (Jellinek 1946, 1957, 1960). Although the AA model of spiritual disease and the disease model of Jellinek have much in common, the disease model did not incorporate the spiritual and moral components of AA. Although Jellinek did not whole-heartedly endorse AA, much of his work was used by those in AA to give the approach professional credibility. The idea of alcoholism as a disease was commonplace in the USA when this conception of addiction received formal respectability through Jellinek's work, popular in the 1950s and 1960s. Max Glatt (1972) developed material based on Jellinek's work that could be used within AA treatment programmes. Jellinek's notion of the "gamma" form of alcoholism became most influential in the field, together with the idea that alcoholism was a unitary disease. These concepts reinforced and maintained AA, but the success of AA itself also helped; it is the mutually reinforcing elements of Jellinek's work and AA that are of interest as it is these that kept the disease model alive.

The basic premise underlying the twelve step approach is that the "alcoholic" is not normal, that she or he suffers from an illness of the whole person. The "alcoholic" is seen as having three characteristics: a physical allergy to alcohol, an "alcoholic personality", and a spiritual sickness. The client is seen as an "alcoholic", rather than a person who has an alcoholic disease. The disease is defined as causing other problems, i.e. it is a primary cause of all secondary problems or "symptoms".

The model of addiction can be applied to families who live with addicts, and separate groups have been developed for relatives and children (Alanon and Alateen). In this way, a client involved in the treatment programme can in effect be surrounded by both family and social groups that concur with the basic beliefs of the programme. This tends to happen with "successful" clients, who socialise more and more with AA or NA members, rely a good deal on their AA/NA sponsor, and try to get their families involved in similar groups.

Various authors have attempted to describe the programme, The most objective account is probably that of Kurtz (n.d.). The majority of the literature is written by adherents of the model such as LeFevre (n.d.) and Anderson (1981).

The twelve steps
Information about the twelve steps is available in the textbooks *Alcoholics Anonymous, The Little Red Book*, and AA leaflets. The quotations given below are drawn from all these sources.

Step one – powerlessness
The essence of the step is that clients should believe or accept that they are an "alcoholic" or an "addict" and that they are powerless over their lives as a result (i.e. admit that their lives are unmanageable). If clients do not accept this interpretation of their experience the treatment programme cannot proceed. This stage is often referred to as "breaking denial".

Step one refers to "the foundation of recovery" and involves AA members coming to an understanding of their own powerlessness.

This emphasis on acceptance of personal powerlessness is an integral part of the notion of alcoholism as a disease and an essential starting point for the programme. The notion of disease and powerlessness is also linked to the notion of responsibility for one's own recovery. This may appear to be paradoxical, but is explained within the AA philosophy in the following way: "Personal responsibility for alcoholism occurs when we have recognized it in ourself, or others have pointed out the symptoms to us, and we realize we are afflicted with a disease. It then becomes our responsibility to start a recovery programme." (Alcoholics Anonymous 1976 : 21.)

Step one then identifies the concepts of unmanageability with the notion of powerlessness as integral parts of the "alcoholic personality" which can only be controlled through adherence to the programme and abstinence. Clients are asked as part of step one to consider personal examples of their own powerlessness and unmanageability.

Step two – hope

This step involves recognising and "coming to hope" that one has the need, and ability, to change, with the help of the programme and more importantly with the help of a "higher power" or "power outside of oneself". This step is a necessary follow-up to acceptance of powerlessness as, without hope and faith in outside help, little progress could be made. The "higher power" can be seen as God or as the Anonymous Fellowship itself, or their therapeutic groups.

Step three – commitment to change

This step involves not only making a commitment to change but also "handing oneself over to others in the programmes, that is, learning to *trust* others." This stage involves an effort on the part of the client to stop "controlling or manipulating others", that is, relinquishing control over both himself or herself and over others.

Step four – the moral inventory

This stage involves the client writing a list of his or her previous character or personality defects prior to treatment. This list is referred to as a "searching moral inventory".

Step five – confession

This stage involves sharing this "moral inventory" with, or telling, someone else. This is often referred to as the "confessional" step. The benefits felt by clients are often described as very similar to religious practices.

Step six

Involves emphasising the willingness to change and to have the higher power to remove defects.

Step seven

Involves putting the initial commitments into action.

Step eight

Involves becoming willing to make amends to people one has harmed.

Step nine

Involves actually making amends, as far as this is practicable.

Step ten

Involves learning to take a personal moral inventory on a regular basis, that is, continually monitoring and evaluating what happens in one's life, admitting when one is wrong, and changing if necessary.

Step eleven
Involves building and improving on faith, and improving one's relationship with one's higher power.

Step twelve
The final step is considered of extreme importance, as it involves helping others, consistently reminding oneself of how bad one was, and reminding oneself of the principles of the programme by teaching them to other alcoholics or addicts. "Twelfth stepping" is thought to give members "a purpose, an identity and self-respect" and is seen as an integral part of recovery and sobriety.

It can be seen from this description of the structure of the programme that a range of therapeutic and "spiritual" components are involved. It appears to be important that a client fully understands and accepts each stage in turn before progressing to the following stage in the sequence. Problems are likely to occur if a client does not fully participate in any one part.

d) A spiritual programme?
Alcoholics Anonymous members would describe AA as bridging "medicine" and "religion"; an incurable disease with spiritual ramifications.

Bill Wilson, the founder of AA, had suggested that alcoholism has a spiritual component and he found this idea reflected in the work of Jung and Aldous Huxley. AA members consistently note that successful affiliation with AA depends upon the capacity of the individual to experience a conversion. However, not all AA members see the programme as inherently spiritual. Kurtz (nd : 4) concludes from his study that the basis of AA is "not God", but the acceptance by the member that he or she is an "alcoholic", "essentially limited, but able to find a healing wholeness in the acceptance of this limitation". This is reflected in Jones's (1965) finding that 88% of AA members interviewed in research admitted to some kind of "conversion".

There are clearly problems in attempting to integrate ideas of spirituality into the dominant paradigms of the natural sciences, psychiatry and psychology. Many professionals and laymen alike do not accept the underlying spirituality of AA and object to the anti-professionalism and anti-intellectualism involved in the approach.

e) Summary
The traditional twelve step model underlies the work of Alcoholics Anonymous, Narcotics Anonymous, and the Minnesota Method. At present we have little understanding of what actually happens in these programmes or why

an approach at odds with both the methods and beliefs of contemporary British academic and professional consensus should survive and flourish alongside its more scientifically credible opponents. Information is usually acquired experientially by "working the programme", with the consequent internalisation of the belief system on which it is based: reports by "insiders" are often more concerned with promulgating this philosophy than objectively analysing the model. Those who have not gone through this process themselves are often critical due to lack of research evidence, but have little understanding of how AA functions. The exception is the work of Denzin (1986, 1987a,1987b) who carried out in-depth qualitative studies of Alcoholics Anonymous. However, the outcome research carried out by "outsiders" has done little more than show that this approach is no more or less effective than any other (Cook 1988).

This model contains elements of significance to the field of drug and alcohol studies as a whole. It deals with the factors known to be correlated with relapse: emotions, relationships, and social norms. It also takes into account the social factors correlated with successful treatment and long term maintenance of change, such as relationships with family and social support systems. Finally, the programme emphasises the importance of the sequential nature of the individual recovery process.

The twelve step model combines those components which have been found to be useful with those which have not. For example, the ideology and dogmatic approach of AA have been frequently detrimental to many. The beliefs of adherents can conflict with those of potential clients, contributing to a 50% drop-out rate (Keene & Raynor 1993) and the moral/spiritual content can also alienate, preventing initial self-referral and non-compliance during treatment (Keene 1994).

In addition, the evidence for the effectiveness of particular elements of the programme is limited; individual counselling (Miller & Hester 1986); group therapy (Frank 1974) and lectures/videos. (Kiner *et al.* 1995). The success of AA and Minnesota is, therefore, as might be expected, limited. There is not enough research to allow clarification of the core components and it is possible that they do not function as isolated elements but as integral parts of a recovery process. Research does not yet allow us to understand these components as a sequence in the context of the individual change process as a whole.

The Current Debate: Physical Addiction, Disease or Behaviour Disorder?

a) Have cognitive behavioural models replaced the disease and medical models?

Epidemiological studies of general alcohol consumption in the population indicate that there are normal (unimodal) distributions. (See, for example, De Lint 1969.) This suggests that there is not a small minority of the population with severe problems, as the disease model would suggest, but a fairly even distribution of dependency across the general population. This statistical information is not, however, relevant to individual drinking careers. It is likely that drinkers fluctuate during their drinking careers in relation to severity of problems experienced. (Edwards 1989, Clark 1976.)

The aetiology of spiritual disease does not fit well with the evidence of drinking behaviours or population distributions. Until recently the disease theory of alcoholism was common-place because the AA methods were seen to be effective for some people; if the therapy worked, people assumed the theory was "right".

This process was, of course, reversed for academics; when the theory was shown to be wrong, they assumed that the AA methods did not work. As the notion of alcohol dependence as a unitary disease is increasingly questioned by both the psychiatric profession and the behavioural psychologists, Jellinek's theory and AA therapy have become less influential and are seldom referenced in contemporary British journals. As Lindstrom (1992 : 54) points out, "Jellinek's working hypothesis had a salutary effect on alcohol research. Today many researchers regard it as a principal obstacle to the advancement of knowledge and the emergence of interdisciplinary approaches to alcoholism".

This is unfortunate as Jellinek had identified important aspects of alcohol dependence and treatment which have been largely ignored in Britain. He focused on the sequential aetiology of the disease and the importance of individual differences. He stressed the need to establish criteria for the suitability of any given method to a given patient, stating that the "criteria so far established are superficial" (Jellinek 1946 quoted in Lindstrom 1992 : 3).

In the same way, the therapeutic methods of AA have been overlooked, particularly the emphasis on initial client attitudes and beliefs and the stages of recovery. However, in the past few years there has been revived interest in both the process of treatment and recovery (Prochaska & DiClemente, 1983, 1986, Miller & Hester 1986) and the importance of individual differences in treatment. Although Jellinek's model of a progressive disease is often criticised, his work is useful in underlining the limitations of a behavioural analysis which ignores physiological aspects of the phenomenon.

Perhaps it is not, then, surprising that an integral part of the development of psychological theories of dependence has been a concentrated attack on the "disease" model of Alcoholics Anonymous. Nick Heather and Ian Robertson are two of the main proponents of this argument, (1981 and 1989). They see the disease theory as a serious threat to the development of a psychological "controlled drinking" approach. "Most influential disease formulations demand abstinence due to the central feature of irreversibility in the theories. The feature has great practical significance for society's response, in that it undermines a 'controlled drinking' approach." (Heather & Robertson 1981 : 161.)

Heather and Robertson propose that the cognitive behavioural model of "problem drinking" is a new model representing a shift from a "pre-scientific" to a scientific paradigm within alcohol studies. They see the old disease model as tautologous and not facilitating the testing of hypotheses. In contrast, Gorman (1993) suggests that the "problem drinking" model of these psychologists incorporates a set of assumptions parallel to those of the disease model and so does not represent the type of change in paradigm that they suggest. He concludes that the "field of alcohol studies" has not yet reached the stage where a "sophisticated understanding of causes has been reached" and he therefore considers it dangerous for the psychologists to make assumptions about aetiological processes when constructing descriptive models.

One of the most vocal critics of the spiritual disease model in the past few years is an American, in whose country, in contrast to Britain, the general consensus is that the disease model is the correct way to conceptualise and treat alcoholism. As a consequence the critic, Fingarette (1988), evoked an angry and emotional reaction from the American public. This is hardly surprising, as Fingarette introduces the book by stating on page 1: "Almost everything that the American public believes to be the scientific truth about alcoholics is false."

Unfortunately there are little research data to substantiate claims of superiority from any particular approach. Data from alcohol treatment studies are often flawed and difficult to compare because of less-than-standardised procedures (Lindstrom 1992). Where results are comparable, studies instead reflect the findings of general psychotherapeutic research, in that few differences can be identified across therapies.

In common with studies of psychotherapy there has been a change in focus, from trying to work out which method is best to attempting to determine which treatment is best for which client. Although retrospective studies have been conducted to compare treatment programmes, prospective studies involving initial random allocation of subjects to services have only recently been undertaken, the most notable being the "MATCH" study in America (Project MATCH Research Group 1993).

It is possible that the proponents of both AA and cognitive behavioural psychology are self-limiting, as each ignores aspects of alcohol treatment which could be effective, so depriving the field of wider research and treatment options. This chapter has emphasised the need to maintain a range of options for different clients. Edwards (1989 : 449) stresses that alcohol studies should remain an area where no one discipline dominates, but where "great varieties of hypothesis, conjectures, models and theories" can operate. Edwards is perhaps one of the most respected critics of the disease model, arguing against the notion of total loss of control and the unitary concept itself, yet he points out that "in the very recent past the received wisdom was exactly the opposite of what we accept today" (Edwards 1989 : 449). He reminds us that in the nineteenth and early twentieth centuries withdrawal symptoms were recognised as a clinical reality and continues: "At some point in the first half of the twentieth Century, clinical awareness of withdrawal phenomena faded . . . an inspection of a few contemporary texts certainly suggests that over the decades the dependence potential of alcohol was generally down-played." Edwards sums up: "How is the ebb and flow to be explained? Without making harsh judgements from the privileged position of hindsight, how is the ability of experts to forget or deny what was known earlier to many shrewd practitioners to be explained?" (Edwards 1989 : 449.)

b) Problems arising from conflicting models
A basic practical problem arising from the theoretical controversy is that communication and co-ordination between professionals, and between professionals and clients, are difficult. The client's view may differ from that of the practitioner and practitioners themselves may differ. The word "alcoholic" can mean different things to different people and likewise the implications for practice may be variously construed. What could have been a healthy academic controversy has become difficult interprofessional working relationships.

The problems arising from this confusion have been highlighted in the literature since the late seventies. The report by a special committee of the Royal College of Psychiatrists *Alcohol and Alcoholism* (1979 : 118) discusses the difficulties of reconciling notions of "illness" and "self responsibility". "A common starting point for any constructive changes in behaviour has to be the individual's personal admission and realisation that he has a drinking problem. This is equally true whether he is going to remedy the matter by his own efforts, or with professional help, or AA . . . (but) with society's present lack of information on the nature of dependence, that person may not even have a clear idea of what he has to deal with, until he can obtain some informed advice."

Griffith Edwards emphasises this point when he states that it "seems probable that terms such as 'alcoholism' and 'alcoholic' are now so lacking in precision as only to be passports to confusion" (Edwards & Grant 1977 : 32). It is clear that if successful communication between referring agents and between different members of any treatment team can greatly increase the efficiency with which the needs of patients will be met, then unsuccessful communication leads to inefficient service provision.

The confusion between professionals is, if anything, surpassed in the relationship between professionals and clients. It is therefore relevant to highlight the discrepancy between academic/professional and lay views about alcohol problems. Although much of the specialist literature in Britain is now based on taken-for-granted notions of behavioural dependency and controlled drinking treatments, these notions are far from those of the general public. Much of the general population view alcohol problems in terms of "alcoholism" though there is some uncertainty as to the exact meaning of the term. This is apparent throughout the media and is also reflected in the few research projects based on consumer opinions. Work in this area is severely limited at present though of intrinsic interest if considering service provision.

Cartwright *et al.* (1975) gathered data on ordinary people's concepts of abnormal drinking. They state that there was widespread token acceptance of "alcoholism as a disease", although little depth of understanding as to what is meant by this phrase. This is borne out in an unpublished Welsh Office survey of people with alcohol problems in south Wales (Keene 1992). A common complaint among clients was that service providers were not themselves familiar with the disease or AA model and often did not refer to AA groups while a criticism of service provision was that workers were not properly trained in different models. Perhaps because there was disagreement as to the nature of alcohol problems amongst their sample, Cartwright and her colleagues concluded: "There is no functionally useful concept of alcoholism latent within our society which can be used when a patient and clinician meet." (Cartwright *et al.* 1975 : 6.)

c) Which approach is best for social workers?

Although there are a range of different approaches to alcohol problems, the most appropriate model for social workers may well be the cognitive behavioural approach. This is partly because it utilises methods and skills that are part of the social worker's repertoire and partly because it is based on a similar professional ethical base, highlighting the values of client empowerment, self-control, responsibility, and choice.

This does not rule out the possibility of referring clients to AA, general practitioners, psychiatric consultants, or to residential services and self-help groups based on different models. In other words, social workers can work jointly with practitioners using the medical or disease models.

The methods described in the following chapters reflect this emphasis and describe how cognitive behavioural theory and practice can best be used by social workers in their own practice. It will become apparent in later chapters how the cognitive/behavioural approach is particularly useful for young people and offenders. This approach has been well developed in those areas where a range of drinking problems occur and physical dependency may be less common. The "controlled drinking" approach can be used with all clients with a range of alcohol problems; it is perhaps only when the physical dependency is particularly severe that either an abstinence-oriented approach or a residential therapeutic programme may be more useful.

Social workers have a range of options, from working with clients themselves to referring them to other agencies (whether specialist residential care or community alcohol teams). Most social workers co-work to some extent with specialist agencies and other generic professionals. In fact, many of the methods described in the following chapter form part of the generic training of social workers. It is, therefore, often the best option for social workers to take an active part in working with alcohol problems at some stage. This may be most appropriate at the initial assessment stage or in the ongoing stages where is is necessary to help clients to maintain behaviour changes over time by improving social skills and developing supportive social environments.

Chapter 3
Community Care and Alcohol Problems

An Introduction to Community Care Developments and the Implications for Alcohol Services

This chapter will give the reader an introduction to the changes beginning to occur in the policy and practice of alcohol service provision within the context of Community Care. It will consider the developing roles of social services and focus on the new social work responsibilities of assessment and care management in this field. It will describe the range of alcohol-related problems and needs, giving a framework for assessment of the former. The two tasks of care assessment and care management will then be examined in detail and a structured purchasing process developed. This will be followed by a brief review of the range of service provision and the roles of different professions, in order to facilitate the co-ordination and management of multi-disciplinary care. Finally, the potential and opportunities within Community Care for improving traditional alcohol services are examined.

Community Care legislation offers care managers the opportunity to make several positive changes in the alcohol field, if early constraints can be overcome. Research in alcohol misuse has indicated that there is a need for a spectrum of different services and different models of work with alcohol problems. It has become evident that no one intervention or treatment model is more effective than any other; different models suit different people at different times. Community Care gives care managers the opportunity to select the most appropriate social care support or treatment at the most appropriate time.

The demands of referral, assessment and care management call for each service to clarify its aims and the methods for achieving them and also for each to provide measurable outcomes to allow evaluation of effectiveness.

A major obstacle to co-operative working in the past has been the dogmatic approaches and controversy between the supporters of different models, each camp convinced that their definition of alcohol problems and their solutions are the only way forward. Their beliefs are implicit within their assessment procedures, so that someone working with a disease perspective would define problems in terms of a disease, whereas one working within a "controlled drinking" perspective would define problems in cognitive/behavioural terms.

The establishment of a theoretically and clinically neutral administrator such as a care manager or independent assessor allows objective assessments of treatment need, independent of a particular therapeutic perspective, and so enables a more efficient matching of clients to a range of different models. Although the criteria to be used for matching a type of problem to a type of agency are as yet ill-formed, it can be seen even at this stage that it is more effective for assessments not to be completed by an advocate of any one model, but by a more objective outsider who can see the benefits of different types of models and can match clients accordingly.

The new circumstances also allow for an assessment of changing social and health care needs within a wider framework. The problems that lead to alcohol misuse and relapse are often social and therefore social forms of intervention and relapse prevention work best. As the responsibility for assessment moves away from medical professions, it becomes possible to look outside the medical treatment perspective in order to understand how best to deal with alcohol problems. Research indicates that the most effective "treatments" are "social treatments", in other words not really treatment in the medical sense at all. Whilst treatment in the sense of therapeutic change is still an important part of dealing with alcohol problems, equally necessary are the development of social skills, the building of relationships, and the development of supportive social environments. So interventions become as much prevention, maintenance, and crisis intervention as treatment. Whilst therapeutic treatment models may be useful to bring about changes in personality or behaviour at particular periods, social and health care support can be used to prevent uncontrolled periods of drinking or relapse at different crisis points throughout a person's life. These issues have been dealt with in more detail in Chapter 2: suffice it to say here that social worker providers may be particularly well equipped with skills and experience to deal with treatment or therapeutic change and in providing the social support necessary for maintaining that change.

Community Care legislation
a) Extending the role of social services
The NHS and Community Care Act 1990 gave local authorities the responsibility for planning and managing Community Care but not necessarily its provision. It was designed, *inter alia*, to reduce the provision of unnecessary residential care and to replace it with support in the community. For social services this places an emphasis on assessment of needs and development of appropriate care plans and it also gives them responsibility for evaluating the quality of care provided by non-statutory specialist agencies.

It is therefore necessary to develop assessment and care management systems and to co-ordinate service provision. There needs to be a careful consideration of how inter agency care packages can be provided, how partnerships between specialist providers and social services purchasers can be arranged and how such service provision can be evaluated.

Alcohol misuse produces both social and health problems. It is correlated with social, psychological and physical problems and has both social and emotional significance. It affects physical and psychological functioning, causing confusion and poor co-ordination and consequent accidents and/or violence. There can be serious long term effects on health. The solutions to alcohol problems vary from help with basic needs for financial and social support to health care and treatment. People with alcohol problems could benefit from a range of generic and specialist support from social, health care, housing and probation workers and various non-residential as well as residential specialist agencies.

However, health authorities have taken the lead in the financing and providing of services in the past. Perhaps as a consequence, alcohol problems have been seen largely as health problems and dependency as a treatable illness.

Social services departments are jointly responsible for funding specialist services, but district health authorities have traditionally funded drop-in and day care alcohol facilities, whereas local authorities now fund residential places. The social care aspects of alcohol problems in the community have perhaps been underestimated and given little priority. Although some local authorities have also contributed funding to specialist agencies and appointed social workers with special responsibilities for alcohol problems, it was only with the advent of the Act that authorities were required to employ or contract out for a specialist alcohol worker to carry out assessments and care plans for residential care. This has provided the incentive for the re-examination of residential services and the review of the respective roles of community-based and residential care.

b) Specialist alcohol service provision
In the 1990 Act, local authorities were given the responsibility for assessing and designing care plans for those people with alcohol problems who require residential treatment. They do not yet have direct responsibility to assess and design care plans for those with drink problems who are in need of other forms of social care to prevent loss of treatment gains or deterioration in social condition or health.

Residential service provision

Community Care legislation effectively then moved overseeing of residential care to the local authorities, giving them the responsibility for the needs of those alcohol misusers who might require such care. The Act obliged local authorities to make plans to assess and meet the needs of people with alcohol problems. Section 47 states: "Where it appears to a local authority that any person for whom they provide or arrange for the provision of community care services may be in need of any such services, the authority, shall carry out an assessment of his[her] needs for those services, and having regard to the results of that assessment shall then decide whether his[her] needs call for the provision by them of any such services."

Clients cannot now, therefore, be referred to residential facilities without a pre-referral assessment by social services, though it may be possible to admit prior to assessment in some cases. A later clause in the section allows for the provision of Community Care services without prior assessment "if, in the opinion of the authority, the condition of that person is such that they require those services as a matter of urgency" (Section 47[5]). This guidance modifies the initial position by stating that local authorities should provide "fast track assessment" in emergencies or in situations where the normal time scales would result in serious deterioration in a person's physical, social and emotional well-being and/or loss of motivation to accept care and treatment.

As with other types of Community Care policy, local authorities were given a great deal of autonomy in developing alcohol services. Some authorities chose to emphasise the single door assessment policy, dealing with all client groups through the same generic procedures. However, as expertise in the alcohol field lay mainly within projects largely funded by or through health authorities, some authorities choose instead to contract out the assessment to specialist alcohol agency staff.

In October 1992 the Government withdrew its commitment to safeguard residential alcohol services through "ring fenced" funding. This had serious implications for residential and non-residential services reliant on local authority funding, partly because authorities were unclear how much funding in fact should be allocated to alcohol services and partly because many authorities did not traditionally see alcohol problems as a priority.

The Government's Community Care policy came into effect on the 1 April 1993, and changed the way registered residential alcohol projects are funded. In the light of their new responsibilities and the lack of "ring fenced" funding for registered care and nursing home provision, the local authorities now had discretionary powers to determine not only whether or not to allocate funding to drop-in day care services instead of residential care but also whether or not to allocate funds to alcohol services at all (90% of residential funding was allocated to working with elderly people and 10% to all other residential groups).

There was much opposition to the lack of ring fencing (Murray 1993, Whitfield 1993) as many thought alcohol problems were seen by local authorities as low priority in contrast to the growing need for residential services for elderly people. However most did reserve funding for residential care, many guessing at the approximate amount necessary for the coming year.

The conditions and constraints of Community Care policy had a detrimental effect on residential service provision, not only through the funding arrangements but also through the emphasis on local service provision. Residential centres traditionally catered for a wide range of clients in geographical terms. Many chose to go outside their local authority area and residential treatment centres needed referrals from more than one authority to be financially self-supporting. This has led to confusion about "cross boundary" funding issues, where clients were not resident in the local authority area or were homeless.

Non-residential service provision
When local authorities became responsible for assessment and placement procedures it was envisaged that the gap between non-residential and residential services would be bridged by the provision of assessment and care plans. This ideal is less than certain in the alcohol field, as an informal split exists between the local authorities, who in effect have responsibility for residential care, and the health authorities who have generally assumed responsibility for day care services.

The emphasis on responsibility for residential services has led many authorities not only to question the effectiveness of different types of residential provision but also to consider the effectiveness of residential help in relation to community-based service provision.

Local authorities do not have a clear-cut responsibility for those who do not require residential care and there is little central guidance regarding the funding of non-residential services. The advice given in *Alcohol and Drugs Services and Community Care* (DoH 1993b) is general, allowing local authorities freedom to develop local policies. These guidelines emphasise the importance of the social service role in assessment for residential care to the exclusion of a clear general policy and practice guidelines. As might be expected, the initial effect was to increase the proportion of funding spent on assessments rather than that on developing services.

Social services do not necessarily fund alcohol day centres or drop-in centres, though they may do so if a particular local authority considers this a priority. Where non-residential alcohol services exist they are often funded from a mixture of different sources, from charities to health authorities and local authorities. These services are often under staffed and may function through short-term funding and/or a team of volunteers.

At present non-residential alcohol services are less affected by local authority policies, though they are often contracted by local authorities to carry out assessments. However, local authorities may work in conjunction with health authorities to provide a joint alcohol service and transfer previous residential funds to community-based projects. Non-residential projects, whilst not affected by local authority changes, have been greatly influenced by changes in funding procedures within health authorities. Projects previously funded by grants from the NHS have instead been contracted to provide specific services.

c) the implications of the wider legislation for services for people with alcohol problems

Models of assessment and care management for elderly people are not easily translated into those for alcohol problems.

Community Care changes were made largely in an attempt to improve services for the great majority of clients, that is, elderly and physically disabled people, those with learning difficulties and those with mental health problems. What is most appropriate for these client groups is not necessarily what is best for people with alcohol problems.

However, although these models are ill-fitting in some ways, they offer many opportunities for developing and improving alcohol service provision in terms of social support and health care in the community. There is an opportunity to make social and health care facilities more accessible to clients with alcohol problems, as resource management allows an overview of both alcohol-related problems and social care needs. The effects of alcohol problems on the carer become highlighted for the first time. Carers of problem drinkers have long remained hidden, the responsibility for care falling almost entirely on the spouse, parent or children, with little acknowledgment or support. The provider:purchaser split will increase understanding of other agencies through the contracting process and developing partnerships, and the increasing emphasis on user involvement may bring to light the needs of a little-understood group of clients. These are only potential benefits at present, opportunities for people with alcohol problems rather than actualities. But it can be seen that Community Care offers ways forward in the future.

The philosophy of support and maintenance in the community is very appropriate for those clients who have been through treatment and need social and psychological support to prevent relapse. In other words, the concept of maintenance may have much to contribute to the narrow and rather old-fashioned, health-orientated concept of treatment in the alcohol field. The previous chapter illustrates that the majority of treatment-outcome gains are lost within one or two years. Research indicates that this may well be due to lack of after-care in terms of psychological skills, emotional welfare, and social support – the traditional areas of social work intervention!

In the alcohol misuse field the social aspects of treatment and maintenance of treatment change are becoming recognised in the research literature. As there is a shift in focus from the medical model to a social support model, so the task of helping people with alcohol problems becomes a social one in the community. This change in focus in the alcohol field itself gives a new perspective on the changes in service provision and the emphasis on community-based services, highlighting new potential and opportunities.

In the drugs field a similar argument is put forward by Sullivan *et al.* (1992), who suggest that professionals should take drug misuse into account in case management by focusing on community functioning and social rehabilitation and in this way help prevent relapse. This would seem sensible in the light of research findings that it is social factors which influence maintenance of treatment gains. The authors outline their plans for developing case management in a later article. (Sullivan *et al.* 1994.)

Despite the research evidence, social work support and domiciliary care are fairly new concepts in the alcohol field, yet community (home based) detoxification is a developing service. Social and life skills, together with anger management, assertiveness training, relapse prevention, and social support networks (rehabilitation) could all be seen within this remit. Social support and maintenance after treatment are increasingly becoming seen as an integral part of treatment, e.g. self-help support groups and home visits during crisis and after relapse.

The alcohol field has traditionally had little user participation in service provision (except where self-help groups such as AA also have members attending statutory or non-statutory organisations) so there are new opportunities for clients to become more involved.

There are therefore several potential advantages for the client in the changes in care provision, not least that day care becomes an option, response time is often improved due to fast-track assessment, and case management means a cohesive approach in which the client has a say.

What are alcohol-related problems and what are the needs of alcohol misusers?

Alcohol-related problems involve health problems, psychological problems and social problems. In this respect, people who drink too much are no different to other social services clients, and consequently the services they require are no different. They may need help with housing and finances, and with child care problems. They may need assistance with anxiety and depression and basic social and life skills. In addition, they may also need "treatment" for underlying psychological problems and alcohol dependency.

Seen through a "treatment" perspective, the needs of alcohol misusers may be narrowly defined in terms of treatment for alcohol dependency. However, if alcohol misuse is understood as a much broader group of issues, including social, psychological and health-related problems, the types of solutions can be seen to be more varied. A useful way of categorising alcohol problems is in terms of those related to intoxication, to heavy drinking, and to dependency. (Also see Introduction). Each of these can have social, psychological and physical consequences and calls for a different type of solution.

It is necessary to distinguish between intoxication, heavy drinking, and alcohol dependency. "Treatment" may be ineffective in the aim of maintaining abstinence or reducing heavy drinking but may still help reduce alcohol-related problems (Emrick 1975). Services for people with mental health problems or those who are elderly include health care and prescribing, social care, continued monitoring, and crisis intervention where necessary. For people with alcohol problems, the key concept is the maintenance of changes in drinking behaviour through social reintegration. The initial changes in drinking behaviour may involve difficulties, but it is the year or two following this change that is important. In common with many forms of physical and mental illness, drinkers may have periods of crisis and relapse and it is then that they need extra support and help.

On the whole, social care involves the maintenance and care of people in the community. The greatest proportion of work with alcohol problems is not concerned with getting people to give up drinking or control the amount they drink, rather it is to do with the long term support necessary to maintain changes in drinking and prevent relapse in the event of a crisis or lapse.

It will become clear that problems can cause alcohol misuse and that alcohol misuse itself causes problems. It is important to distinguish between cause and effect in order to aim any intervention at the cause rather than its symptoms.

For example, if a client is depressed or anxious and uses alcohol to self-medicate , it will be constructive to deal with the underlying depression or anxiety. Many people use alcohol as a solution or a means of coping. However, alcohol misuse can also cause depression and anxiety. If a client stops using alcohol or controls his/her use it would effectively deal with psychological problems caused by the drinking itself.

a) Alcohol-related problems

Alcohol misuse and related problems vary during the course of a client's life. There will be times when s/he uses less alcohol or drinks in a non-problematic way and there may be periods when s/he gives up altogether. It is probably necessary to continue to work with clients through several periods of problematic alcohol misuse. It is now generally accepted that the relationship can last a long time and workers help support the client through periods of crisis in their lives when they may drink more or when they lose control of their drinking.

In order to deal with alcohol misuse it is necessary to provide support to prevent the kind of problems that cause it (such as stress and depression), help with the kind of problems that arise from it, and to deal with physical and psychological dependency.

The table below gives a structure for understanding, identifying and assessing different types of alcohol problem. The table is designed to be used as an assessment grid to be repeated at each stage of the helping process as the client's problems and needs change.

Examples of the types of problems to be found in each category are outlined below;

Assessment grid

PROBLEMS	intoxication	heavy use	dependency
social	relationships	financial problems	isolation
psychological	mood swings	depression	depression
physical	accidents assaults	ill health	withdrawal symptoms

N.B., many of the symptoms of heavy use are also present with dependent use.

Social problems
Social problems include those of a legal nature, criminal offences, occupational difficulties, and unemployment. Social isolation is not uncommon, or there may be relationship problems and/or sexual problems. Self-neglect is common. There may be child care problems, and possible abuse. Finally, there may be a lack of social and life skills and possibly also homelessness.

Psychological problems
A similar broad range of psychological problems are related to alcohol misuse, such as variations in mood, disinhibition and aggression, and problems of depression, anxiety, and poor self-esteem. Longer term problems can include excessive feelings of guilt, hallucinations, paranoia, and suicide attempts.

Physical problems
Short term physical problems associated with misuse include blackouts, hangovers, lack of motor co-ordination, and accidents. Long term physical problems include vitamin deficiency, impotence, muscle degeneration, liver damage, cancers, anaemia, fatty heart, and, eventually, possible brain damage. Finally, physical dependency itself brings tolerance of large quantities of alcohol, craving for alcohol, withdrawal symptoms, shakes, delirium tremens, and epileptic fits.

b) Social and health care and/or treatment?
Community care means the provision of social and psychological services and support to enable people to live as independently as possible in their own homes. Alcohol "treatment" research indicates that clients benefit if this type of support is given to them at critical times in their lives, when they are ready for change and particularly in the year following treatment and at any point where relapse is likely.

It can be seen then that the social services approach to support people with mental health problems and those who are elderly is, in one way, ideally suited to working with alcohol problems, as it emphasises the need for ongoing maintenance support in the community. Whilst there may be a need for in-patient detoxification or supervised out-patient detoxification and basic brief interventions (cognitive/behavioural skills), the main tasks are to support clients at particular times before and after treatment and prior to the problems developing at times of stress and pressure.

The helping process is dealt with in the following chapters: the details of the provision of care and provider tasks are dealt with here, together with a brief outline of needs. It is important to point out that the type of help and support needed by a client will vary depending on what stage he or she has reached.

i) Service provision without treatment or before treatment
For those clients who are waiting for treatment, or for those who are not prepared to (or cannot) change their drinking at the time of assessment, there is a need for support to prevent excessive drinking through periods of severe emotional problems.

ii) During treatment
During treatment and detoxification (if required) there are additional needs for health care and medication; there may also be a need for child care, domiciliary care, CPN monitoring, meals on wheels, etc., and for intensive social support in the period immediately after detoxification when relapse is most likely.

iii) After treatment
The critical stage is after treatment, when there are needs for support to prevent relapse, in order to maintain treatment gains: this is best done by social care workers, who can offer regular support and crisis intervention if necessary. There is also a need for intervention in the event of a crisis that might precipitate relapse and in the event of a lapse.

c) What services are necessary before, during and after treatment?
Dependency treatment, social, psychological and health care needs all require different types of intervention. Chapter 4 deals in detail with how to provide different types of intervention at appropriate times; however, an indication of the range and type of useful provider input is given below.

i) Before treatment.
Prior to treatment it may be necessary to provide help with housing difficulties and with legal and financial problems. Health care may be a priority but perhaps the most important pre-treatment issue is child care support and help, and support for the carers, if they are required.

ii) During treatment
Social and health care services remain important during treatment and services such as home care and "meals on wheels", together with child care provision during crisis periods and periods of detoxification, may be vital to successful treatment completion. Treatment services themselves include detoxification prescribing at home, monitoring and support, individual counselling, and short term cognitive behavioural programmes to learn to control drinking.

iii) After treatment

The most important help to maintain treatment gains include the setting up of self-help groups and developing or establishing social support networks in the event of stressful situations and crisis points. In addition, individuals can be helped to develop new skills for themselves, such as stress, anxiety, and anger management, together with relaxation and cognitive behavioural coping skills. It may also be necessary to provide treatment for depression and/or anxiety. This may involve psychological interventions and/or a drug prescription. Finally, an intervention service in the event of a relapse or other crisis may be necessary at any time. This can include cognitive behavioural programmes of relapse prevention and relapse intervention.

It can be seen that it is useful to divide alcohol problems into treatment, health and social care needs. The Community Care assessment and care management procedure can then be used to assess and manage provision of social and health care needs before, during and after treatment. The procedure can also be used to identify needs for treatment and further clinical assessment. It then becomes easier to determine which professionals are the most appropriate providers of which services at which times. (See below.)

Community Care: Assessment and care management process

It is important to distinguish between the social work role in terms of purchaser and provider. This chapter is concerned with assessment and care management within the Community Care remit of purchasing and managing care. Chapter 2 is concerned with treatment models and chapter 4 with social work provision of both treatment and social care.

a) Assessment of alcohol problems: the issues

There are many areas of assessment which remain unclear in the early stages of Community Care. For example, there are difficulties in determining what should be assessed, how it is to be assessed and who has the expertise necessary to carry out the assessment. The timing of assessments is particularly pertinent in the alcohol field where speed of referral can be crucial.

These issues are as relevant in the management as in the assessment of care. It is, for example, often unclear what type of expertise is necessary for the effective design and monitoring of health and social care plans and what type of knowledge is required to be able to match clients' needs to the many different kinds of treatment provision.

Local authorities have developed different types of solution for the lack of in-service expertise. First, by creating new posts for specialist alcohol workers, and second by the development of contracting arrangements or partnerships with specialist alcohol agencies and/or health authorities (Murray 1993.) The NHS and Community Care Act allows for local authorities to contract out assessments to specialist agencies. Voluntary agencies can be involved not only in preparing care provision but also "in addition have a role in providing expert advice in assessment:" (DoH 1993 : 32).

Specialist assessment and support are necessary if there is the possibility of a need for detoxification (in-patient or out-patient), that is, if the client shows signs of withdrawal or has been drinking heavily and regularly for a long period of time. It may also be necessary for a specialist to assess treatment needs and match them to the range of different types of treatment facility, but it is debatable whether a specialist is essential to provide an assessment of social, psychological, and health care needs. It is possible that a generic social worker is equally capable of assessing and making the appropriate provision, though some knowledge of the short and long term effects of alcohol and an understanding of physical and psychological dependence would be useful. In the same way, general health assessment and care may well be sufficient for health-related problems and GP supervision and general domiciliary nursing adequate during periods of detoxication and withdrawal. Specialist involvement can therefore function in partnership with other agencies rather than as a sole provider. There is an opportunity for the care manager effectively to manage resources by co-ordinating short term specialist treatment with longer term non-specialist health and social care.

What kind of assessment is most appropriate for alcohol problems and who is the most appropriate assessor?

Alcohol problems are traditionally seen as an illness or behavioural disorder and therefore suitable for diagnosis or clinical assessment and treatment. This clinical assessment procedure and therapeutic process must be distinguished from the assessment and care management task required in Community Care purchasing. Specialist alcohol agencies have traditionally carried out both forms of assessment together and integrated them into the therapeutic task itself. In other words, assessment is seen by treatment providers as an essential and continuing part of the clinical treatment process.

However, alcohol problems can also be defined in terms of needs for social support, health care, and personal skills training. Much recent research suggests that the most important aspects of recovery are social rather than therapeutic. These needs can be assessed without clinical input or expertise. The confusion in the alcohol field concerning the nature of dependency and alcohol problems and the most effective kind of intervention exacerbates the problem of what should be assessed and by whom.

As a basic minimum it is useful for an assessor to have some knowledge of alcohol-related problems and dependence together with knowledge of generic and specialist service provision in order to enable assessment and the matching of needs to available services.

In order to deal with the problem of assessment, local authorities have developed two different ways of responding to alcohol problems. Some local authorities nominate an in-house social worker to make a "purchaser's" assessment of need for residential care and others contract work out to "clinical" or provider specialists. This split in local authority responses highlights a difficulty in distinguishing between an administrative assessment of social and health care needs and a therapeutic assessment of treatment needs.

The theoretical problem of who should carry out this assessment is often determined pragmatically: the degree of expertise the care assessor has determined how much of this assessment he or she carries out and how much is left to the specialist alcohol agencies themselves.

b) What kind of management is most appropriate for alcohol problems: social and health care support and/or counselling and treatment?
The confusion about different types of assessment is again reflected in the controversy concerning whether "treatment" is necessary for alcohol problems or whether health and social care support is sufficient. It is clear that health care support is necessary for detoxification, whether in hospital or supervised in the community by GPs and CPNs. Research indicates that social support is necessary to maintain treatment gains.

Chapter 2 highlights the dual nature of alcohol problems. While both social and health care support is necessary, it is not necessarily sufficient. Health care is necessary for detoxification and social care to prevent relapse, but these may not be effective without therapeutic intervention in between. Research shows that while relapse rates are high, especially, as noted previously, within the first two years following treatment, treatment itself can be effective in one-third of cases, irrespective of the model used. This was discussed in more detail in Chapter 2.

Treatment therefore has a place in the management of alcohol problems, but so do health care and social care, before and after treatment. So it becomes clear that both kinds of management, and therefore also assessment, are necessary:

the administrative kind for assessing social and health care needs before treatment; the clinical kind for assessing treatment needs; and the administrative kind for assessing post-treatment social and health care needs.

c) Community Care, assessment and care management tasks: the purchaser MACAM

The process of assessment and care management will be described in five steps: motivation, assessment, care planning and care management, action, and monitoring. The acronym MACAM will be used to describe the process. This will be referred to as "the purchaser process" in order to distinguish it from the provider task which will be called "the provider process". The latter will be described in Chapter 4.

i) Motivation

Motivating clients and other professionals to use community care procedures involves publishing and making accessible information about available services and the rights of individuals to access these services. This can include health education and health promotion literature, leaflets and information booklets, but perhaps most importantly the ability of care managers to communicate effectively with clients.

There is a lack of specialist knowledge among statutory social workers and care managers alike. Training and information about the needs of people with alcohol problems are therefore essential in order to motivate staff to consider the types of services available and how they locate their clients' needs.

ii) Assessment

Assessment of those with alcohol problems for care in the community is not yet seen as part of the Community Care remit; however, individual authorities are collaborating with health authorities to develop joint working practices.

Assessment is seen as a local authority responsibility within Community Care. The provision of residential care for people with alcohol problems may be regarded as a form of health and social care, as for elderly or disabled people. However, most residential establishments for people with alcohol problems are therapeutic communities often with intensive therapeutic programmes. Assessment is not therefore of the need for residential care but often for a programme of treatment within a structured therapeutic community.

The practical consequences of the conceptual confusion between treatment and other kinds of care have resulted in an anomaly in Community Care assessment as a whole, where people with alcohol problems are assessed in terms of social or health care needs yet destined for intensive therapeutic interventions.

One of the major problems arising as Community Care procedures were applied to residential alcohol treatment centres was that social workers lacked the expertise to determine which clients needed residential care and which did not. Social services' criteria for assessment give guidance concerning who is entitled to assessment, assessment of needs and an assessment of the services necessary to meet these needs. It includes information from a formal assessment interview, the accumulation, with client consent, of previous records and files from other agencies, together with the client's own views and the views of any carers.

The assessor then constructs a care plan based on this assessment, clarifying what services will be provided and how progress will be reviewed. The decision about residential placement will depend on the local authority criteria of resi-dential care and the budget available at that time. The client is then allocated a care manager who will plan and review care. There is much confusion in the alcohol field itself concerning what type of client should be referred to residen-tial care and which should receive help in the community. Some local authorities will assess most referrals from alcohol agencies as entitled to residential care, others are more cautious. The following criteria are those commonly used among alcohol workers themselves to determine suitability.

Failure to modify drinking in previous serious attempts to change drinking in the community is the a major determinant, but social problems such as home-lessness or extensive criminality often serve as motivating factors. The need for a different, structured or drink-free environment or the need for removal from the present environment are often cited, together with the need for stabili-sation (which could be provided by a residential environment). Finally, the need for a supportive, structured group setting and therapeutic support are more specific reasons for referring to residential care.

The range of service provided in residential communities can vary from little more than simple bed-and-breakfast accommodation to intensive therapeutic regimes. The length of stay varies : many will accept clients for more than one period and some also offer temporary, half-way house accommodation and some form of after-care support.

iii) Care planning and care management
The care plan consists of the care the assessor considers necessary in the light of the needs assessment. It can be prepared in discussion with the client, the client then being entitled to this service. If the care plan includes treatment from

a specialist alcohol agency it is likely that the agency will itself carry out a further assessment and care plan for treatment. The care manager also has responsibility to review the service provided to ensure that the client is receiving services outlined in the care plan. She or he is also responsible for ensuring that changing needs are assessed and the care plan consequently updated. This latter responsibility is particularly important when dealing with alcohol problems, as the needs of a client will change before, during, and after treatment.

Care planning involves taking the needs identified by the assessment, agreeing practical objectives to fulfil these needs, and determining how to achieve these objectives efficiently. The implementation of the care plan includes arranging resources and purchasing the appropriate services.

Care managers can be seen to play a supportive or controlling role. The care manager's assessment, care plan, monitoring and reviews should provide a framework for providers. Providers of treatment can then work within this framework to devise and carry out a similar treatment process or "MACAM" involving their own assessment, care plans, action and clinical monitoring and review.

iv) Action
Action involves purchasing and co-ordinating care. It may include purchasing basic health and/or social care, further assessments, and treatment itself. The alternative models and methods of care provided are discussed in the following chapters.

v) Monitoring
Monitoring involves the continued surveillance and support offered by the care manager in order to maintain quality of the delivery of the care plan. The rationale for Community Care planning and management is to introduce a structure into assessment and ongoing care. The structure should be apparent in the recording of cases over time.

Review involves reassessing needs at particular points in the provision of services in order to revise the care plan at specified intervals. This is particularly relevant at treatment completion, where there is an increased need for social support.

Monitoring and review of client progress
Monitoring and review are a particularly crucial part of working with people with alcohol problems because their needs may constantly change. Effective care management would involve an initial assessment of social and health care need followed by the monitoring of progress and a review of changing needs at each stage of the helping process.

Because clients may need health care or social support to stabilise their alcohol use, reviews of social and health care problems give greater understanding of the degree of motivation and the problems underlying alcohol misuse. They should include a review of available resources during detoxification and treatment where appropriate. During detoxification and treatment themselves clients may need specialist medical support, whether on an in-patient or out-patient basis. This is also a period where clients are less able to cope with normal routines and may need basic home help or child care support.

After treatment, clients need a further Community Care assessment, as their social and psychological support needs will increase. This is the stage at which a review is most crucial because, as therapeutic support is withdrawn, social supports are necessary to fill the gap. Relapse is commonplace and gains will be lost if support is not available for a year or so after treatment, particularly at periods of stress and crisis. A review procedure at the end of treatment will help determine whether a further Community Care assessment and basic social and health care provision in the community should form an integral part of the treatment programme. This can involve basic support and maintenance facilities during and after withdrawal or more-complex social support networks and psychological back-up.

Finally, a review of needs in the event of a lapse or relapse can avoid the complete regression to old patterns of drinking behaviour.

Monitoring of agency process

Care managers have a role and responsibility as purchasers and contractors to determine the effectiveness of services. These entail identification of performance indicators and client satisfaction measures. Outcome measures are difficult to determine in the alcohol field as "success" for one agency may be seen in terms of abstinence and for another in terms of controlled drinking and for yet another in terms of improved quality of life and fewer social and health risks.

The outcomes expected by purchasers are often unrealistic if they are not familiar with the rates of successful outcome, relapse and attrition, all of which are considerably higher than for most treatment interventions (see Chapter 2). It is therefore extremely important that care managers have discussions with treatment specialists in order to negotiate acceptable goals and establish acceptable attrition rates. For example, it may be considered enough for a client to attend on a fairly regular basis and that there be an identifiable change in his or her health and social welfare, or drinking patterns.

The priorities of care managers have not necessarily been in harmony with those of agency providers, and the need for accountability to care managers under the NHS and Community Care Act has brought about changes in statutory and non-statutory alcohol agencies. They include changes in aims and objectives, in management, and in monitoring and evaluation. It can be seen that care managers and purchasers require contracting skills, must be able to design a service specification, cost a service, and provide quality assurance, monitoring and evaluation. As many alcohol services are based on models of care that are unknown to non-specialists and are often provided by non-professionals or volunteers the quality of the service becomes particularly relevant.

Care managers therefore have a responsibility to work closely with alcohol agencies to establish agreed goals, to ensure monitoring and evaluation of client progress, and develop agreed outcome and follow-up measures in order to develop competent evaluations of service effectiveness. These data-collection and monitoring systems should be standardised as far as possible to allow comparisons with other agencies and integration with local authority and health authority data. Confidentiality is a particular area of concern in the alcohol field, particularly for those clients with children, and consequently there are serious problems in the development of multi-agency databases.

As care assessment information for residential care remains on local authority records, clients with children can remain very apprehensive about giving information or seeking help if they are not convinced of the confidentiality of the records.

Care managers should monitor the quality of staff performance. Quality of performance can be gauged partly in terms of training and supervision strategies. (It should be noted that recently the quality of training for voluntary counselling in the alcohol field has been improved and this is often linked to local participation in the VACTS scheme for volunteer counsellors and training through local councils on alcohol.) Formal practitioner guidelines outlining the roles and responsibilities of staff in particular situations also give indicators of quality and effectiveness.

Perhaps most importantly, voluntary agencies in the alcohol field should provide clear outlines of policy. Long term agency plans should include developmental strategies to clarify the values and priorities of the agency and outline future directions. The agency policy should also inform purchasers of the management structure and responsibilities of steering/management group members.

Community Care stresses the importance of user involvement and user rights. Care managers should therefore ensure agencies adhere to clear rules of confidentiality and access to information, that they develop literature outlining clients' rights and appropriate mechanisms for user feedback and complaints procedures.

Care management: co-ordinating and managing multidisciplinary care

The new care managers have responsibility for organising care from a range of disciplines, which requires greater knowledge of what might be available for people with alcohol problems and the roles and responsibilities of different professional groups.

The aim of effective co-ordinated multidisciplinary working is particularly important for this client group as alcohol misuse causes a range of different social, psychological and physical problems. Care managers are involved in the co-ordination of other professionals to fulfil care plans; they can mobilise resources and co-ordinate and monitor care.

Working with generic professionals

There is a need for generic professionals to work in conjunction with each other and specialist alcohol agencies. Social and health care workers can provide support facilities ranging from child care, transport, and housing to health care and mental health problems. Specialist agencies can provide treatment and after-care services. (See Chapter 2.)

The following professionals have skills and resources which can be mobilised for working with people with alcohol problems.

a) Generic professionals

The health care profession deal with health problems related to alcohol, including GPs, accident and emergency departments and other acute facilities. The police deal with alcohol-related disability, and hostels for homeless people help accommodate a proportion of clients with alcohol-related problems. The prison service sometimes offers alcohol education groups but perhaps the Probation Service does most to support people with alcohol problems on a long term basis, offering continued monitoring and support and crisis intervention when necessary. Many probation agencies are developing assessment of alcohol problems as an integral part of their overall assessment procedures. In effect, probation could be seen as offering a social work service providing social and psychological support for clients with alcohol problems. (Also see Chapter 8.)

In contrast, as noted earlier, social services have not traditionally played a large part in dealing with alcohol problems. Social workers can offer education, motivational interviewing, and counselling. They can help to motivate clients and teach social and psychological skills, such as relapse prevention. They can also provide advice regarding welfare rights, housing, child care, and financial problems. Social workers, together with health visitors, may also be best placed to identify initial problems and provide support at times of crisis to avoid relapse, as they are among the few workers who visit people in their own homes.

Information about alcohol problems for professionals and clients is available from health promotion officers. There is often a specialist in alcohol problems within each health authority area.

The most important contact for health care is, of course, the local GP who will provide a health check, health care and a prescribing service. The GP may also be able to arrange for a community detoxification to be supervised by him/herself or a community psychiatric nurse.

There may be a specialist psychiatrist available, either attached to a community alcohol team or simply a psychiatrist with an interest in alcohol problems. This is an extremely useful resource as these professionals can also offer detoxification and withdrawal programmes and psychiatric assessment and care. Specialist community alcohol teams often have a psychiatric consultant who will carry out psychiatric and health assessment.

Community psychiatric nurses, health visitors and other qualified nurses provide health care in the community. Some can give prescriptions to clients at home, and a CPN is therefore useful for visiting clients attempting a home detoxification. (This service may also be available through community alcohol teams and health centres.) Psychologists are another appropriate professional group for referral, not only to assess and work with underlying psychological problems but also to develop structured cognitive/behavioural programmes.

b) Specialist care
Specialist care is available from a range of residential and non-residential agencies. Non-residential agencies vary from informal "low threshold" non-statutory provision to statutory community alcohol teams.

A range of services may be provided including:
assessment; health care; social and welfare advice concerning housing, employment, and legal issues; individual counselling; psychotherapeutic interventions;

cognitive behavioural interventions; group work; relapse prevention and after-care; prescribing for withdrawal and/or maintenance; consultancy and co-working.

Community alcohol teams are more likely to provide health and psychiatric care and have a doctor present to prescribe for withdrawal and possibly on a long term basis. Staff may include psychiatrists, doctors, psychologists, social workers, probation officers, and other – unqualified – specialists. They may also use volunteer counsellors. These teams offer a support and training service to generic professionals including social workers. The teams offer to liaise closely with the social service specialists employed to co-ordinate care resources for residential, rehabilitation, and other services. They provide a range of services to clients, though some may concentrate only on referrals.

Non-statutory alcohol services are perhaps more likely to provide social and welfare advice related to housing, employment, and legal issues. The emphasis at most agencies is on one-to-one counselling; "drop-in" clients, assessment and counselling form the major part of the work-load. These agencies also operate as "low-threshold" entry points into other services.

c) Specialist residential services
Many local authorities have drawn up contracts with particular residential services but others are more flexible. There are different kinds of service provision utilising different treatment models. Certain alcohol projects simply offer overnight accommodation whereas others offer highly structured pro-grammes of therapeutic and practical activities, these being interspersed with educational input such as lectures and videos. A few services have a strong Christian element and others are less intense and therapeutic. Many take both drug and alcohol misusers, whereas some specialise in the latter only. Some are based on either the "Twelve Step" or Minnesota model (see Chapter 2) or a form of intense group psychotherapy and counselling. The more therapeutic environments may present a regimented and intrusive regime with little privacy; this does not suit all clients. It is therefore very important to be aware of the type of programme and the content of each service before deciding to refer a particular client. There is a high drop-out rate from these services, espe-cially in the first few weeks. It is therefore essential to inform the clients themselves what to expect before they go and, if possible, arrange preparatory visits.

The length of stay varies from a few weeks to several months or a year or more. Some projects insist on abstinence, requiring that clients are detoxified prior to arrival, others offer detoxification as part of their service. In some instances couples and mothers and children are accepted. The issue of resettlement is important to many, who will offer half-way houses, shared flats and/or continued after-care support. The staffing of these services varies from consultants, psychologists, qualified nurses and social workers to ex-users and volunteers. Most will have access to medical support. As with all residential facilities, levels of staffing often reflect the levels of funding allocated.

It can be seen that the central role of care managers within social services departments is the assessment and co-ordination of client care. Work with people with alcohol problems takes place within a multidisciplinary context, with professionals from health care, social services, Probation Service and non-statutory services working together. Knowledge of different skills, roles and interdisciplinary working relationships is necessary. Each separate discipline will approach problems of alcohol misuse in different ways depending on the objectives and priorities of its particular profession. For example, a general practitioner would concentrate on the health care aspects, whereas a probation officer would concentrate on the implications for offending. These differences in focus and priorities also exist within each profession, thus a member of a child care team in social services would be likely to focus on different aspects of drug and alcohol misuse than those from a member of a mental health team.

In summary, to repeat, it can be seen that it is useful to divide alcohol problems into social and health care needs and treatment needs. The Community Care assessment and care management task can then be used to assess and manage provision of social and health care needs at various stages. The procedure can also be used to identify needs for therapeutic treatment and match clients to the range of models available before further clinical assessment within a particular approach.

Community Care: the way towards an improved alcohol service
a) Assessment and matching clients to a range of services over time
Two conditions are necessary for an effective and comprehensive alcohol service to be developed. First, as recommended in the majority of professional reports, a range or "spectrum" of services is necessary. Second, an independent assessor or independent method of allocation is necessary in order to match the needs of individual clients to the services of different agencies to ensure that the theory and therapeutic approach "fit" the understanding and needs of clients.

Unfortunately, in the past in many local areas there existed one specialist service for people with alcohol problems. This service would work with a specific theoretical model, use a specialised therapeutic approach, and assess all potential clients in terms of its own particular treatment model. While any one particular service is likely to be appropriate and useful to many clients, it does not fulfil the role of a range of services, dealing with different problems.

Research indicates that a variety of theoretical interpretations of problematic drug and alcohol use can offer a range of social and therapeutic "tools" with which to facilitate and maintain therapeutic change. Although it is necessary to provide a structure for assessment and allocation of clients to particular social and health care services, to limit this range of options by theoretical commitment to a limited "treatment" approach, or worse, one particular treatment model, seems nonsensical. A single, dogmatic approach fails to help some people, whereas a more eclectic one allows a "fit" between service provision and different problems in a wider range of situations. The range of services must of course be limited to those with demonstrable effectiveness in the context of recent research.

b) Client choice.

The term "addiction" or dependency means different things to different people: they interpret and experience the phenomenon differently, and therefore it should come as no surprise that no one theory will "fit", or adequately interpret, the different groups or clusters of behaviours and experiences variously described as "addiction". This issue was discussed in more detail in the previous chapter: suffice it to say here that the answer is that some models of addiction and some forms of intervention are useful for some people, but not for others. It can be useful to believe in the disease model if this leads to commitment to abstinence; or alternatively it may be useful to believe one can control one's drinking if embarking on a controlled drinking programme. In the same way, if clients believe their drinking is a response to stress, it may also be useful to receive social support at these times, rather than refer the client to a treatment agency.

Sociological studies have illustrated that imposed "diagnosis" excludes the client from having any influence on the definition of his or her own problem. Diagnosis that purports to be a scientific act could equally well be construed as a social act of assigning people to categories and exercising over them the power of classification. It is implicit in Community Care that clients should have a say in assessments and a choice of service. It is suggested that clients exercise this right in the social assessment procedure in the selection of an approach chosen from a range of services and models of intervention. This is part of the philosophy and understanding of social care, assessment, and care management. When clients are given a clinical assessment or diagnosis for treatment they may be given less say.

It is not unknown for those professionals who adhere to a particular approach or dogma, to oppose alternative forms of treatment and this is the source of their confidence and to some extent their effectiveness; but their activities must be constrained and limited by a more sceptical and pragmatic approach by those in a position to determine the overall pattern of service delivery.

It is fairly clear that it would be extremely difficult for a particular theorist or therapist to place themselves within a larger framework together with other theoretical positions which contradict their own. Therefore it is necessary for an individual "outsider" or "assessor" not working with a particular theory or set of constructs to create and apply a set of criteria for categorising each of the theoretical positions.

c) Care management

Care management and resource allocation depend on clear understanding of a range of models together with an assessment of the relevant individual characteristics, problems and needs. In addition, there is a need for a practical system of administration.

There are serious difficulties in defining the role and necessary credentials of an effective assessor and these have caused some controversy in local authorities across the country. There is clearly a need for some form of an independent assessor to match the models and methods of a range of services to the beliefs and problems of a range of clients. In this way cost effective services can be developed which are appropriate to the needs and likely response of the clients. The task of assessing these needs will clearly be difficult, as it involves both initial assessment and continued monitoring.

For effective matching, the main priorities are understanding and clarification of alternative models and research into individual differences to allow an understanding of criteria for selection and the design of an assessment instrument. Research into the latter is only slowly developing. (See Chapter 2.) However, this is not the only difficulty; there are both bureaucratic and professional constraints. In administrative terms there are extra costs in implementing extensive assessments. In professional terms there are difficulties in achieving assent between existing agencies and professionals to the idea of an external assessor taking over what has been seen for some time as a purely "clinical" role. In practical terms there are also difficulties in training competent, yet neutral, assessors. The difficulties of any one individual making "objective" assessments independent of particular theories are clearly problematic in themselves. There are nevertheless many advantages to a system that allows a choice of social care and treatment interventions.

d) Matching client to services

From the evidence available it seems as if the idea of matching or "fitting" particular theories and methods to particular clients may prove practically and administratively useful. Marlatt (1988: 475), in an article considering the possibilities of matching, has noted two possible advantages of matching clients to interventions. First, this "may enhance motivation for treatment and/or compliance and adherence to the treatment programme, regardless of the eventual outcome", and second, that matching may "enhance treatment efficiency or cost-effectiveness, criteria that have important economic implications for health care delivery".

There are also practical advantages. In Britain today different models of social care and treatment flourish side by side. The Community Care system allows for the best possible use of all by effectively allocating the most suitable clients to each. Whilst matching research is still in its infancy, in the future there is likely to be increasing research evidence for care managers to use to determine the best matches.

Different models suit different clients and have different advantages – for example, the disease model of AA and the Minnesota model provide in-depth counselling and self-help groups which offer consistent ongoing relapse prevention support (see Chapter 2); AA support is free, in the form of a countrywide network of self-help groups. On the other hand, the "controlled drinking" approach may be more accessible to many clients, and the simple provision of social and health care support may be preferable to any treatment.

e) A choice of treatment models

The disadvantages to using any one treatment model are, of course, the constraints that this places on alternative options. The basic premise of AA rules out possible alternatives which theoretically may be equally viable and perhaps with a greater "fit" for some individual experience. If these basic beliefs are accepted, alcohol problems cannot be seen as a disorder of behaviour, so excluding methods which involve helping individuals to learn to control and modify their own behaviour. The same is true for the behavioural approach. If clients accept the initial premise that they can control their own behaviour, they cannot then admit powerlessness and hand themselves over to a "higher power" – which is part of the AA philosophy.

It is likely that, for each particular therapeutic programme to work effectively, clients must believe one interpretation. For cognitive/behavioural programmes clients may need to believe that they have the capacity to control their drinking behaviour. For AA clients, involvement entails belief in their individual pow-erlessness in the face of a disease. If clients at AA continue to believe that their problems are the cause of their alcohol use and that they do not have a primary disease but have merely developed (controllable) drinking behaviours, they are unlikely to benefit from the service offered.

This is not to say that either of these theoretical interpretations is more accurate, useful or "true", but that the addictive-disease model will be of no use unless it is construed by the client as accurate and "true". There is no doubt that the treatment programme carried out by each of the treatment models described in the previous chapter is useful and beneficial to those clients who believe its basic premises and work through the prescribed programme. Though in any treatment regime it is likely that only a third will actually work through the therapeutic programme successfully. (Lindstrom 1992.)

If there is only one alternative for people in any geographical area, or if the system of allocation is fairly arbitrary, it is possible that there may be serious disadvantages for some clients if allocated to particular "badly matched" models. For example, the disease model may reinforce failure, and a "slip" becomes defined as a "relapse" rather than a lapse to be used as a learning experience. Similarly, behavioural/cognitive models may fail to take into account the seriousness of a lapse for someone with an advanced physiological addiction or someone with a strong belief in the disease model.

In order to take advantage of many different solutions we repeat that it is important not to be constrained by any one theoretical or professional approach. To do this it would be necessary to categorise theories within a larger framework, in terms of the appropriateness of each for particular psychologi-cal, social and health problems, including dependency.

At present we have limited information about the range of models or the signif-icance of individual differences. Information concerning process and outcome would allow greater awareness of the clinical and social advantages of different models. Researchers will also then be in a better position to clarify and classify models and so study the relevance of individual differences to each.

The implications of these conclusions for policy development can be seen in terms of the avoidance of rigid ideological or theoretical commitments. The role of the care managers makes them ideally placed to institute a system of assessment and allocation of clients to treatment (independently of the beliefs of particular therapists).

Although it has been argued here that a broader approach to understanding and managing addiction would be useful, this area has only recently become the focus of research interest. It would therefore be foolish to dispense with notions of treatment. If the field of drug and alcohol use dispenses entirely with the concepts of diagnosis and treatment it is doubtful whether there would be an adequate theoretical structure for the identification, assessment and allocation of clients to replace them. Community Care assessment allows for the development of a procedure preceding and perhaps following the specific treatment assessment. It is this new framework that provides an opportunity to develop a comprehensive system integrating social care and social theories of addiction with treatment and medical/therapeutic approaches.

Chapter 4
The Social Work Provider:
A Therapeutic and Social Care Role

Introduction: helping people with alcohol problems
This chapter is concerned with methods and processes in helping people with alcohol problems. These methods can include the health and social care needs of clients, and the more complex therapeutic needs. Social work providers are ideally placed to contribute both aspects of a comprehensive alcohol service, as their education, training, and experience includes both social support and a counselling function.

There is no doubt that social workers have the appropriate skills for working with people with alcohol problems, but research has indicated that there is a lack of confidence among generic workers as a whole in this field. An important study carried out by Shaw and colleagues has identified three areas of concern amongst generic professionals working with problematic drinkers. The first was "role adequacy", professionals felt they lacked the information and skills necessary to respond to drinkers. The second was "role legitimacy", they were uncertain as to what extent it was their task to deal with these clients. Third was "role support", they were unsure where to seek advice and where and how to refer for specialist help (Shaw *et al*. 1978).

The majority of social workers have a good understanding of short-term crisis intervention, task-centred work, systems thinking, and structured counselling skills. These skills can be used as an integral part of working with clients who misuse alcohol. What is needed is an awareness of which generic skills and methods are appropriate for working with this client group. If social workers apply their own education, training and experience to work with clients with alcohol problems they will find they can develop effective change programmes themselves.

In order to work with clients as a provider, the social worker needs an understanding, not only of different models of therapeutic change, but also of which general social work methods and skills can be most helpful at different times in the helping process; whether before, during, or after treatment, if treatment has been offered.

Many of the methods used by specialist alcohol workers will be familiar to social workers. They can therefore effectively utilise the skills they already have in this setting. The sequence of intervention is dependent on bolting on two elements to the beginning and the end of general counselling practice: first, at the beginning, motivation; and second, at the end, maintenance or relapse prevention.

These elements are critical when working with people with alcohol problems. Clients are likely to fail to change in the first place if counselling takes place when they are unmotivated and they are likely to relapse if there is no relapse prevention, in terms of developing social support networks and coping skills.

Two effective methods have been developed to deal with these two problematic areas. The Motivational Change Model of Miller and Prochaska and DiClemente, and the Relapse Prevention Model of Marlatt and colleagues. Both have been developed specifically for work with substance misusers and can be used independently of any particular model or aim of intervention.

Assessment:distinguishing between assessment for (Community Care) purchasing and assessment for treatment

Two forms of assessment can be used when working with clients with drinking problems.

Assessment for care management: the care plan

It is possible that an initial assessment and care management plan has been prepared in advance by social services within the Community Care framework (see Chapter 3). It is also possible that a social worker could refer the client for guidance on eligibility for assessment. If a Community Care assessment is available it is useful, but not in itself sufficient, for provider purposes. It is therefore necessary for social workers to carry out a further assessment in order to inform the counselling change process itself.

If a Community Care assessment has not been carried out, this may be because the client was not considered appropriate for residential provision. In many local authorities, social services involvement with alcohol misuse largely focuses on those clients who require residential care and those drinkers whose children could be at risk. It may be difficult to obtain social and health care support in the community in some areas through this route. In some localities specialist alcohol services are financed by local authorities and staffed by social workers; in other areas all specialist services are health authority based and/or located in voluntary agencies with little funding or expertise. Health authority based services tend to be referral only, whereas those financed by social services or voluntary agencies are perhaps more likely to take self-referrals. (See Chapter 3.)

If a Community Care assessment of need and care plan are available, they provide a useful foundation for therapeutic assessment at each of the four stages of the therapeutic process.

a) Motivation
A review of social and health problems gives a greater understanding of the degree of motivation and the problems underlying alcohol misuse.

b) Treatment
A review of social and health care needs and resources will include social support available during detoxification and treatment, but more importantly identify particular needs during detoxification, if that is required.

c) Maintenance
This is the stage at which a review of the need for health care and social support is most crucial. As therapeutic support is withdrawn, social supports are necessary to take over this role, particularly in the first year or so. Maintenance therefore involves offering social and financial support and helping clients develop effective social supports themselves. It is as important to strengthen clients' skills as it is to strengthen the supports in the environment. This involves helping clients develop behavioural control skills, particularly those of relapse prevention, together with anxiety and anger management.

d) Relapse intervention
At times of crisis or in the event of a lapse, immediate support can avoid the often rapid relapse to old patterns of drinking.

Effective care management would involve an initial assessment of need followed by the monitoring of progress and a review of changing needs at each stage of the process. It is possible that clients will not have the benefit of a care manager, especially if they have not been referred for residential care.

Assessment for therapeutic change: the treatment plan
The second form of assessment is a therapeutic one. This can be carried out by a social worker or specialist alcohol agency. In the past, the Community Care assessment and care plan formed an indistinguishable part of the therapeutic assessment and care process. In many authorities these tasks are still carried out together by specialist alcohol workers. However, the Community Care procedures described in the previous chapter indicate changes in this approach, highlighting the role of social services in assessing social and health care need. It is therefore necessary to emphasise that, although an assessment of both therapeutic need and health/social care need is necessary, neither alone is sufficient. It is essential that both aspects of care are available throughout the helping process and therefore that both types of assessment take place at each of the four stages. If a care manager does not carry out half of this assessment, it is necessary for the social work provider (or specialist) to carry out both parts.

The sequential social work provider process: a framework for action

This chapter offers a simple, straightforward framework for intervention. This helping framework will be labelled the "provider process" in order to distinguish it from both the purchasing process (Chapter 3) and the treatment component in isolation (Chapter 2). The provider process incorporates the treatment component of care but involves the social work provider in the provision of a much more comprehensive service. This service includes therapy and continuing social care, in order to provide an overall package for the management of alcohol problems in the community.

The provider framework consists of a sequence of four stages. Each stage has an integral assessment. The first, *motivation*, consists of an assessment of motivation and motivational interviewing. The second, the *treatment or counselling for change process*, includes assessment of change and action for treatment or counselling for change. The third stage is *maintenance*, which includes *assessment* for maintenance of change and the *actual* maintenance of change. Finally, *relapse intervention* consists of assessment for intervention at relapse and return to change, and maintenance of it.

As shown in the following framework there are four main components in the treatment process, each involving the preparation of therapeutic intervention plans to help people change and/or maintain change. Each intervention plan should be based on a separate assessment. The assessment grids for each phase are illustrated on the right of the framework. These help clarify the client's needs and potential resources at each stage.

FRAMEWORK

INTERVENTION	ASSESSMENT GRID
a) Motivational interviewing	Assess for motivation
b) The treatment/ counselling for change process	Assess for treatment/ counselling for change
c) Maintenance of change	Assess for maintenance of change
d) Relapse intervention	Assess for reintervention and return to change

Practical guidelines: an overview of the assessment and helping process
These four stages of intervention and the methods used at each stage are based
loosely on the counselling frameworks of authors such as Truax & Carkhuff
(1967), Kanfer & Gaelick (1986) and Egan (1990); together with the motivational and process theories of Prochaska & DiClemente (1982, 1983, 1986,
1994) and Miller (1983); and the relapse prevention and intervention strategies
of Marlatt & Gordon (1985) and Wilson (1992).

The first three sources emphasise the need for a structured counselling process
and highlight consecutive stages of help. Specialists working with people who
experience problems with drinking and smoking have added two important
stages at the beginning and end of the general counselling framework. Prochaska
& DiClemente and Miller emphasise the need at the very start of the process to
motivate and assess motivational stage; Marlatt & Gordon and Wilson stress the
need at the end of the process to support and maintain clients and intervene
promptly after a crisis or lapse to prevent a complete relapse. At each stage a
distinct type of counselling, care, and support is required and is a prerequisite to
a separate assessment.

A useful counselling framework is that of Gerard Egan (1990). Egan's general
model of counselling provides the basic core tasks for working with people
with alcohol problems. The two additional components are preliminary motivation and post-treatment maintenance.

a) Motivation
Prochaska & DiClemente's model of motivation and that of Miller's motivational interviewing can be used to help assessment and increase motivation in
the early stages.

b) Treatment (counselling framework)
This involves the definition and clarification of problems, using the counselling skills of listening, reflecting, paraphrasing, open-ended questions, and
appropriate body language and eye contact. This is then followed by the development of goals and the planning of strategies, using the counselling skills of
confrontation, challenging and suggesting different frames of reference,
keeping communication concrete and to the point. Finally, the action phase
involves using the counselling skills of support, advice and encouragement,
and practical help. (Egan 1990.)

Egan's three stages also correspond roughly to the different stages of motivational interviewing, with the earlier reflective and non-directive counselling
preceding the more confrontative later stages. (Prochaska & DiClemente 1986.)

c) Maintenance (relapse prevention)

Models of relapse prevention and community support can be used to help develop the skills and social networks necessary to maintain treatment change.

d) Relapse intervention

Procedures for prompt intervention in the event of a crisis or lapse can help prevent complete relapse.

This sequence, or continuum of change, will probably occur more than once in the course of a client's life; research is limited but estimates vary from three to seven as an average number of times to complete the cycle before achieving permanent change. (Prochaska & DiClemente 1982.)

Generic counselling skills are familiar to social workers. These can be used for different tasks: for the motivation stage, when attempting to understand the client and develop a working relationship; for assessments when understanding problems and needs; for helping clients to work out what choices are available to them, making decisions about which goals to choose and develop strategies for achieving these goals; for helping clients change cognitions and control behaviours; and finally, for teaching social and relapse-prevention skills and for helping the client put these plans into action.

It is important to note that motivation and motivational assessment should occur before assessment for change. It is also possible that assessment and preparations for maintenance of change will need to take place before change itself.

The process does not end when the change has been achieved. Clients should return for regular follow-up sessions and also when they relapse or have difficulties that may lead to relapse; this must be seen to be expected and is an integral part of helping. A working relationship may involve supporting the client through this sequence many times.

THE FOUR STAGES

The four stages of the sequential framework will be dealt with in turn. The type of assessment appropriate to each stage will be outlined first, followed by an overview of intervention methods.

a) Motivation

This is the first step of the four-stage process. It involves linking the client in and should take place before assessment for change, in order to ensure co-operation. Linking in and motivating the client involves clarifying the service to be provided, that is, saying to a client "these things are available if you have a problem and want to take advantage of them."

Prochaska first published "Systems of Psychotherapy: A Transtheoretical Perspective" in 1979. This was followed by his work with DiClemente to develop the idea of Transtheoretical Therapy (Prochaska & DiClemente 1982) and in 1983 they produced their much quoted paper "Stages and processes of self-change of smoking: Toward a more integrative model of change". At the same time W. R. Miller developed the concept of motivational interviewing. Both concepts were based on ideas about change processes and stages of change. Miller's work was published in Behavioural Psychotherapy in 1983 and again (with Sovereign and Krege) in 1987.

Miller *et al.* (1988) suggest that motivation can be increased by enhancing the client's self-esteem and self-efficacy and highlighting discrepancies between the present and how the client wants things to be. Basic client-centred counselling skills of unconditional positive regard, understanding and empathy can help increase self-esteem, and cognitive skills of providing alternative frameworks or scenarios can help highlight discrepancies.

Miller & Sovereign (1989) describe several counselling techniques useful for motivating people to change, from giving feedback to clients, giving them responsibility for their own decision to change, taking a non-confrontational stance and providing pragmatic alternatives. Miller discusses the means of increasing motivation in terms of eliciting self-motivational statements from the client. (Miller 1983.)

These methods of interviewing and counselling in the field were developed in the 1980s using notions of individual change processes, apparently in the absence of any coherent theory or testable hypotheses (*British Journal of Addiction* letters and articles 1992-3), yet they were tremendously popular among practitioners and spread rapidly in the early 1990s. These ideas were popularised and now form a base for specialist and non-specialist training in Britain (Aquarius, "Managing Drink") and in counselling techniques themselves (Davidson *et al.*). The two main criticisms of this model are the lack of a theory of motivation and difficulty in distinguishing the particular stages of change.

i) Motivational stage: assessment.
The aim of an assessment at this stage is simply to determine level of motivation for change: the process also serves to link a client into the change process and motivate further. In other words, this initial stage of the change process involves identifying the degree of motivation and if possible increasing it. Both of these objectives can be achieved by utilising the techniques of motivational interviewing described in the "change process" by Prochaska and DiClemente. This model of change involves determining if the client is in the "pre-contemplation",

"contemplation" or " action" stage and tailoring the counselling response accordingly. The use of this method can increase both understanding and motivation prior to assessment. See Chapter 5 and Barber (1995) and Velleman (1994) for an indepth discussion on these stages.

ii) Motivational stage: therapeutic intervention
The main task at this stage is to build understanding and trust. This is done by listening to clients' views of their problems and being clear-cut about one's own professional position.

It is particularly necessary to develop the relationship between yourself and your client by clarifying what you can and cannot do. This stage should be designed to remove any blocks to client help-seeking by establishing rules of confidentiality and clarification of professional responsibilities regarding children or criminal activities.

The first step is to greet the client non-judgementally and make them feel at ease. This is particularly important with alcohol problems as many clients do not recognise their drinking as a problem and may be reluctant to involve social workers in this area of their lives. As Prochaska and DiClemente point out, it may be necessary for the worker to raise the issue and lead the client to consider possible links between drinking and other problems. This shift from general social topics to alcohol consumption could be made by discussing the possible contribution of alcohol to the overall picture of general problems, so raising awareness of the issue and the social worker's involvement.

It is also useful to give clients education materials and encourage them to weigh up the pros and cons of alcohol use and come to a decision to change their behaviour as a consequence. It is important to give clear information about services and resources available and the punitive or controlling elements involved in the professional relationship.

In essence, the motivation stage includes demonstration of the qualities of empathy, respect and genuineness, together with active listening, feedback, and encouraging the client to disclose information. It involves non-confrontative body language, appropriate eye contact and reflective body language.

It is important to concentrate, to ask open-ended questions, identify significant issues, ask for specific detail, and prevent too many deviations in the conversation. An integral part of the early non-directive stage is to remain silent for much of the time and allow the client to fill awkward pauses. Feedback involves paraphrasing what the client has said and it is most effective when it is specific and identifies significant issues. The object of paraphrasing is to avoid misunderstandings and to clarify issues; it also serves as a clear indication to the client that you are listening and taking seriously what is said. Feedback also includes positive and empathetic responses in terms of attempting to understand what the client may have felt in certain situations and asking specific questions about emotional states. Summarising is similar to paraphrasing but can be used specifically to clarify what has occurred so far and to determine what issue or direction should be pursued next.

It can be seen that much work on motivating clients focuses on non-directional or reflective counselling styles, emphasising client-centred techniques. These facilitate the next step of treatment itself.

b) Treatment.

Having assessed the client's motivation it is then possible to start the beginning of "treatment" or counselling for change, if this is felt to be appropriate. Models of treatment have been discussed in the previous chapter; the methods of achieving therapeutic or behaviour change are however often similar across different models, both AA groups and controlled drinking groups using cognitive behavioural techniques of change.

i) Treatment stage: assessment for therapeutic change.

This assessment requires a further assessment grid (see p72) in order to determine the ability of the client to change, obstacles to change, and the client's own resources for change. This assessment will need to include identification of what the client will need in order to change. This is a longer assessment of the client's needs and his or her personal resources. It is used to establish both the client's problems and needs and his or her capacity for change and consequent needs.

This assessment is then used as the basis for negotiation of aims, client and worker agreeing on short and long term objectives. The plan includes prioritising needs and setting practical goals within the resources available. It includes developing alternatives to present drinking, for example, offering alternative solutions to problems such as depression, loneliness or boredom by providing the necessary resources and developing different social support networks.

Although a Community Care assessment may well have been carried out before assessment for treatment needs, it is important to stress that this procedure relies on the client's participation and involvement. This takes time when working with alcohol-related problems, where "denial" or disagreements between clients and professionals are not uncommon. It has therefore been recommended that assessment of motivation should take place before an in-depth assessment. It is also possible that part of assessment will consist in self-monitoring and this too requires co-operation and motivation by the client.

Assessment not only comes after motivation but also continues throughout the helping process. In other words, it is an integral part of that process as a whole. It contributes to motivation by enabling the client to understand their problems better; it encourages the identification and understanding of alcohol use as a problem and/or the recognition that it causes other problems; it helps the client to understand the reasons for alcohol use and the problems that underlie and perpetuate it. Assessment can include interviews, questionnaires, diaries and observation.

The main focus of assessment is traditionally seen in terms of amounts drunk and frequency of drinking as these are perhaps the easiest variables to measure. However, patterns and context of drinking may be far more significant in explaining or predicting problematic use. A comprehensive drinking history should also provide information about patterns and the context of drinking. In this way a picture can be assembled of the kind of alcohol misuse that has occurred in a person's life and an indication of the antecedents and consequences of periods of problematic misuse.

Assessment for cognitive/behavioural control programmes covers three main areas: the events that lead up to episodes of alcohol misuse (antecedents); the behaviour beliefs or cognitions that mediate use; and the consequences of misuse. Each individual assessment should therefore include a detailed review of the client's drinking behaviour in the context of the individual and social factors that cause and reinforce drinking behaviour. This is probably best achieved by asking a client to keep a diary of a week's drinking and then discussing each drinking episode in some detail. (See also Chapter 8.)

In addition, assessment should include the psychological, social and physical problems that may be related to alcohol use and an indication of whether these are a consequence of misuse or actually contribute to the drinking. Finally, an assessment should identify if there are signs of physical and psychological dependence. This will encompass: present drinking (amount, frequency, patterns, context, social and individual antecedents and consequences); the history of drinking (amount, frequency, patterns, context); problems leading to alcohol misuse (social, psychological, health); problems arising from alcohol misuse (social, psychological, health); and finally, level of dependency, if any.

If health care needs are identified at the assessment stage, a referral to a GP is the essential first step. The GP is likely to provide a useful contribution to the overall assessment, particularly if blood tests identify health problems, and may also be prepared to prescribe or provide community detoxification or refer to a detoxification service.

Detoxification

If necessary, social workers should refer clients to their GPs or a specialised alcohol team for detoxification. It may be necessary for some clients to be detoxified before using help effectively. This is, of course, only necessary for those who are physically addicted. The aim of detoxification is usually abstinence or at least a period of abstinence. Detoxification regimes can also be used to transfer the client from alcohol to benzodiazopines or simply to reduce the tolerance levels and amount drunk.

If a client has been a heavy drinker over a long period of time, it is safer to admit for in-patient detoxification, but there is increasingly an option of supervised community detoxification, involving an out-patient prescribing regime.

It is important to note that assessment at this stage should be designed to achieve a plan which results in identifying achievable practical short term goals. Progress should be monitored and short term goals renegotiated on the basis of progress made or of failure to achieve these goals and client readiness for decisions and action.

Finally, an integral part of assessment for treatment is helping the client decide on treatment goals. The changes clients' choose to make to their drinking habits can vary from giving up alcohol completely to trying to control their use. Clients will also need to make many other changes to their lifestyles, learning new skills and constructive coping strategies (not involving alcohol). A range of needs should be identified at this stage including necessary changes to drinking behaviour, changes to lifestyle, and improvements in personal coping skills.

(ii) Treatment stage: therapeutic intervention

There are a range of possible interventions for treatment and they can involve the structured treatment programmes discussed in the previous chapter, or a structured programme of therapeutic change, supervised by the social worker. If social workers decide to refer clients for treatment, they are still likely to be involved in the motivation stage and in the maintenance and relapse intervention stages after it. It is often assumed that a specialist agency, GP or psychiatric consultant will provide an overall package, but it is unusual for motivation and relapse prevention to form an equal and integral part of the treatment programme itself.

i) Cognitive/behavioural techniques and psychotherapy
Social work education and training includes a basic grounding in psychology and counselling skills. In addition, most social workers have experience of working with clients under stress and at periods of crisis in their lives.

Social workers are therefore ideally placed to structure and support a client through the therapeutic change process and to help teach new behaviours and new skills. They are familiar with assessment and setting a series of concrete goals. Some social workers use cognitive behavioural techniques to change attitudes and beliefs, modify behaviours, and for monitoring behaviour and behaviour change.

ii) The 12 step programme
This is not designed as a professional intervention and if social workers feel that this is best for their clients they should refer to a Minnesota treatment agency or advise the client to attend AA. The average length of attendance at AA is six years, so it is clear that the programme itself is orientated towards after-care and relapse prevention. The social worker can co-work with AA and Minnesota agencies to ensure that the client has further social, health care and counselling support.

iii) Skills teaching
Social workers often have practical experience of a range of useful techniques for teaching new skills to clients, such as anxiety management, anger control and helping clients how to control thoughts and behaviours and develop new coping skills for living without alcohol.

iv) Practical help
Social workers have expertise in social care: housing liaison work, welfare rights, assisting with financial problems, and in linking clients with a wide range of resources in other agencies. Systems thinking and network approaches encourage wide-ranging and effective use of available resources. Social workers are therefore ideally placed to help the client solve underlying problems which may be contributing or maintaining alcohol use.

Monitoring and review of client progress are an integral part of all stages, but are particularly necessary in the treatment stage as the client may not be able to make changes immediately or achieve goals set. It is often necessary to re-negotiate goals and this can only be done effectively if set objectives are closely monitored.

c) Maintenance

The change process should not be undertaken without the inclusion of an integral maintenance plan. These processes overlap as the maintenance of change is intricately interlinked with the change itself: first, planning for maintenance of change must take place during the initial change phase; second, the client is likely to relapse and return from the maintenance to the change phase several times. The maintenance plan must form a continuation of the change process or relapse is the most probable outcome within two years.

Maintenance of change is concerned with preventing the situation deteriorating again. After-care maintenance consists in making the most of the client's coping skills and social supports in the environment. Preparation for maintenance of change often takes place before the end of intervention. (See also Chapter 3.)

i) Assessment for maintenance

This is a secondary assessment of social support systems and other individual resources/skills. It is carried out in order to establish the client's needs after changing behaviour. It also includes assessing progress made in treatment to make sure that the client has solved any underlying problems contributing to drinking and has a clear understanding of vulnerabilities to alcohol misuse in the future.

Continued assessment (monitoring and review) is essential to enable early intervention if the client's situation deteriorates. Monitoring also allows the worker to evaluate their own work. Monitoring of progress is essential at this stage, to enable preventive action or early intervention to prevent full-blown relapses.

Monitoring can involve self-monitoring by the client and/or worker monitoring the client's progress in order to modify interventions, change goals, and increase support and resources, where necessary. It should also include the worker monitoring and evaluating their own input (with individual clients, with the agency population, and with the targeted population as a whole).

ii) Interventions for maintenance

Following the assessment of personal needs and skills and social resources this stage then consists in preparing the client's social environment and developing personal skills (including cognitive/behavioural relapse prevention).

The treatment stage usually involved changes, not only in clients' drinking but in other aspects of their lives. The social worker will help clients develop a new lifestyle to prevent relapse; the worker will then monitor clients' progress in order to offer ongoing support and to be available quickly in case they lapse or relapse to dangerous patterns of alcohol use. Action here therefore involves a regular series of contacts and appointments to support and monitor the client's progress.

A programme of after-care support

Therefore a good programme could include ongoing support on a regular basis and clear guidelines for a repeat care plan, if the client lapses or relapses. It may involve the development and maintenance of family, social and community support systems and alternative occupations. It should incorporate the identification of potential high risk relapse situations, cognitive behavioural techniques for relapse prevention, and social skills training. Finally, it should encourage diversionary activities and the development of new social networks such as the development of leisure interests and social contacts.

Cognitive behavioural methods can also be used to maintain change and prevent serious relapse after a lapse. That is, they can be used to help maintain abstinence within a 12 step approach or to maintain controlled drinking. These involve the setting of a series of concrete goals, monitoring behaviour change and self-monitoring by the client. They also include identification of high risk potential relapse situations, cognitive behavioural skills for coping, and avoiding relapse and actual relapse intervention.

For a full description of the role of cognitive behavioural techniques in relapse prevention and relapse intervention see Marlatt & Gordon (1980), Marlatt & George (1984), Marlatt & Gordon (1985).

d) Relapse intervention

The immediate necessity in the event of a crisis or relapse is to be available to the client and offer the same services as before. This can then be followed by the opportunity to re-enter the change process. Relapse can mean anything from a single drink to a complete return to old drinking lifestyles and patterns of behaviour and physical dependencies. It is therefore important to determine its extent before acting further. A reassessment of the client's behaviour and circumstances is necessary.

i) Assessment

Assessment should be immediate and focus on the seriousness of the event; relapse is an extremely vague overarching term. It is essential to assess the type and seriousness of the "relapse" before intervention. The assessment should also include a review of the situation and reasons for relapse; the event can then be seen and used by the client as a learning experience, rather than a failure.

ii) Relapse interventions

Speed is the essence of effective relapse intervention; the earlier a situation is recognised the less likely the client will have completely relapsed. It should have been emphasised in the earlier stages of the therapeutic process that relapse is not a failure but an expected part of the change process. The client will then be more likely to turn to the worker quickly if they need help.

This continued support (regular phone calls, meetings and/or group support) and immediate availability at relapse should be built into the after-care phase. At present it is not uncommon for client and worker to see the end of a treatment phase as the final "outcome", and therefore feel any relapse is a failure and should be disguised from the worker. This mistake stems from the notion of "treatment" as a distinct programme with a clear end point, rather than treatment for a re-occurring problem, where there is no "outcome" as such, only a continued monitoring of progress and availability of support when necessary.

A summary of relevant social work skills

a) Counselling and cognitive behavioural techniques.

Counselling and cognitive behavioural techniques are an integral part of social work. These can be used at all four stages: firstly during motivational inter-viewing, secondly as part of the change process itself, thirdly for maintenance of change, and finally for relapse intervention.

b) Dealing with social problems

It may be useful at different stages in the helping process, though perhaps most helpful at the maintenance stage, to deal with social problems, because the majority of relapses are associated with social factors.

As noted previously the strategies include support and help with housing issues, welfare rights, child care problems, and developing contacts with agencies that have appropriate resources, together with helping the client solve practical underlying problems which may be contributing to or maintaining alcohol use. Also helping the client to modify their own environment so it becomes less stressful and to reduce the number and frequency of known antecedents for relapse. Finally, an integral part of dealing with social problems includes the development of new leisure facilities, social contacts, and support networks.

c) Helping to learn new social and life skills

Again this is probably most useful for maintaining change, as relapse often occurs when clients cannot cope with problematic relationships or emotions.

It is therefore useful to help the client learn skills and strategies for coping without alcohol and to develop self-confidence and self-control. These skills and strategies could include assertiveness training, anger control, self-control skills, and stress-management techniques.

Chapter 5
Young People

Adolescence and Attitudes to Youthful Drinking

Adolescence has been described in a variety of ways, but it is generally seen as a "period of psychological development unique from other developmental phases" (Muisener 1994 : 58). It is seen as spanning the time from puberty – often generalised as beginning around 12 – to incorporation of an adult identity which occurs somewhere after the age of 19 (Cole & Weissberg 1994, Reilly *et al.* 1994). Definitions include biological, social, cultural and developmental factors. Biologically, adolescence involves physical development such as the production of secondary sex characteristics. Socially, adolescents are experiencing changes related to differences in expectations of children and adults. Peer relationships take on added significance and, psychologically, adolescents are adjusting to changes in their bodies and in social expectations, while adult cognitive processes are beginning to develop (Reilly *et al.* 1994).

Opinions vary as to whether adolescence is a time of deep emotional upheaval or a more "normal" stage of psychological development, with behaviour seen as little different to that of adults (Ostrov & Howard 1981, Hodgman 1983). What is clear is that use and misuse of alcohol by adolescents is a multifaceted matter. As Muisener succinctly states:–

"Teenagers with [alcohol] problems vary in gender, psychological make up, family background, peer affiliation, ethnicity and socio economic status. . . . Due to this heterogenity there is a need for diversity in ways of understanding adolescent [alcohol] use and a need for translating these diverse understandings into relevant [helping] approaches."
Muisener 1994 : XV)

Because we believe that:–

"Alcohol use and abuse among adolescents has [sic] been well documented, as have the behavioural, psychological and social consequences. Yet, much less attention has been paid to specific adolescent needs. . . . There has been little recognition of the differences between the needs of adolescents and those of adults, with much less research in and . . . attention to adolescent alcohol [use and] abuse."
Rickel & Becker-Lausen 1994 : 75)

When considering adolescent drinking in the United Kingdom it is difficult to avoid media hype which has clamoured for many years about "tipsy teenagers", "teeny tipplers", and "boozing kids" (Dorn 1983). "The impression is given that 'the problem' is increasing in size and is one in which youthful drinking and public disorder are closely linked" (Dorn 1983 : 4). Therefore, "moral panic" sees adolescent drinking as part of an overall breakdown in discipline and in the fabric of society (Cohen 1971). However, such fears are not new. Consider this:

> *"Legislation at the turn of the century signalled widespread worry about the exposure of children to alcohol. The very purpose of the formation of the Band of Hope was the instruction of boys and girls on the properties of alcohol and its consumption and by 1901 it was reported that in the United Kingdom there were 28,894 local societies, with a total member-ship of 3,536,000 boys and girls."* (BMA 1986 : 1)

Well, if concern about youthful drinking is not new then the availability of relevant research evidence is a recent phenomenon. There has been a tendency to see *all* youthful drinking as problematic, especially that which takes place collectively and in public places. However, recent research has rightly located youthful drinking "in the more general context of the use (and misuse) of . . . substances by society at large" (Plant & Plant 1992 : 13).

Alcohol is a legal drug. It is readily available to all adults; it costs relatively little and prices remain relatively low; it is used by adults to celebrate the happy occasions, to drown sorrows on the sad occasions; it is used to relax either at home or by a visit to the local pub or club. While legal restraints are imposed upon when and where adolescents may drink alcohol, they grow up in a drinking society, a society "in which drinking is both widely practised and generally regarded as a legitimate and enjoyable activity" (Plant & Plant 1992 : 19). The mass media actively promote the use of alcohol; it is often associated with power, status, conviviality, sexuality, attractiveness, popularity, and achievement. On television, elaborate and well-researched adverts extol the virtues of drink, while drinking occasions are regularly portrayed positively and at length in both drama and soap opera. Sports teams regularly wear strips sponsored by lager and beer firms. Almost all adults drink on at least an occasional basis. Most young people in Britain have parents who are drinkers and they are likely to come into contact with other adults who drink. Drink is readily available to them. However, it is perhaps appropriate to recall Ritson's wise words when he states:–

> *"We should remember that the vast majority of adolescents acquire responsible, pleasurable drinking and that literature throughout history is scattered with references to the deplorable behaviour of the younger generation which often reveals more about the memory and selective perception of adults then it does about the young."*

Ritson 1983 : 108-9)

Indeed, there is evidence that the "moral panic" about drinking by young people does "not reflect significant increases in levels of alcohol related problems amongst the young. Sometimes they even occur at times when youthful drinking habits are stable or when alcohol consumption may be declining" (Fossey *et al.* 1996 : 54). In fact, the overall evidence indicates that the majority of young people consume alcohol in moderation and "that drinking habits amongst British teenagers have remained relatively stable during the past ten years" (Fossey *et al.* 1996 : 61).

Children's Perceptions of Alcohol, Adults Attitudes to Children and Alcohol

Studies have suggested that most young children learn about alcohol at home and many have clear impressions of alcohol well before they start school. In 1972 Jahoda and Cramond studied a group of 6- to 10-year-olds in Glasgow. Two-fifths of 6-year-olds could identify alcoholic drinks by their smell and three-fifths could do so before the age of 10. These children also could perceive drunken behaviour in a film as being associated with alcohol. Most of them had had contact with intoxicated adults, while girls received less adult encouragement to drink than boys (Jahoda & Crammond 1972). More recent studies in the early and mid-1990s by Fossey confirmed these findings, but indicated that young children aged 5 to 10 years had developed greater knowledge and awareness in identifying alcohol and in recognising drunken behaviour. The children equated consumption of alcohol with drunkenness, regardless of the actual amount consumed, and disapproved of such behaviour (Fossey 1994). Interestingly, adults seem to underestimate children's understanding of the distinctiveness of alcohol and its effects, believing that this occurs at, or above, the age of 12 (Aitken & Leathar 1981).

Adults seem to have harsher and more restrictive attitudes to the age at which children should drink which do not match their actual actions. "In one study, for example, almost half [of the adult sample] said children under 18 should not be allowed to taste alcohol drinks and [between a half and one-third] said children under 18 should not be allowed drinks of their own at home with their parents. Given that most children have at least tasted alcoholic drinks in the company of their parents by the age of 10 and the majority have had small drinks of their own in the company of their parents by the age of 14 these findings point to an inconsistency between actual and recommended parental practice." (Aitken & Leathar 1981 : XIV.)

Teenage Drinking Habits

Aitken (1978) examined the drinking habits of 10- to 14-year-olds in the Central Region of Scotland, with most of these children having consumed alcohol and having done their first drinking at their parents' homes, while girls reported their first drinking experience at a later stage than boys. Thus for most adolescents the family exerted a strong influence on their use and perception of alcohol (Swadi 1988).

Davies and Stacey (1972) conducted a study of 14- to 17-year-olds in Scotland. This revealed that, by the age of 14, almost all of the boys and the vast majority of girls had tried alcohol. By 17 only 2% of boys and 4% of girls had not tried alcohol. Attitudes towards alcohol were positive: taking it was seen as a "grown up" and prestigious thing to do. By 17, most boys and girls had drunk alcohol in pubs or dance halls. Drinking was approved of by peers and seen as "tough", "mature" and "sociable". Hawker's (1978) survey of over 7,000 young people aged 13 to 18 in England confirmed Davies and Stacey's findings, with many young people becoming regular drinkers in their early teens. Other, more recent studies have confirmed the earlier findings, indicating that around one-third of boys and girls are drinking regularly by the age of 14 and 15 (Marsh *et al.* 1986, Plant *et al.* 1990, Plant & Foster 1991, Loretto 1994, Newcombe *et al.* 1995). This is not necessarily a cause for alarm because, in Ritson's words:–

"Adolescence is a time of transition and experiment. The young person tries out various forms of identity and is strongly influenced by his/her peers and the images around him/her. He or she naturally experiments with alcohol because it is part of the adult world". Ritson 1983 : 109)

A study was undertaken in the Lothian Region of Scotland of over 1,000 young people who were school-leavers aged 15 and 16 during the initial phases of the work (Plant *et al.* 1985). Hardly any young people reported never having consumed alcohol and over 60% of those who had, being given their first experience of alcohol by a family member such as a parent or guardian. Almost a half of the boys and a third of the girls reported having drunk alcohol in the previous week, usually at home. Almost one-fifth experienced their last intake of drink in a pub or hotel. A study in north-west England of over 700 14- and 15-year-olds revealed that drinking at parents' homes (71%), friends' homes (58%), or public places such as streets or parks (58%) and pubs (39%) were the most popular locations for drinking (Newcombe *et al.* 1995).

The group in Plant *et al.*'s (1985) study were reinterviewed, then aged 19 and 20, as compared with 15 and 16 at the initial interviews. The most common location for drinking, as one might expect, had changed from the private sphere – the home, to the public sphere – the public bar, and there had been a move from drinking with parents to drinking with friends. However, the heaviest drinkers at 19 to 20 were different to those who had been heavy drinkers when 15 to 16. Other studies in Britain by Ghodsian and Power (1987) and Bagnall (1991) over seven years and 10 years respectively, revealed only low levels of association between teenage drinking habits and later patterns of alcohol use (Fossey *et al*.1996). In addition, a review of international evidence by Fillmore (1988) of individual drinking habits over time concluded that drinking patterns change considerably with increasing age. The findings of these studies indicate that social workers should be wary of assuming that problem drinking in adolescence will necessarily continue into adulthood, and also confirm that, for many adolescents, problems with drink are a temporary phenomenon.

It is important to note here that very few young people are convicted of buying intoxicating liquor "under age". In Scotland numbers of young people convicted for under age purchase of alcohol fell from 1,242 in 1973 to only 44 in 1991, while in recent years in England and Wales fewer than 2,000 young people have been convicted annually for under age alcohol purchase, the numbers falling to 370 in 1993 (Lister Sharp 1994). Furthermore, since 1981, fewer than 500 shop owners have been convicted annually of selling alcohol to young people in England and Wales with the figure falling to 240 in 1993 (Lister Sharp 1994). Very high percentages of the 14 to 15-year-olds in Newcombe *et al.*'s (1995) study had ever been refused a sale of alcohol. All this suggests there are obviously great difficulties in restraining young people from buying alcohol and in discouraging vendors from selling it to young people. Presumably economic reasons dictate these trends. Off-licence owners, shop-keepers, and supermarket managers are more concerned with profit margins than questioning and restraining under-age drinking, while resource-stretched police forces have other priorities in their minds way beyond under-age drinking. The point is reinforced that young people have very easy access to drink. It is easy for them to purchase alcohol.

Also there are indications that the mid-1990s have seen an increase in the choice and availability of drinks with high alcohol content which have been marketed specifically to appeal to young people, both girls and boys. These are readily available in bars, supermarkets, and off-licence premises. They include bottled strong lagers and ciders, such as Diamond White, K and TNT Liquid Dynamite, aperitifs, and fortified wines (with over 13% alcohol content) such as Thunderbird, MD 20/20, and Bacardi Breezers. In addition there are alcoholic colas, alcoholic lemonades – such as Hoopers Hooch and Two Dogs – and alcohol "crushes" such as Tilt available in chiller cabinets alongside ordinary lemonades and cola-type drinks, with alcohol content ranging from 4.2% to 5.5%.

The development and availability of these drinks are likely to result in higher consumption levels by young people on each drinking occasion and hence per week, with a corresponding increase in actual frequency of drinking. In other words, higher alcohol intake is likely, either with deliberate intent or on some occasions, without young people being aware of the high or actual alcohol content of particular drinks.

Intoxication and Adverse Consequences of Alcohol Misuse
High percentages of young people had experienced intoxication in the sample of 15- and 16-year-olds in Lothian Region studied by Plant *et al.* (1985). Over a third of the males and a quarter of the females had been very drunk in the past six months. Around a quarter to a third had experienced a hangover in the past six months; around a third had undergone an "upset stomach" due to drinking; about a fifth had disagreed with their parents because of drinking with the parents believing they had spent too much on drink. Newcombe *et al.*'s (1995) study revealed that almost a quarter of the sample of 14 and 15-year-olds in the north-west of England had been drinking on the last occasion of shoplifting, vandalism, or threatening or hitting someone. There were notable gender differences in deviant behaviour following drinking, with boys more likely to be involved in physical violence or vandalism and girls more liable to be noisy and to steal from home. In fact, a quarter of Newcombe *et al.*'s (1995) sample of drinkers had been stopped and questioned by the police after drinking and a third of those arrested had been drinking. The study by Marsh *et al.* (1986) found that almost one-third of their male sample of 17-year-olds had fallen over at least once after drinking and a half had been sick. The more the adolescents in Marsh *et al.*'s sample enjoyed themselves, the more likely it was that difficult consequences followed, such as feeling guilty, being sick, and feeling incapable. Clearly it is possible to suffer from occasional intoxication, to have an alcohol-related problem, without being a heavy drinker. A young person may get drunk only twice in a year but on one of those occasions a car may be crashed, and on the other a job may be lost, even though they may be abstinent for the rest of the year.

As teenagers grow older, so adverse consequences are likely to increase. Plant *et al.* (1985) in their follow-up study of the 15- to 16-year-olds in Lothian Region at the age of 19 and 20 years found that males in particular were more likely to suffer alcohol-related consequences on account of their higher consumption levels. 25% of the males in the sample had been involved in a fight after drinking and half of those had been injured, 15% had been asked to leave somewhere on account of intoxication, while 16% had had arguments at home linked with their drinking. Both sexes frequently regretted comments they had made whilst drinking, felt bad about having been loud and noisy, being sick or collapsing in the presence of other people, and being unable to recall events.

Nevertheless, it should be made clear that very few young people die in Britain from clearly and specifically alcohol-related disease and their numbers barely reach double figures even when the statistics include those aged between 15 and the mid-20s (Plant & Plant 1992). However, larger numbers do die following alcohol-related accidental injuries and in accidents on the roads. The proportion of drivers killed in such a manner declined over a 10-year period between 1979 and 1989, so that deaths of riders and drivers in the late teens fell by 50%. On the other hand, almost one-third of pedestrians killed in the same period were aged 16 to 19 and had elevated blood alcohol levels. (Office of Population Censuses and Surveys 1990, Registrar-General Scotland 1988.) Also, approximately 1,000 people aged 19 or under still die each year in road traffic accidents in Britain and evidence suggests that many of these fatalities are alcohol related (Fossey *et al.* 1996).

These kinds of incidents are associated with the effects of alcohol as a depressant and as a disinhibitor. Response times are slowed down and mood changes are associated with disinhibition, which in turn has been defined as the "activation of behaviours normally suppressed by various controlling influences" (Woods & Mansfield 1983 : 4). In western culture alcohol is associated with disinhibition, clumsiness, and the removal of social constraints. One becomes more affectionate and sentimental and/or more aggressive, and mean. However, it is not just learnt, acquired behaviour that is significant, but the setting for that behaviour. For many young people, alcohol is associated with enjoyable music and the sociability of peers, which are found in most lively pubs in town centres. These acquire reputations as good places to have a great time. Young people can "let their hair down" and easily get drunk in these exciting settings, some of which can become "trouble sites", with disorder likely to occur outside the premises. Everyone leaves at closing time, looks for more excitement, may seek fast food and cluster around the streets (Hope 1985, Ramsay 1982, Tuck 1989). Disorderly incidents are likely for some and

> *"participants in disorder are more likely to have unskilled jobs or to be unemployed . . . and to have left school at sixteen. These are young men who have not found their role in society. They may not have enough money to get on to night clubs after an evening in the pub . . .; they cluster outside take aways unwilling for the evening to end, still looking for excitement. It is these gatherings which are the characteristic focus of disorder".* (Tuck 1989 : 66)

Arguments are more likely to occur and violence may take place, with the victim as well as the attacker likely to have been drinking at the time of the assault (Myers 1982).

Heavy Drinking Amongst Teenagers

Definitions of what constitutes "safe" and "heavy" drinking in one week vary and different studies have used different measures. The royal medical colleges have provided guidelines for "safe" and "sensible" levels for *adult* alcohol consumption *each week* (Royal College of General Practitioners 1986, Royal College of Psychiatrists 1986, Royal College of Physicians 1987). These are as follows:–

ADULT MALES (Units per week)	ADULT FEMALES (Units per week)	
1 - 21	1 - 14	Light Drinking
22 - 35	15 - 21	Moderate Drinking
36 - 50	22 - 35	Regular Fairly Heavy Drinking
51+	36+	Regular Heavy Drinking

It should be stressed that these are general guidelines and need "to be related to specific people such as pregnant women and to specific situations such as drinking and driving" (Plant & Plant 1992 : 51).

If the unit levels for adults are applied to adolescents then there are likely to be some problems in that alcohol consumption affects people in different ways. For example, body weight is a significant factor, as heavier people can absorb alcohol more readily into the body than those of lighter weight. Hence, as the majority of adolescents and females are of lighter weight than most adults and males, then alcohol is likely to have a more significant impact upon them. In addition, some adolescents may be unused to alcohol, be relatively inexperienced drinkers, and have low tolerance of alcohol compared with more experienced adult drinkers. Therefore, again, alcohol is likely to make a bigger impact upon adolescent drinkers. Other factors are also influential, such as the environment, the situations, in which drinking is done. For example, drinking alone or in the company of friends in a bar can have a significant influence on the impact made by alcohol (Coggans & McKellar 1995). Hence the same amount of alcohol ingested may have different effects according to the setting in which it occurs.

Weekly Consumption and Last Drinking Occasion

Equally, in any one week the quantities consumed can be spread out over several days in that week or they can be concentrated into one or two occasions or days around the week-end, resulting in "binge" drinking, with the likelihood of more serious consequences. For example, in Marsh *et al*'s first UK survey of 5,000 13- to 17-year-olds:–

*"On week days and Sundays between 1% and 2% claimed to have drunk
more than the equivalent of five pints of beer on any single day.
On Fridays this rose to 5% and on Saturdays to 9% amongst the English
and Welsh adolescents and to 14% amongst the Scots."*
Marsh et al. 1986 : 31)

Goddard (1991) carried out a survey of 16- to 17-year-olds in England and
Wales. It was discovered that 13% of the males and 8% of the females were
consuming more than the recommended levels of 21 units per week for males
and 14 units per week for females; 2% of the males and 1% of the females were
drinking at very heavy levels, in excess of 50 units per week (for males) and 35
units per week (for females). Plant *et al.* (1985) found that in Lothian Region,
Scotland almost one-quarter of the 15- to 16-year-old males were drinking in
excess of 21 units per week, with 7% exceeding 50 units per week, while 12%
of females were drinking in excess of the recommended 14 units per week.
Also, significantly, on average, all the young people in the study had consumed
over half their total week's intake in one day (Plant *et al.* 1985). Therefore, it
can be seen that alcohol made a considerable impact upon some younger
teenagers and this is a considerable cause for concern.

In the later teenage years these figures reach even higher proportions for males,
but female "heavy" drinking declines. For example, in Plant *et al.*'s (1985)
follow up study of 19 and 20-year-olds, weekly consumption by males was up
by a third, while female consumption per week remained similar to that when
aged 15 and 16 years old.

Plant *et al.* (1990) discovered a substantial proportion of heavy drinkers in their
survey of over 6,000 14 to 16-year-olds in England. Heavy drinkers were
defined as males consuming 11 units or more on their last drinking occasion
and females consuming 8 units or more on their last drinking occasion.

Percentage of Heavy Drinkers		
Age	Males	Females
14	5.4	7.1
15	10.7	10.1
16	13.5	15.5

(Plant *et al.* 1990 : 688)

A similar survey of 14- to 16-year-olds in Scotland of 7,000 teenagers revealed that 18% of males and 10% of females had consumed more than 11 units on their last drinking occasion (Plant & Forster 1991). Furthermore, a recent survey of 700 14 and 15-year-olds in Merseyside and Manchester found that as many as 30% of the boys and 33% of the girls, using the same criteria, could be classified as "heavy drinkers" (Newcombe *et al.* 1995). Again, these figures are a cause for serious concern and show a clear *increase* in the quantity of alcohol consumed *per drinking session*.

In fact, it is the frequent, heavy drinkers who are likely to encounter most problems with alcohol that is, those who drink *frequently each week* and who consume *considerable quantities on each drinking occasion*. They tend to drink in bars, with friends and older people, are far more likely to have been "deviant", involved in accidents, stopped by the police, arrested, convicted, or to have experienced negative consequences after drinking (Newcombe *et al.* 1995).

Heavy Drinkers and Risk Taking

The attitudes of 14 to 16-year-old heavy drinkers have been examined by Plant *et al.* (1990) in contrast to those who drank less or who were non-drinkers. The heavy drinkers were more likely to endorse positive reasons for drinking. These included the belief that alcohol helped to make it easier to mix at parties, to talk with members of the opposite sex, to calm anxieties, or alleviate boredom. Friends of heavy drinkers were more likely to be heavy drinkers themselves and to be more likely to smoke and use illicit drugs (Plant *et al.* 1985). In fact, there is much evidence to associate together adolescent drinking, drug use, and risky sex. Such risk taking has been seen as a natural, "normal", commonplace, and widespread feature of adolescent behaviour, although clearly there are social, cultural and ethnic differences (Plant & Plant 1992). Many young people may see themselves as invulnerable, may get positive benefits from risks, and see themselves as immune to negative consequences of risk behaviour as they search for independence and identity (Elkind 1985). Indeed, "the greatest level of risk is experienced by those who are the most 'extreme' cases such as the heaviest drinkers . . . such individuals place themselves at a high level of personal risk [and] . . . may be difficult to detect, contact and influence" (Plant & Plant 1992 : 142).

Young People, Alcohol and Crime

The survey of more than 700 14 and 15-year-olds in north west England by Newcombe *et al.* (1995) revealed that 80% of the sample had been involved in incidents of "deviant behaviour". These were defined as shouting in the street at night, threatening people, fighting, stealing from home, smoking cannabis, shoplifting, or vandalism. Boys, working class respondents and black or white young people reported more deviant acts than girls, middle class, and Asian respondents. One-third of the sample said their most recent example of deviant behaviour had been at a time when they had been drinking. Those who drank more frequently committed significantly more deviant acts than those who drank less frequently. Therefore, the authors concluded: . . . "for this [sample] deviancy . . . is significantly related to both more frequent and heavier sessional drinking" (Newcombe *et al.* 1995 : 340).

As regards involvement with the police, 21% of boys in the sample had been convicted or cautioned for a criminal offence, compared with 2% of the girls. Interestingly, 25% of the weekly drinkers and 15% of the monthly drinkers had criminal records compared with only 6.5% of the occasional drinkers and non-drinkers. Criminal damage, disorderly behaviour, and thefts from shops were the most common offences.

Around 6% of those cautioned or convicted of drunkenness offences in England and Wales in 1989 were 17 years old or younger and 15% were aged 18 to 20, with the peak age for offending for drunkenness being 20 years (Home Office 1990). However, as Plant and Plant (1992 : 57) have stated plainly, "Neither feelings nor behaviours are found in a bottle. Drinking does not by itself produce criminal behaviour." Thus it is problematic to suggest drinking "causes" crime. It is more appropriate to suggest that drinking is associated with crime, where the characteristics of the person, the nature of the drinking, and environmental factors all interact. Studies on young offenders have revealed that significant percentages are seen as heavy or problem drinkers. The figures vary over a number of studies from 15% to 40% (Hollin 1983, Fuller 1979, Heather 1981). Average weekly consumption rates of young offenders are very high, varying from 58 units to 84 units per week in two samples (Sleap 1977, McMurran & Hollin 1989). Many young offenders themselves perceive a relationship between their drinking and offending. In one study, over one-third of Hollin's (1993) sample of young offenders thought that their drinking and delinquency were related. Also McMurran and Hollin (1989) found that most young offenders thought the effects of alcohol and its social context directly influenced their behaviour, leading them to be involved in actions that they would not do when sober. For further information about adult offenders see Chapter 8 .

Implications for Helping Young Problem Drinkers

If we have masses of statistics and if we are clear that alcohol does cause problems for young people what can be done about those problems? If we have considerable evidence of the impact of alcohol upon young people what are the implications for prevention and intervention?

First, it is perhaps helpful to clarify that there are very few, if any, "alcoholic" young people. It is clear that while almost all adolescents drink most do so sensibly and moderately; some are intoxicated on occasions and an important minority drink heavily.

Alcohol misuse by young people is a serious problem in that most teenagers experience intoxication and negative consequences as a result of drinking, while the minority who drink heavily are particularly at risk in relation to more negative consequences, such as accidents, road injuries, and offences. Therefore, most of the alcohol-related problems experienced by adolescents relate not to dependency on alcohol but to heavy drinking and episodes of intoxication, linked to experimentation and recreational use. It is in these areas that help is required.

As with other adult problem drinkers it is likely that ambivalence will be present in young people when considering a reduction of intake or giving up problem drinking. Drinking can have negative consequences, but it also brings rewards and benefits, such as feeling happy, having a good time, and feeling at ease with friends. For instance, in one sample of over 600 14 and 15-year-old drinkers in Newcombe *et al.*'s (1995) study, 56% did not want to change their behaviour, 28% didn't know, while 15% (110) indicated that they wanted to change their drinking patterns. Of those wanting to change, 27% wanted to drink more, while 60% wanted to drink less or give up.

It should be emphasised also that what is perceived as an alcohol problem by others may not be regarded by the user as a problem. For instance, in the studies undertaken of 15 and 16-year-olds by Plant *et al.* (1985) very few respondents thought they had experienced alcohol-related problems – even though negative consequences had been encountered. In addition, very few young people were worried about their drinking. At the follow-up stage when respondents were aged 19 and 20, despite a high level of negative consequences for some, including criminal involvement, in fact, only one male and four females had looked for help for their drinking problems from a sample of around 1,000. Therefore, many young people may feel they do not have a problem with drink and may be reluctant to accept help that is offered.

Alcohol Education
At the same time, alcohol misuse by young people causes considerable alarm to the media. Amidst the "moral panic", demands are made for action to be taken, remedies to be sought and answers to be provided. One approach that has been suggested as being of value to young people with drink problems is alcohol education. However, unfortunately, to date, despite beliefs that alcohol education is valuable and notwithstanding the fact that many initiatives have not been

evaluated, a large number of studies have concluded that alcohol education with adolescents is not successful. While levels of knowledge can be increased, providing information on alcohol issues and problems does not lead to behaviour change. Indeed, behaviour change that follows can be negative. For example, Stuart's (1974) study of drug education and junior high school pupils revealed that a group that had received drug education did display increased knowledge of drugs, but at the same time reported significantly greater levels of alcohol and drug use compared with a "no education" control group. A survey of drug and alcohol education programmes by Kiner *et al.* (1980) and also Plant *et al.*'s (1985) work revealed that this was not an isolated finding. Another study of over five and a half thousand junior high school pupils showed that a control group who had received alcohol education displayed a significantly greater increase in knowledge about alcohol, but no differences in actual alcohol use compared with a control group who had received no education (Dielman *et al.* 1986). A large scale study in 1988 by Hopkins *et al.* produced similar conclusions. In fact, very few studies have noted less frequent alcohol use and fewer behavioural changes in resisting social pressures to drink following alcohol education courses. (Bagnall 1991, May 1993, Plant 1994.)

So, overall, it appears that alcohol education courses are ineffective and may even be counter-productive. Many alcohol education programmes may be ill-directed and will include many non-problem-drinking young people. Indeed, these people may curiously explore to test out information provided about drinking. Also, crucially, alcohol education has tended not to provide information and skills about how to moderate, change, and lower consumption. Raising awareness is not enough; information about how to deal with antecedents and consequences of drinking would be more appropriate. Therefore, more-specific target audiences of much younger children or particular groups of young people, giving more appropriate messages, allied to back up skills training to effect behaviour change are more likely to be successful (McMurran & Hollin, 1993). Furthermore, "low threat", moderate messages giving guidelines for sensible drinking are more likely to succeed when presented to specific categories of drinkers in a non-threatening manner, rather than "high threat" exhortations to abstain altogether (Bensley & Wu 1991).

At present, the most promising educational approaches with young people are aimed at those for whom drinking is causing some tangible and present problem, and who are likely to respond because they can see an immediate reason to follow the advice given (Heather & Robertson 1989). There are clear implications here for social workers who may well come into contact with young people at the court report stage or already be in contact with young people who are experiencing tangible and current problems with alcohol.

Social Work Intervention, Knowledge, and Skills

It is plain, then, that many young people do not view themselves as having problems with alcohol, even though this may be clearly the case. Social workers are not likely to find young people presenting alcohol problems as a difficulty but adolescents may well present other difficulties at home or work, associated with or underlying which may be alcohol problems. Hence social workers need to be sensitive to this point, to be ready to consider, to explore, to question a young person's drinking patterns and possible consequences. It is easy for social workers to work in ignorance of an alcohol problem. If they lack training, confidence and support in intervention with alcohol-related problems (Harrison 1992) then this is even more likely to be the case . work with young people when less obvious drink problems will be presented, where overt dependency is most unlikely, where intoxication in particular and heavy use are much more common problems.

Assessment is a key skill in working with young people experiencing problems with alcohol. Social workers are familiar with this skill from their qualifying courses and from their experiences in generic practice which they can transfer across to work with problem drinkers. In addition, assessment of alcohol problems requires some more specific specialist skills, built upon a well-established generic base. These skills surround the need to inquire in an open and non-judgmental way to obtain information from the young person about, for example,

- Amounts of alcohol consumed.
- Types of alcohol consumed.
- Length of time that alcohol has been consumed.
- Frequency of alcohol consumption.
- Setting/location for drinking.
- Companions for drinking
- Physical effects.
- Psychological effects.
- Social/relationship effects.
- Legal/financial effects.

It is by exploring these areas and broader aspects, such as family history and relationships, education background, and present or past contact with other agencies, that social workers and young people would be jointly in a better informed position to assess strengths, weaknesses, stage of change, possible tasks for intervention, and targets for change.

It is important for social workers not to underestimate their own existing, valuable, transferable knowledge and skills in working with youthful problem drinkers (Collins *et al.* 1988). All social workers have knowledge of adolescent developmental patterns and needs, having followed courses on human growth and development at the qualifying stage of social work training. Also many of them have extensive experience of working with adolescents. Furthermore, they all have basic interviewing and counselling skills at their disposal. Skills in Rogerian counselling should be well established. Genuineness, positive regard, and empathy provide an invaluable foundation for working with young people experiencing drink problems (Collins *et al.* 1988). Interview skills focusing upon explaining and questioning, and confrontation based upon a foundation of empathy are additional valuable resources, while the importance of careful, sensitive listening can never be underestimated in work with young people. Also see Chapter 4.

Task centred and contract based approaches offer clear opportunities for short term, goal oriented, well-focused interventions, based upon the wishes and wants of the young person with the benefit of review and monitoring after several weeks of contact, to evaluate achievement and aims (Collins *et al.* 1988, Leckie 1990).

Social Work Intervention and The Stages of Change
Prochaska and DiClemente's model has been examined in depth by several writers (Barrie 1990, Baldwin 1990, Barber 1995). Many young people may well be in Prochaska and DiClemente's (1983, 1986) stages of pre-contemplation and contemplation rather than being ready to actually act on their problems when they meet social workers.

F e-contemplators generally see the positives, the rewards, and the benefits of drinking as outweighing the negatives, the costs and drawbacks occurring as a result of drinking. Many young people in the pre-contemplation phase may not feel they have problems which require help, may prefer to see the difficulties they experience as being related to another person or some other aspect of their lives. They may see little point in seeking out help for their drinking or in using help. Yet a social worker can help young people to reassess their situation. There are three aims here:–

> *"First, the opportunity is given to offer information on the impact of alcohol . . . and of the social and legal consequences related to drinking. Given that drinking behaviour is likely to continue, the second aim is to*

enable individuals to examine their health and social situation, thus reducing or limiting the damage which might accrue through continued drinking. The third aim is to attempt to alter the client's motivation by identifying possible reasons for drinking and establishing links between that behaviour and any difficulties or life events which may have been experienced (e.g. court appearances, health problems. . . .)"

(Barrie 1990 : 160).

Contemplators are young people considering the need to act, to change, to do something about their drinking. The young person may be drinking quite heavily, but will not be happy with that situation. Information will be looked for. There may be some regret and disappointment about their behaviour and some willingness to change, perhaps to weigh up the positives and negatives of drinking. Hence the adolescent may be willing to become more conscious of problems, to change attitudes and beliefs about drinking before actually changing behaviour. The aims are:–

"1. Providing information on alcohol and related problems as well as advising on . . . help available and what such help consists of.

"2. Identifying problems which individuals experience in relation to their drinking and considering the costs and benefits of continued or changed behaviour. The aim being to increase the individual's perception or belief that there is a need to change their behaviour."

(Barrie 1990 : 160-1)

In the *action* stage the young person's disappointment about their behaviour will be evident, as at the contemplation stage, but now the decision to stop, or change, will have been made. The young person's attitudes, opinions and beliefs will be actually changing, there will be a commitment to change, and alternative activities to drinking will be or have been taken up. The aims here will be:–

"Maintaining and increasing an individual's commitment to his or her changed behaviour . . . strategies to help change behaviour e.g. by problem solving and realistic goal setting." (Barrie 1990 : 161)

If crises occur such as negative events involving injuries and frightening incidents then it is at those times that the young person may be more ready or willing to act upon, use, and accept help (Fanti 1985). Social workers can be ideally placed to provide such help as they may well be already in contact and available. This seems especially important as we have emphasised that research evidence suggests young people are unlikely to seek out helping agencies for assistance with problem drinking (Plant *et al*. 1985). Furthermore, it is hoped that the social worker would be seen as a trustworthy figure, with a sound relationship with the young person. This should assist him or her in disclosing anxieties about alcohol problems, as it is clear that people experiencing difficulties prefer to relate their concerns and worries to a trusted helping figure who is already known to them. This appears to hold true whatever the nature of the difficulties the young person is experiencing, be it mental health, alcohol, physical or sexual problems, or problems in behaviour at school.

In the *maintenance* stage the young person will have changed their drinking behaviour for some time. There will be a vigilance about risky situations such as meeting previous drinking companions, or visiting sites or settings for drinking such as pubs, clubs or other meeting places. The young person should try to avoid such problematic locations when they wish to relax or socialise; they should be involved in alternative activities to heavy drinking.

The aims at the this stage would be:–

> *"To maintain commitment to the changed behaviour or way of life and, by implication, to prevent relapse and plan the management of relapse. Focusing much less on drinking behaviour results in overall lifestyle change being a major aim . . . changing relationships and creating a new way of life."* (Barrie 1990 : 161 - 163)

Again a social worker can be ideally placed to help during the maintenance stage, especially when a young person is subject to a supervision order which ensures long term continuity of contact. The social worker can provide reassurance, praise, reinforcement and support for the changes achieved in behaviour, such as the continued avoidance of previous drinking companions and risky meeting places.

Relapse should always be seen as a probable stage in the cycle of change especially where young people are concerned. The likelihood of relapse amongst all problem drinkers is quite high. When resolution has broken down and a bout of drinking has occurred then then relapse should not be seen as a "failure" and the young person is not necessarily back to "square one", because they can still use change strategies (Allsopp & Saunders 1987 and 1989).

The aims at the relapse stage would be:–

> *". . . a combination of those used in both contemplation and action . . . to move individuals from thinking about changing their drinking behaviour to doing something about it [again]"* (Barrie 1990 : 163).

Once more, social workers in contact with young people via statutory orders can react with empathy and reassurance, acknowledging that their relapse is an almost universal experience. Also by encouraging the young person to reframe their perceptions, to renew commitment to change after a "slip" or "accident", enabling perception of this as an experience that can be a source of learning rather than an occasion for negative over-reaction (Marlatt & Gordon 1985).

Involvement of Other Agencies

The social worker may wish to involve a helper from an alcohol agency for consultation, assessment or ongoing counselling (Leckie 1990). Such decisions are not easy to make. If joint ongoing work is agreed, then it is important for the social worker to clarify what roles each worker will be undertaking, with regular review and monitoring arrangements, built into the process. As regards ongoing counselling other "specialist" alcohol agencies rarely work with young people. Although Alcoholics Anonymous have expanded to include "Alateen" groups for teenagers in some areas, in order to widen their core population beyond adult clients mainly in their 40s, some young people may find the emphasis on abstaining difficult to meet and follow through. However, the "golden rule" for social workers should be to use whatever assistance will be of most help to the young person at that particular time. For some, AA may be the most appropriate agency, if there is a thriving and appropriately oriented group within the particular geographical area.

Councils on alcohol also rarely work with adolescents, but again if the social worker feels particularly insecure about working with a teenager experiencing drinking problems, then a referral may be appropriate for ongoing counselling. More likely, perhaps the social worker may wish to refer to a council on alcohol for an assessment of the young person's problem drinking or may wish to seek information, consultation, or advice from that agency (Collins *et al.* 1990).

As stated above, given that the social worker may have an already established relationship with the young person and his or her family, there is a great deal to be said for the same worker continuing with the intervention rather than referring on to voluntary agencies. Voluntary workers while feeling confident about working with alcohol problems may feel insecure about working with teenagers and associated legal, emotional, mental health, sexual, or behavioural problems.

Adolescent Alcohol Misuse and Other Problems

It is perhaps rare to encounter a youthful problem drinker who experiences problems only with alcohol. It is important to consider the adolescent drinker who, in addition to experiencing problems with alcohol, may have other difficulties. There can be overlap, for example, with a concurrent psychological disorder, the experience of child abuse and having grown up with other family members with drinking or drug problems, especially parents. In such situations some teenagers unfortunately struggle with multiple jeopardy and it is not easy for workers to intervene for a variety of reasons. Often much emotional damage may have occurred during early-development years and there may have been considerable ongoing stress during earlier ma   ative stages. The adolescent boy or girl who has gone through severe emotional traumas, as well as experiencing problems with alcohol, can prove to be even more difficult to engage in the helping process. An excessive focus upon alcohol problems can result in the risk of rejecting other important aspects of an adolescent's functioning. Equally an over concentration on psychological disorder or physical or sexual abuse can lead to a neglect of problematic drinking. Sometimes child psychiatrists and clinical psychologists may be required who are particularly expert in childhood traumas, or working with the children of parents with serious drink problems, in order to clarify assessment and intervention plans to determine appropriate prioritisation of problems and focus for helping. If coexisting problems are not worked upon, then the young person who is attempting to stop misusing alcohol, or reduce intake, can be subject to overwhelming pressure and may be very likely to continue with episodes of intoxication or heavy drinking. There is no easy answer to "chicken and egg" questions about the exact nature of the relationship between adolescent problem drinking and psychological disorder. Furthermore, each family with a so-called specific psychological disorder is unique and will have unique needs. Sensitivity and a wariness of excessive confrontation are important prerequisites for the social worker (Singer & White 1991).

In work with adolescents who have been misusing alcohol and have been victims of abuse, the social worker needs to create a safe environment for helping and careful awareness of the dangers of overpowering the young person (Muisener 1994). It seems there is no direct causal evidence linking parental alcohol abuse with child abuse but there is strong evidence of an associative and correlative type (Abel 1983, Law *et al.* 1983, Creighton 1984, Mather 1988, Schmidt 1991). For example, in Great Britain, alcohol misuse is one of the most frequently cited factors in the family backgrounds of cases involving child abuse, including sexual abuse. An NSPCC study of a five year period of referrals to their child abuse register found one in five to have alcohol use as a stress factor (Creighton 1984), while a study of family cases in a social services department in Bristol found one in five to have alcohol problems, and a third of those families with alcohol problems were on the "at risk" register (Abel 1983). Also, a study by Devon County Council (Mather 1988) found that a quarter of registered child abuse cases were from families with drinking problems. These figures would indicate that many children who have been placed on child abuse registers have come from families where alcohol is misused.

Therefore, social workers are likely to find themselves engaged with adolescents who, in addition to alcohol problems, may well have been the victims of physical abuse, and clearly the workers need to be aware of, and very sensitive to, these matters. Where teenagers have been physically abused in the past the adolescent may not yet have disclosed such abuse and this can be an extremely painful experience. In turn, young people who have been the victims of physical violence can become aggressive themselves when intoxicated or involved in heavy drinking (Cavaiola & Schiff 1989).

A young person who is on supervision and appears to have a drink problem also may have been sexually abused and it may be only after some time that the young person feels safe to disclose such experiences to the social worker (Harrison *et al*. 1990). Moving at the young person's pace is very important and he or she should feel empowered and actively part of goal setting in the helping process. Feelings of shame about sexual abuse and alcohol misuse will require slow, careful, thoughtful, empathic consideration (Coons *et al*. 1989). If adolescents are receiving help for problem drinking, failure to understand and work with sexual traumatisation can result in a continuation of, or swift return to, problem drinking.

The Family
Social workers do not always work with adolescents within a family context, but this is often the case. Again, social workers have usually studied family interactions as part of their basic qualifying courses, but may rarely have considered working with families where the adolescent boy or girl is a problem drinker. The impact of the family upon the young person who drinks heavily and the effect of the young person's drinking upon their family is likely to be profound. The family has been described as a "holding environment" for the young person (Winnicott 1965, Foxcroft and Lowe 1991, Muisener 1994) that should provide emotional cohesion, safety, control and support for facilitating healthy psychological development, and as Carter and McGoldrick (1980 : 14) have emphasised, "adolescence is something that happens to a family not just to an individual child".

In relation to alcohol use the teenager's family system can interact in three different ways:–

1.   Collaborate to protect the teenager from developing problems with alcohol.

2.   Influence a teenager's use of alcohol by enabling, precipitating, and perpetuating an environment for the teenager's drinking.

3.   May act as a resistance and buffer to peers' influence towards alcohol involvement.

(Adapted from Botvin & Tortu 1988)

It is suggested that "a high degree of parental nurturance along with low coercive punishment and clear expectations for adolescent behaviour appear to be salient factors for the prevention of alcohol . . . abuse . . . in adolescence" (Barnes & Windle 1987:17). Yet, if a family becomes overwhelmed by stress (which could include that of the adolescent's alcohol abuse), it can become a less than adequate holding environment for the adolescent's developmental needs, and a precipitating environment for problematic behaviour, including alcohol abuse. Families can precipitate or enable alcohol abuse by the young person in a variety of ways.

Uninformed or Unaware Enabling
The teenager conceals alcohol abuse from the parents and the parents are unaware or, at most, only mildly suspicious of their child's use of alcohol.

Alcohol and Avoidant Enabling
Parents have concrete evidence of their teenager's abuse of alcohol but choose not to intervene, often because of ignorance of the problems alcohol abuse may cause or because they see alcohol abuse as a life stage event that will be outgrown.

Aware and Disempowered Enabling
Parents have different opinions about how to handle the teenager's alcohol abuse or take only inconsistent half-measures, often feeling powerless about influencing or altering their teenager's alcohol abuse.

Aware and Indulgent Enabling
Parents may abuse alcohol and supply alcohol as well as use alcohol with the teenager, knowingly promoting ongoing alcohol abuse.

(Muisener 1994).

Young Drinkers and Parental Misuse of Alcohol
Overall, young people whose parents have been involved with alcohol abuse represent another vulnerable group. Some of them may have developed coping mechanisms and are not severely affected by the parental drinking problems. Others may be mildly affected. For some teenagers the stress and pressures of growing up in such a situation are considerable. They can lead to an adoption of patterns of intoxication and heavy drinking. Some parents with drink problems act as a "precipitating environment" for the young person's alcohol misuse by exposing the young person to their own heavy or dependent drinking, and possibly encouraging imitation of it, where the young person strongly identifies with the parents (Muisener 1994).

Many children of alcohol-abusing parents can grow into adolescence with a number of concerns. These include feelings of anger, insecurity, guilt, fear, and distress (Black 1981, Morehouse 1984 and 1986, Rivinus 1991). There is difficulty in asking for help. Trust is a particularly important issue. This will need to be addressed by the social worker by being consistent, reliable and dependable over a period of time (Black 1981, Fanti 1990). An adolescent problem drinker who has grown up with alcohol-abusing parents may often compare himself or herself with parents when seeking help. In addition to a more usual tendency to minimise problems, they may regard themselves as "not as bad" as their parents. Hence it is important for the social worker to maintain a focus upon the adolescent's drinking and associated behaviour and not get drawn into excessive comparison with parental drinking habits (Muisener 1994). On the other hand, a desire not to be like the parent can be a strong motivation to stopping or reducing the adolescent's drinking, but underlying this may be considerable feelings of anger towards the parent. For many children of alcohol-abusing parents the idea of reducing, of abstinence and sobriety may seem undesirable, especially if their parents are unhappy "dry drunks". Furthermore, adolescent children may identify positively with their alcohol-abusing parents, feel loyalty to them in their own alcohol misuse, may not want to reduce or give up their own drinking. Their strong identification with parental behaviour patterns may be greater than any difficulties caused by their own substance abuse.

In working with an adolescent and families where parents have been or are misusing alcohol there are particular difficulties and issues for social workers. In those situations in families which are misusing alcohol and parental misuse is hidden it will be very difficult to engage the family in helping. Efforts will be made to sabotage any progress made by the adolescent in order to keep him or her as the problem rather than uncovering and dealing with the parent's alcohol misuse. In situations where parents are still drinking, but the drinking is openly acknowledged, the timing for addressing parental misuse is crucial and again there is a need to focus on the adolescent's needs and not to become too involved with parental drinking concerns.

It is perhaps those families that fluctuate between being "wet" and "dry" that are perhaps the most challenging. In other words, the parents move between drinking and non-drinking, with constant shifts and, on occasions, chaotic situations. Sometimes the parents will support their teenager with love and affection, but may then become preoccupied by their own need for more drink (Rivinus 1991). Such situations can be bewildering for the young person who is trying to reduce or stop drinking. At such times they will require maximum support and consistency from a social worker.

Therefore social workers attempting to assist an individual adolescent who is abusing alcohol can be faced with particularly demanding scenarios and difficult work when parents are secretly or openly misusing alcohol or are fluctuating between giving up and continuing with their drinking. For further material about working with the family see Fanti (1990).

Clearly the most positive environment for working with the adolescent problem drinker in a family setting is those situations where the parents do not abuse alcohol or no longer do so and there is active effort by them to resolve the impact of alcohol misuse on the family. Openness in such families and the desire to change and move on are positive indicators for the healthy progress of the adolescent drinker.

Other Stresses in Family Life

Stress and problems in family life can arise from a number of sources which precipitate adolescent alcohol abuse. For example, factors such as isolation, expected and unexpected bereavements, alcohol abuse by older brothers and sisters, racism experienced by black families, poverty, unemployment, and poor housing (Preto & Travis 1985). Within families there can be problems in internal dynamics (Fleck 1980) which enable alcohol abuse. For example, leadership issues when parents are split and either over-authoritarian or excessively *laissez-faire* attitudes prevail, thus leading to inconsistent limit setting. Also *family and generational boundaries* can become blurred and diffuse, when one parent may be under-involved and the other over-involved with the adolescent alcohol abuser. Hence:–

> *"Whenever there is an acting out adolescent and especially where*
> *alcohol . . . is involved, there [may be] an exaggerated and unhealthy*
> *parent coalition. . . ."*
> (Huberty & Huberty 1984 : 133)

The family member who is often closer to the adolescent can take on an enabling role, supporting the young person in their drinking, often covering up for their drunken behaviour and not helping them to face the consequences of that behaviour (Wegscheider 1981).

The idea of family triangles perpetuating alcohol abuse has been described by Fanti (1990) in adapting the work of Karpman (1968), while Schaefer (1987) has further adapted the model in relation to work with adolescent alcohol abusers. A regular cycle of persecutor, rescuer, and victim roles is played out by the family. The dysfunctional triangle may usually include an over-involved parent (a "rescuer"), an under-involved parent (the "persecutor") and the adolescent (the "victim"). Muisener (1994) provides a useful practice example of a male adolescent occupying the victim role in a family. The father worked protracted hours, was very distant from his son and was in the persecutor's role, regularly imposing strong and excessive punishments for his son's alcohol abuse, which had led to problems at school and arrests by the police. The mother, in turn, acted as the rescuer, intervening regularly to moderate, to "water down" her husband's harsh punishments. As they became locked into operating in these roles the parents experienced a breakdown in family leadership. They were enabling the alcohol abuse of their son by failing to apply appropriate limits and consequences for his abuse of alcohol.

Other family members, brothers and sisters, can also function in one of the three roles of rescuer, persecutor, or victim. The triangle needs to be effectively interrupted so as to prevent further alcohol abuse, with the parents giving up their position in the triangle in order to take on board a more active role in changing their adolescent child's alcohol abuse. In ongoing work with those under supervision the social worker is in danger of becoming a regular part of the family's pattern. For example, with the social worker becoming a participant, stepping in for an absent "rescuer" or "persecutor". The worker may continually strive to "save" the adolescent alcohol abuser and the family from chaotic situations, perhaps sooner or later persecuting or berating the adolescent drinker for problematic behaviour, eventually becoming emotionally exhausted by the family. There is clearly a need for social workers to discuss such situations with an informed consultant or supervisor in order to avoid the pitfalls of these interactions.

Family crises are likely to occur in families where an adolescent is abusing alcohol (Steinglass 1987, Fanti 1990). As Fanti has pointed out, "the repeated use of alcohol by an individual family member, should be seen as not only negative in effect. The use has a positive effect that the user values over and above the cost of resulting damage. This balancing act fluctuates with time. There will be occasions when the consumer feels that their alcohol use is causing difficulties which far outweigh the benefits of use. It is at these crisis points that the individual is susceptible to change" (Fanti 1990 : 127).

A crisis has been defined as "an upset in a steady state caused by a stress for which the system does not have a coping response. . . . Thus a crisis related to alcohol use can be a major opportunity for a family to change" (Fanti 1990 : 134). The involvement of a young person in an alcohol-related accident, an alcohol-related problem at school, a police caution, an appearance at court after a drink-related incident, or a violent argument at home following drunkenness can all lead to a family crisis and an opportunity for change in the use of alcohol and the family functioning. Therefore social workers can use family crises caused by drinking in a positive way. Fanti has expressed this most succinctly when stating "crises are the way in" (Fanti 1990 : 151).

Stages in Family Change

1. Engagement and Disengagement by the Social Worker

This is the stage when a family has expressed a willingness to use help so that it can move from a pattern of enabling drug use towards attempts to change the enabling pattern. "The family crisis at this state is the crisis of unbalancing. By beginning to interrupt or stop a family pattern, such as enabling, the family's homoestasis becomes unbalanced [thus creating] the recovery crisis" (Muisener 1994 : 183). Family goals at this stage include, firstly, moves to transform itself away from denial of the adolescent's alcohol problem by becoming aware of its pattern of enabling and how it has related to the young person's substance misuse. Secondly, the family learns about the process of intoxication and heavy drinking and factors that may influence the process of adolescent alcohol use (Muisener 1994).

Parents are likely to struggle with bad feelings such guilt and pain about the young person's misuse of alcohol (Robinson 1990). They may find it very hard to accept this pain, fearing change and resisting help. In engaging so-called "resistant" families several general principles have been suggested (Steinglass 1987, Fanti 1990). These include:–

- The social worker should decide which members the family to include in helping.

- Early interviews should be arranged with the family, as close as possible to the initial contact with the young person.

The worker should:–

- show considerable interest in the family and be flexible in ways of including it.

- approach families with a rationale for work that is non-pejorative and non-judgmental and does not blame the family for the problem.

- adapt to the family needs and goals for future work,

- strongly believe in the help provided and convey this sense of conviction to the family.

2. Empowering

At this stage family members are actively working to avoid enabling the adolescent's problem drinking. Members of the family are actively pursuing strategies to help the young person be accountable for their use of alcohol and the consequences of behaviour associated with it. The crisis now is one of risking change. The unbalancing of the homoestatic process is continuing, despite attempts to return to previous patterns of enabling. The goals now are firstly, for parents to exert greater control within the family though effective setting of limits. Secondly, for parents to be more in control of their reactions towards the behaviour of the adolescent. Thirdly, for the parents to communicate with the young person as someone who is moving away from problem drinking and becoming more aware of his or her needs during this period (Muisener 1994). Again, many parents may fear change, still feeling doubts about their abilities and uncertain about making demands upon the young person.

Workers need to provide considerable empathy and guidance at this stage. Treadway (1989) has suggested:–

> *"The two key elements for empowering parents are for the [worker] (1) to communicate to the parents that they represent the core of the solution rather than the cause of the problem and (2) to help them learn how to pick their battles carefully. Parents cannot truly control adolescents, but they can learn how not to be controlled by them."* (Treadway 1989 : 149)

3. Integration

At this point, when the young person does not use alcohol or makes only limited use of it, families move through a period of addressing unresolved crises. Having stopped enabling, or having achieved a diminishing of enabling the adolescent's drinking, the family may still need help other areas. The family recovery crisis at this stage can be the crisis of revelation in that longer-standing problems may emerge and require attention. These may provoke considerable grief and anger. The primary goals are now, firstly, to continue family recovery work while turning attention towards the unresolved family crises and, secondly, to begin to come to terms with and heal the "legacy" of unresolved crises (Muisener 1994). Again, dramatic family events such as separations, death, divorce, and "family secrets", such as parental alcohol abuse or physical or sexual abuse, can be amongst the unresolved legacies which the family needs to confront – a difficult and frightening prospect for many family members. Individual help may be needed to struggle with the impact made by family crises and grief work can become a common focus on these occasions.

The Social Worker's Knowledge of Alcohol Use, Adolescent Development, and Family Dynamics in Helping with Families

It has been noted already that social workers have knowledge of family interaction patterns and skills in engaging families in the helping process. In addition, the worker can provide the family with knowledge and skills to assist their understanding of alcohol misuse, and coping strategies to deal with its impact on the family. The family can be encouraged to learn about adolescent intoxication and heavy drinking, including information about pre-contemplation, contemplation, action, maintenance, and relapse. The needs of younger brothers and sisters can be highlighted when an older child is abusing alcohol. For instance, issues about the anger surrounding chaos and confusion that has occurred in the family as a result of heavy drinking, anxieties about the reasons behind alcohol abuse by a brother or sister, and feelings generated by continuing use of alcohol in the past are all appropriate topics for consideration by the social worker.

Furthermore, family members can be helped to learn about adolescence and possible stresses on family life during adolescence. Promoting awareness of the meaning of adolescence to the family is a useful approach. Information about the sexual, cognitive, moral, and emotional changes that the young person is going through can assist parents in their work as parents. Additionally, increased awareness of parents mid-life experiences and changes in their relationship with each other can help to "normalise" transitions for anxious parents and assist them in coming to terms with such transitions.

In actively intervening with family dynamics social workers can stimulate leadership by encouraging parental teamwork, emphasising the importance of a consistent and balanced approach to the adolescent alcohol abuser and the importance of providing supportive authority and appropriate limit setting in consultation with the teenager. The worker can also encourage "the natural delineation of the generations . . . and help parents to be parents and teenagers to be teenagers" (Muisener 1994 : 191). Thus, well-defined and appropriate relationships are maintained with emotional separateness and the appropriate degree of intimacy, thereby, hopefully, avoiding over or under-involvement in parent: adolescent relationships. Finally, the worker can model and encourage active, effective, positive communication of feelings and open discussion of issues in the family, so that the attribution of blame is avoided. Nowinski (1990) has expressed most clearly the need for families with a substance abuser to improve mutual communication:–

"We must look closely at communication. Substance abuse . . . represents an attempt to cope with issues and emotions without communicating about them therefore communication becomes vital to recovery."
(Nowinski 1990 : 202)

The Peer Group – Preference and Support

If families play an important part in adolescent alcohol abuse then consideration should be given also to the place of the peer group in influencing adolescent behaviour. As with many other aspects of adolescent alcohol misuse, considerable debate surrounds the impact of the adolescent's peer group. Some – for example, Davies and Stacey (1972) – have highlighted the impact of the peer group, while others, such as Dorn (1983) and Coggans and McKellar (1995), have urged caution in such matters. It is nevertheless helpful for social workers to give some consideration to the role of peers. Muisener (1994) suggests:–

"The teenager's peer relationships are his second family. Peers are a transitional or secondary holding environment to the primary holding environment of family during adolescence. . . . Emotionally disruptive peer relationships during adolescence can thwart adoptive psychological development and leave the young person vulnerable . . . to drugs."
(Muisener 1994 : 91)

A young, moderate drinker who is only occasionally intoxicated may *prefer* to be with, and feel most "at home" amongst, a group of other moderate drinkers, while a young, heavy drinker may *prefer* the company of, and feel most "at home" with, a group of heavy drinkers. The group can offer *support* and *acceptance*, meeting needs for security and identity. Drinking can be one of the unspoken rules for inclusion and provide "ties that bind"; feelings of rejection or alienation may decrease as feelings of acceptance and belonging increase. At the same time, the drinking group can act as a "perpetuating environment" for continued drinking, encouragement of drinking, facilitating denial of problems, and establishing drinking as a primary social activity (Shilts 1991).

The implications here for social work are that the role of the peer group is an important factor in assessment of adolescent drinking and in helping. Reducing intake or giving up alcohol may well involve a challenge of not seeing, or seeing less of friends who abuse alcohol and developing new relationships with those who do not abuse it. This is a far-from-easy task. It can involve feelings of hurt, betrayal, and loneliness.

Group work can assist in examining these matters, if such a group is available in the local area. Negative behavioural patterns can be considered in it.

Identification, clarification, and sharing of problems can take place with those who are going through similar experiences (Bratter 1989, Myers & Anderson 1991). To look for alternative activities, avoiding heavy drinking friends and risky situations where heavy drinking typically occurs are examples of areas than can be worked on in such groups.

In addition, group work can help members give feedback to, and receive it from their peers; assist reinforcement of positive attitudes and behaviours to drinking; and monitor progress that is made. For a more detailed account of work with groups of problem drinkers see Barrie (1990). However, it is important to note that the social worker may not find it easy to set up or discover an appropriate group for teenage drinkers, although there may be better access for "older" teenagers with drinking problems who have offended, via groups run by the local Probation Service. For details about such groups see Chapter 8.

Conclusion

It is clear that there are no easy answers to the complex and multifaceted nature of alcohol misuse by adolescents. Each young person will encounter unique problems with alcohol that are the product of community, group, family, and intrapersonal pressures. Intervention by social workers is usually, with individuals, families and groups. There are well-established transferable knowledge and skills that social workers can draw upon in working with adolescents who misuse alcohol and their families, while some specialised skills are required. Social workers have a lot to offer in their work with young problem drinkers and, with appropriate training and support, they can intervene confidently, purposefully, and effectively. It is important not to over-react to young people's drinking, but, at the same time, when drinking problems do occur social workers should be able to identify them and act to effect a remedy in a variety of ways with a combination of care, confidence, and conviction.

Chapter 6
Elderly People

Introduction

The later stages of life have been seen from a variety of perspectives and there are various interpretations as to when one becomes an "elderly person". There is some agreement that the age of 60 or 65 is seen as the beginning of another life-stage, often, but not always, following retirement. However, as Marshall (1983) and Froggatt (1990) have pointed out, the label "elderly person" could be applied to people who vary in age by as much as 25 years! Hence attempts have been made by these authors to distinguish between the "young old", those under the age of 75; the "old old"; ranging from 75 to 85; and the "very old", aged 85 and beyond.

We must be very clear that each elderly person is unique and special. Overall, each has experienced and will experience their life in different ways, based, for example, upon their earlier developmental patterns and upon social divisions such as class, "race", and gender. Nevertheless, it is perhaps useful also to consider the experiences that older people may have had in common. One experience is likely to have been the loss of several significant people or several significant roles – in some cases these might be parental or work roles. Other shared experiences include a likely decrease in income and some decline in physical health; ageist attitudes will make an impact and there may be a movement from independence to interdependence with others or dependence on others (Scrutton 1989). At the same time elderly people can have more space available to them and opportunity to express themselves, to fulfil their own needs and the needs of others.

Yet what is also clearly evident is that neither the literature on social work and older people nor that on problem drinking and social work gives much time, space or attention to examining problem drinking amongst elderly people (Hunt 1982, Marshall 1983, BASW 1989, Collins *et al.* 1990). Indeed, there have been few studies of problem drinking amongst elderly people either in Europe or the United States. This is in contrast to the amount of attention given to other groups of problem drinkers, such as young people. A variety of reasons have been put forward for this neglect. These include assumptions that excessive drinking is not a particular difficulty for elderly people, with lower levels of consumption and fewer problem drinkers in older age groups (Atkinson & Kofed 1982, Mishara & Kastenbaum 1980, Office of Population Censuses and Surveys 1990, Goddard 1991). Some studies of problem drinkers have even excluded those above the age of 60 or 65 years, as it has been argued that alcohol problems amongst elderly people were self-limiting because of changing psychological, social and economic factors (Drew 1968). For instance, it has been claimed that elderly people drink less as they grow older, have fewer financial resources to purchase drink, have less easy access to it, are more likely to abstain from alcohol, and if they had experienced serious problems with alcohol when younger they would either have died or no longer have the energy to continue with their drinking at the same level (Cahalan & Room 1974, Johnson & Goodrich 1974, Anderson 1980). So, the general tendency has been to "play down" problem drinking amongst elderly people and, if older people do drink, so what! They had experienced long and demanding lives. They were entitled to have a few drinks, which do no harm and can have positive value in promoting relaxation and health (Malcolm 1984, Smith 1988, Goodman & Ward 1989). Let them get on with it and enjoy themselves!

Ageism and Discrimination Against Elderly Problem Drinkers

At this point we should acknowledge that ageism permeates our society and, for instance, may even be inadvertently present in this chapter. Ageism can easily lead to the marginalisation of issues relating to old age and particularly to the problems of old age (Pitt 1982 in Thompson 1993). Thus problem drinking by elderly people is likely to be an issue that is well down the list of priorities of many helping agencies in view of the way in which ageism permeates society's institutions.

A number of "common assumptions . . . reflect and reinforce ageism" (Thompson 1993 : 84). For example, older people can be seen as:–

- "Past it", a burden, and a drain upon existing resources and hence other client/user groups should have preferential help.

- Patronised and have their decisions made for them by workers without proper consultation or consideration of their rights.

- "In decline", as "ill" – the "what can you expect at your age" syndrome.

- Lonely and alone, rather than alone and perhaps content or with a wide social network of contacts and also content.

- Poor and with financial difficulties.

(Thompson 1993)

These assumptions can easily lead to stereotyping when assessments are made and ageism can make a profound impact on the life of an older person, leading to feelings of being a burden and of having low self-esteem. The stereotypes of ageism are often internalised by those suffering discrimination. Therefore, those receiving strongly negative messages will often see themselves negatively, and experience lower morale and eroded confidence (Thompson 1993). There is also a need to consider the fact that elderly problem drinkers may also suffer from "double jeopardy". That is, they can be labelled and stereotyped as "old" and "past it" as well as "alcoholic". Thompson has expressed this most concisely:–

> *"When two or more such oppressions combine or intersect their impact*
> *can be even more significant and the resulting disempowerment even*
> *more far reaching."* (Thompson 1993 : 99).

In the situation of the elderly female problem drinker, then "triple jeopardy" is likely to be the case with the person labelled as "past it", "alcoholic" and likely to suffer from sexism. It is acknowledged that women problem drinkers are subject to particular stigma in a way that male problem drinkers are not (Kent 1990, Ettorre 1992). Older female problem drinkers will suffer additional disadvantages on account of low status, restrictions imposed by traditional roles, loss of these traditional roles and loss of economic power. The protracted experience of sexism experienced and suffered over a lifetime can make it even more difficult to maintain feelings of dignity and self-worth. Hence the criticisms aimed at, and the shame felt by, an elderly female problem drinker may be particularly problematic, discouraging efforts to seek help.

The attitudes of some workers may be open to criticism as well. For instance, Marshall (1989 : 109) points out:–

> *"Social work with elderly people . . . is littered with unchallenged,*
> *usually negative received ideas. These ideas are often not put into words*
> *but are carried into social work from society generally."*

Also, if workers have negative stereotypes about problem drinkers (Collins *et al.* 1988) then they may be likely to have even stronger ones about older problem drinkers. For example, Carruth *et al.* (1973) and Googins (1984) "found that older problem drinkers were viewed least favourably by community care providers and these attitudes presented considerable barriers to [helping]" (Pruzinsky 1987 : 89). Thus it is clear that workers need to be very aware of, and sensitive to, their own attitudes in working with elderly problem drinkers.

Countering Ageism in Working with Elderly People who are Problem Drinkers

It is clear that one important task is to counter ageism that inevitably will always be present in work with older problem drinkers. This will include maintaining an awareness of the structural context, the economic and political setting for one's work (Phillipson 1982). In order to fight against ageism we should:–

- Avoid depersonalising myths or stereotypes.
- Recognise and act upon associated, interwoven, and multiple oppression, including racism and sexism.
- Beware of excessive reliance on medical models which may emphasise pathology or disease.
- Avoid restricting any service on account of age "limits".
- Avoid becoming entangled in backing up any negative images.
- Recognise that elderly people are still moving onwards, still in the process of learning, still developing.
- Provide positive feedback that enhances dignity, rights, self-identity and self-esteem.
- Be wary of creating dependency and move towards inter-dependence.
- Empower elderly people to look to choice and find meaning in their lives.
- Avoid excessively "separating off" elderly people from ourselves and others, when we are all involved in the reality of ageing.

(Kuhn 1986, Townsend 1986, Bytheway & Johnson 1990, Thompson 1993)

The Effects of Alcohol on Elderly People and Misdiagnosis

In several respects, elderly people are more vulnerable to the effects of alcohol and are more susceptible to its impact on their bodies (Black 1990). Body water content declines and body fat increases with age, while lean body mass decreases by about 10% between the ages of 20 and 70. The combined reduction of body water content and lean body mass probably accounts for higher blood alcohol concentrations in elderly people than in younger people after the intake of alcohol (Hartford & Samoraishi 1984). Also the liver and kidneys take longer to break down alcohol; it remains in the body longer and is more likely to affect the brain and liver. Hence alcohol is likely to affect older people more readily than those who are younger; smaller doses of alcohol produce more rapid intoxication for longer periods of time as the body has a decreasing ability to process alcohol (Rosin & Glatt 1971, USDHEW 1971, Carruth *et al.* 1974). As a result some authors have argued that, with this increased sensitivity to alcohol, different "sensible limits" for drinking should be used in work with elderly people, rather than those applied to the general population (Graham 1986, Saunders *et al.* 1989).

Also symptoms of intoxication sometimes may be disregarded because they closely resemble other ailments which may affect elderly people – for example, the symptoms of Organic Brain Syndrome include impairment of orientation, memory, intellectual functioning, and judgement and shallowness of affect. Intoxication often produces the same symptoms, but if a patient is elderly, then they may be likely to be diagnosed as suffering from Organic Brain Syndrome (Pruzinsky 1987). An elderly problem drinker visiting an out-patient or accident and emergency department can stagger, have slurred speech, or be incoherent and confused. This can be seen as evidence of senility rather than an alcohol problem (Sherouse 1983). In fact, it has been suggested that at least 10% of patients presenting with dementia have alcohol-related brain disease (Dunne & Schipperheijn 1989).

The general point is that alcohol problems in elderly people are "often missed because many signs are attributed to ageing, rather than alcohol use. For example, symptoms of confusion, paranoia, disorientation, memory loss, depression, anxiety, aggressive behaviours and social isolation are often ignored for this reason" (Blackmon 1985 : 192). Thus, it is recognised that many hospital doctors and general practitioners have difficulties in identifying alcohol-related problems and, therefore, in working with elderly people; misdiagnosis and masking of symptoms can be a frequently encountered problem (Shaw *et al.* 1978, Cartwright 1980, McInnes & Powell 1994). Hence, the appropriate identification and diagnosis of alcohol problems by medical personnel are particularly important in working with elderly people because alcohol abuse, in addition,

> *"may be present in non specific ways such as falls, accidental hypo-*
> *thermia, malnutrition, . . . confusional states and decreased self caring*
> *skills, although classical presentation with both physical . . . and*
> *psy-chiatric symptoms does occur"* (Crome 1991 : 176).

In fact, Wright & Whyley (1994) identify alcohol as one of the three main causes of falls, which are a significant cause of mortality and morbidity in older people, because it slows down reactions, weakens judgement, balance and self-control. Woodhouse (1987) implicated alcohol in nearly 50% of cases of hypothermia because many older people drink alcohol to warm themselves up and keep fuel bills down, when, in reality, alcohol speeds up the loss of body heat and increases the risk of hypothermia.

Incidence of Alcohol-Related Problems Amongst Elderly People
We know that all studies indicate that problem drinking is, or becomes, a well-established behaviour pattern amongst some elderly people. In the United States it has been estimated that between 2% and 12% of elderly people are problem drinkers (Rathbone-McCuan *et al.* 1976, Schukit 1979, Atkinson 1984), while studies in Britain have suggested that between 9% and 15% of the elderly population are problem drinkers (Moss & Beresford Davies 1967, Smith 1980, Bridgewater *et al.* 1987, Saunders *et al.* 1989). It is estimated that in

England and Wales at present half a million men, 15% of the total population, and a quarter of a million women, 5% of the total population, over 65 are drinking in excess of recommended limits (Alcohol Concern 1996). Therefore, Wesson (1992) suggests that overall alcohol consumption by older people has increased by one-fifth in the past decade. In hospital populations, studies of medical admissions over the age of 65 have revealed between 5% and 9% of patients drinking above the recommended levels (Naik & Jones 1994, Bristow & Clare 1992, Mangion *et al.* 1992). It is not easy to make direct comparisons between studies because of differences used in the definition of alcohol problems, in the samples studied and in the data collection procedures (Saunders *et al.* 1989). However, two studies in Britain have produced important findings. Firstly, in a study in Liverpool of a large sample of GP patients, it was discovered that 20% of elderly males and females who were drinking regularly were exceeding recommended sensible limits of alcohol consumption (Saunders *et al.* 1989). Secondly, another study of GP patients in central Newcastle revealed that 27% of elderly men and 9% of elderly women in the sample were heavy drinkers, while 13% of the total number of respondents drank enough to put themselves at risk from alcoholic liver disease (Bridgwater *et al.* 1987). What emerges also is that other figures may well be underestimates of the prevalence of problem drinking, for a number of reasons. For example, traditional approaches to estimates of drinking prevalence may not be applicable to elderly people. Arrest statistics may not indicate the extent of the problem because of possible reluctance to charge elderly problem drinkers, while hospital statistics may reveal, as already noted, a tendency to misdiagnose alcohol problems or to protect older patients from a diagnosis which specifies alcohol as a contributory factor (Rathbone-McCuan & Hashimi 1982).

It is also particularly significant to note that, in the light of future projections, by the year 2000 elderly people will constitute an even larger percentage than the present 20% of the overall population and hence the figures quoted earlier are likely to increase proportionally. Therefore, the number of elderly people with alcohol-related problems is likely to grow in proportion to the increase in the elderly population as a whole. Also, UK *per capita* consumption has increased by 60% in volume during the past 30 years and, at present, people in the middle years, i.e. their 50s, are consuming far more alcohol than their parents did at the same age. Thus, "middle aged" people at present are likely to continue consuming alcohol when they in turn become "elderly" people, with a proportionate increase in alcohol-related problems (Robinson *et al.* 1989).

Four Groups of Elderly Problem Drinkers
Researchers in the field of alcohol problems amongst elderly people have classified these groups:

1. Long term problem drinkers who started early in life.

2. Those problem drinkers who started later in life.

3. Those who have had intermittent problems with drinking.

4. Those combining alcohol with other drugs.

(Hubbard *et al.* 1979, Malcolm 1984, Pruzinsky 1987, Crome 1991)

1. Long Term Problem Drinkers Who Started Drinking from Early in Life
This group of people will have survived into old age and continued drinking, despite expectancies that they might spontaneously give up their excessive alcohol intake, or die as a result of their long term problems. It has been suggested that this group of elderly problem drinkers would be more likely to have physical complications such as liver and heart problems and would be more likely to have underlying personality problems (Crome 1991). Some writers describe these drinkers as chronic long term "alcoholics" who were in the greatest danger of institutionalisation or death (Hubbard *et al.* 1979). Hubbard *et al.* found that the long term problem drinkers in their study all lived alone and were either divorced or widowed and most of their support systems had "given up" on them (Hubbard *et al.* 1979).

Their children and former partners were very resentful and abusive of these "alcoholics", fed up with disappointments about, and deceptions from them – often culminating in a total lack of communication. Likewise, community/ helping agencies such as AA, detoxification units, and social service workers were highly resentful as a consequence of previous negative contacts, lies, deceit, refusals to accept help, and accusations against staff.

These older problem-drinkers were themselves extremely vulnerable to abuse and likely to be victims of crime. They were exploited by "friends". They were often victims of stealing, or attacked while drunk. Often these clients lived in the poorest accommodation – in low cost hostels, in the poorest areas – with high crime rates. They were perceived to have the following "basic styles of adaptation" (Hubbard *et al.* 1979 : 167) :–

(i)   Withdrawn, depressive, characterised by hopelessness, suicide attempts, and great problems in community living. These drinkers were said to be apathetic about receiving help and all had histories of hospitalisation, due to alcohol problems.

(ii) Hostile paranoia, vacillating between demanding agency services and then accusing agency workers of forcing them to accept services or treating them badly. They were often involved in fights or arrests for drunk and disorderly offences.

(iii)   Manipulative, deceptive, being very adept at getting services, while denying any problems with alcohol and maintaining heavy drinking. Their resourcefulness improved their quality of life but at the same time provided them with considerable resources for drinking excessively.

2. *Later Onset of Problem Drinking*

In these situations the elderly people concerned had started problem drinking later in life. They were likely to have shown no previous evidence of problems with alcohol and seemed to be responding to the losses and stressors of ageing and used alcohol to cope with, or escape from, their difficulties (Pruzinsky 1987). Some elderly people medicated themselves and used alcohol to alleviate pains associated with a physical illness, such as arthritis or rheumatism. In fact, the relief obtained was short term but the condition causing the pain was often made worse (Sherouse 1983). A chronic pain cycle became established, with drinking used as a relief, and if no medical remedy for the cause of pain was provided then the cycle of pain and relief drinking continued.

An accumulation of losses is a common feature amongst elderly people. For some, loss of employment through retirement can lead to an increase in alcohol consumption to relieve negative feelings, tension, and stresses if appropriate alternative leisure interests or voluntary or part time work have not been found to meet the person's needs. Losses of partners and friends can also have a negative effect. An individual may have problems in coping with boredom, loneliness, hopelessness, depression, and anxiety, turning to alcohol as a cry for help (Zimberg 1974, Butler & Lewis 1977). Sometimes alcohol problems may have become established as a result of a specific trauma or loss such as that of a particular job or of a long term partner, the onset of serious physical disability, and, as a consequence, lack of meaningful roles and positive self-esteem (Roisin & Glatt 1971, Hubbard *et al.* 1979). When Leigh (1980) interviewed 200 elderly people about what contributed to their need for, and use of, alcohol or medication one-half of the men and a quarter of the women gave loneliness as the major reason. In their attempts to deal with loneliness 13% "took a drink" (Leigh 1980). Some writers have concluded that elderly women are particularly at risk (Carruth *et al.* 1974, Blose 1978). It has been pointed out that older women frequently live longer, live alone, have been widowed and generally, having suffered the loss of various significant roles, turned to alcohol as a way of coping alone with the stresses of ageing (Pruzinsky 1987).

Family members could tend to deny the existence of alcohol problems in their elderly parents, rationalising that they had "always liked a few drinks", or describing drinking as a help in overcoming physical ailments such as constipation and memory loss. The elderly people themselves had a tendency to use such explanations as well (Hubbard *et al.* 1979).

3. Intermittent Problems with Drinking

These elderly people may have had intermittent problems with drinking over the years, in that they may have had occasional episodes of heavy or problem drinking, but experienced considerable periods of sobriety as well. In old age they may have been less successful in controlling their drinking because of the removal of constraints such as the need to maintain involvement in regular employment (if employed) and a reduction or ending of family commitments, ties and obligations alongside the appearance of physical strains and additional blows to their self-esteem.

4. Combining Alcohol and Other Drugs

Over 75% of those aged over 75 in Britain receive prescribed medication. Hence, elderly people, particularly females, consume more medication than any other age group. They are a high risk group which is likely to suffer negative effects from the combination of drugs and alcohol (Gomberg 1982). Dependence on alcohol and one or more psychotropic drugs was found in 14% of elderly patients in one study (Finlayson *et al.* 1988). Alternatively alcohol may only be used infrequently or in small amounts, but can be dangerous if taken in conjunction with a number of prescribed drugs, affecting memory, mobility, feelings, and a host of other cognitive and physical functions (Hubbard *et al.* 1979). Clients mixing alcohol and drugs could display symptoms of diffuse, organically related dementia but, in fact, were victims of the combined effects of alcohol and "over the counter" medication. Physical problems for these elderly people could include poor nutrition, dizziness, fainting, and injuries from falls, based on their reactions to a progressive "overdose" of alcohol and drugs (Hubbard *et al.* 1979).

These elderly people tended to attribute the decline of their abilities to the "normal ageing" process and were likely not to inform their general practitioners of the amount and extent of their alcohol use, nor the total number of drugs they were taking, as they were often seeing several "specialists" in addition to their own general practitioner. In most cases improvement was swift when alcohol intake and drug use were closely monitored (Hubbard *et al.* 1979).

In turn, there is some evidence in Great Britain that elderly people may be taking drugs and do not realise the use of alcohol is contra-indicated. Cartwright & Smith (1988) note that, in their study, 78% of the elderly people receiving medication had no recollection of being given advice that they should not take alcohol when, in actual fact, it was prohibited because of their prescribed drugs. Furthermore, GP's were frequently inaccurate in assessing the drinking habits of elderly patients, even when prescribed drugs mixed badly with alcohol (Cartwright & Smith 1988).

Helping Elderly Problem Drinkers
Generally there is cause for optimism about helping older problem drinkers especially those whose drinking problems are of recent onset. At the same time there are several caveats.

Some elderly people may be less likely to reach out for help. It has been suggested that they are more likely to hide their drinking for a variety of reasons and to be unwilling to admit to having drinking problems. Over half of the sample "cases" in a large scale study in Liverpool did not admit to having problems because of alcohol (Saunders *et al.* 1989), which reflected earlier reports that elderly people may be more prone to denial than younger people because of feelings of shame, "moral failure" and the high social stigma attached to drinking problems in this age group (Haberman 1970, Barnes 1979). Accusations of "weak will", immorality, and having lost control of one's life may be very real fears for this particular generation. Also they are less likely to be referred to helping agencies, as younger people are, because of job pressures and legal requirements such as those contained in a supervision or probation order. These elements are not usually present in the life of the older person (Pruzinsky 1987). Furthermore, there may be genuine fantasies and uncertainties about the role of helping agencies such as alcohol advisory services, and fears that difficulties with drink problems will be inevitably resolved by drug treatment, hospitalisation, or harsh, combative attitudes from the helper (Goodman & Ward 1989).

In turn, there are indications that social workers may underestimate the prevalence of problem drinking amongst elderly people. Social workers' attitudes may well often involve seeing drinking as a pleasurable activity and a consolation for the elderly person. They may well feel "generally uncertain about how they should respond, if at all, to evidence that an elderly client was drinking to excess, but not to a point at which his or her health was immediately at risk" (Smith 1988 : 350). In fact, Lawson's (1994) study in Hounslow indicated that even when alcohol abuse *had* profoundly affected an elderly person's health, the workers concerned did not offer any intervention. Social work employees in this study were more likely to underestimate the prevalence of alcohol problems among elderly people than with any other client/user group. On average only 4% of elderly people on social work caseloads were *reported* as being affected by alcohol abuse compared with the much higher rates of prevalence of alcohol problems amongst elderly people generally that were noted earlier in this chapter. In Lawson's study one social work respondent, in reply to a non-response to an older drinker's problems, claimed, "He's in his 70s, why shouldn't he do what he wants?" The overall feeling amongst social work respondents seemed to be based on the ageist assumption that elderly clients/users with drink problems were too old to change the "habits of a lifetime" (Lawson 1994 : 337).

In general, social workers interacting with problem drinkers find it hard to achieve a balance between the desire to respect client/user rights and privacy, and at the same time not avoiding discussion of problems with drink. This is particularly the case with older problem drinkers (Graham & Romaniec 1986). Confidence, combined with sensitivity, is important in intervening and assessing problem drinking, as we have seen in earlier chapters. However, in work with elderly clients this difficulty is likely to be "compounded by higher numbers of untrained workers, lower awareness of the possibility of alcohol problems and a lack of expertise in assessment" (Simpson *et al*. 1994 : 585).

We have noted that both in the past and in the present there has been little consideration of the needs of elderly people with drinking problems. Indeed, even now in the era of Community Care and care management,

> *"there is a general lack of appreciation that older people may have*
> *alcohol problems . . . few community care plans see them as a group that*
> *need identification by virtue of their alcohol related problems".*
> (Harrison *et al*. 1996 : 89)

A basic dilemma is "whether older people with alcohol problems should be encapsulated within services for older people or whether services for people with alcohol problems should include adults of all ages". (Harrison *et al*. 1996 : 89)

Surprisingly, the debate about priorities or appropriate access routes by care management services for elderly people with drinking problems has not really started. However, for the moment, social workers can continue to make important contributions. There are important and particular messages about avoiding excessive confrontation in the early stages of helping an elderly person with drink problems and of the need to bear in mind the significance of motivational interviewing approaches, based upon understanding and empathy (Miller 1983). Furthermore, Prochaska and DiClemente's (1983, 1986) work on the stage the drinker has reached in considering giving up drinking, be it pre-contemplation, contemplation or action, is equally as relevant to work with older problem drinkers as in work with other groups (see also Chapters 4 & 5).

Identification and Assessment of Elderly Problem Drinkers

A key point to be borne in mind is the importance of a whole range of workers involved with elderly people in identifying problem drinking. This includes, for example, social workers, general practitioners, hospital based doctors, health visitors, community psychiatric nurses, ministers, ambulance drivers, home helps, and providers of meals. For example, it is interesting to note that a study of

50 home help clients in a London borough showed that 28% of them had asked for drink to be brought to them on a weekly basis and half of these consumed up to three bottles of spirits a week (Longman 1985). Also, another survey of elderly people receiving a regular home help service found that 12% drank every day (Fanti 1985). This is not to say that all these home help clients actually experienced problems with drink, but work by de Sauza in Edinburgh indicated that 7% of the home helps in her study reported having clients with an alcohol problem (de Sauza 1991). However, it is also known that, in general, professionals working with older people, from social workers to home helps to chiropodists, are unaware of the fact that limits for "sensible" drinking for the general population may be inappropriate for older people (Wesson 1992). Wesson's survey revealed that 90% could not recall even having seen information related to older people and alcohol. Thus it is important for all workers interacting with elderly people to be aware of warning signs that an alcohol problem might exist. There are the more obvious points such as the presence of bottles, the smell of drink, drinking in the worker's presence, being intoxicated when the worker is present, frequent comments about alcohol, and requests for alcohol to be bought. In addition, the person may seem unkempt, have slurred speech, forget medication and appointments, and lose money (Luthringer 1973). These are just some of the warning signs. Without "going overboard" or becoming paranoid about possible drink problems, it is important to consider the amount of alcohol being consumed and its possible contribution to the elderly client's psychological and social situation (Hubbard *et al.* 1979).

Skills used in assessing the drinking problems of elderly people are usually similar to those used in assessment with other problem drinkers (Hunt & Harwin 1979, Hunt 1982, Leckie 1990). As Hunt (1982 : 41) states, "the knowledge and skills employed are those the social worker would expect to use in the course of the initial assessment of any referred client". The skills emphasised are listening, collecting information, sensitive follow-up of relevant issues, appropriate but not excessive reassurance, open-ended questioning, explaining, information giving, and the sharing of assessment. The assessment of drinking itself would require specific details as outlined in earlier chapters. The focus would be upon identifying the relationship between the client's drinking and problems being experienced. In assessment, in working with elderly problem drinkers, as noted earlier, the relationship between alcohol and physical health in old age is crucial. Many older clients may face serious health problems caused or aggravated by their use of alcohol. Saunders *et al.* (1989 : 107) have expressed this succinctly:–

> *"Deterioration in health whether a consequence of alcohol abuse or an incidental accompaniment of ageing, is likely to be an important factor in the natural history of problem drinking in later life."*

Recognition of high risk crisis situations is also important when assessing elderly people's drinking. Amongst elderly people with alcohol problems it is acknowledged that in the United States between 5% and 15% suffer from a pre-existing depressive disorder while it has been estimated that alcohol is an important factor in about one-third of suicides in elderly people (Schuckit 1979, American Medical Association 1977). Older problem drinkers have higher rates of suicide attempts than those elderly people who are not problem drinkers (Mishara *et al.* 1973, Schuckit 1979). It is in these situations that, when required, social workers should be prepared to act quite quickly and decisively. Of course, knowledge and experience of crisis work are invaluable as noted in earlier chapters (O'Hagan 1986, Leckie 1990, Fanti 1990). The crisis can be viewed not only as a traumatic event but also as a situation where normal problem-solving or coping mechanisms have failed. Both worker and client can work together to help the client regain equilibrium, re-establish problem-solving mechanisms, and develop possibilities for growth within the crisis. But, at the same time, the elderly client experiencing a crisis with alcohol problems should not be asked to take too much responsibility too quickly (Hunt 1982).

Use of Transferable Knowledge and Skills in Intervention

As we have seen already, social workers have transferable knowledge and skills to assist them in their work with elderly problem drinkers, based upon individual counselling, family and group interventions, and in linking people with available resources. In relation to the last-mentioned point, knowledge and use of systems approaches can be invaluable in making contacts with formal and informal organisations (Pincus & Minahan 1973). Many elderly problem drinkers may lack information about available resources, but wish to make use of them. Social workers can act as brokers and advocates in such situations: for example, helping to link elderly people with volunteers, to provide opportunities to attend day centres and lunch clubs in order to combat loneliness or isolation if they are required or, for those with more prominent drink problems, to develop an involvement with Alcoholics Anonymous. AA can offer a social network and a fellowship for elderly problem drinkers, which may have been missing. AA tends to attract "more mature" problem drinkers and their "one day at a time" approach can be extremely effective with an older person experiencing drink problems, stressing the quality of each day of life rather than the quality of life that may be left (Pruzinsky 1987).

The need to maintain manageable, achievable targets and aims in work with individual, older problem drinkers is clearly necessary. The use of contracts, problem solving, task centred, cognitive behavioural and social skills approaches are familiar to most social workers, with their clear emphasis on achievement of specific goals and requirements for review at regular intervals

(Collins *et al*. 1988, Leckie 1990). Furthermore, all social workers should be familiar with the challenges which elderly people may face at this life stage, as a result of teaching and learning sequences on elders which form part of human growth and development sequences that lie at the core of most social work courses.

General Guidelines for Intervention in Helping Elderly People with Drink Problems

Some general guidelines can be provided in helping elderly people with drinking problems, based on the ideas of Richard Goodstein (1978), summarised thus:–

1. The help offered to an older problem drinker would be similar to that offered to someone younger. Too often, drinking problems experienced by elderly people are dismissed under the assumption that they are complaining unreasonably, are unlikely to benefit from help, or wouldn't appreciate the help offered.

2. In working with elderly problem drinkers it is important to bear in mind that they are survivors and have many strengths which have been built up over many years and can be built upon again. It is all too easy to exaggerate problems and undervalue strengths, good qualities, assets, and positive elements.

3. There is obvious value in reaching out, showing active interest, and responding positively to elderly problem drinkers.

One practical point is that some elderly people may not be willing or able to leave their homes to participate in office-based interventions, so there is a need to reach out, when necessary, to offer help that is home based (Mishara *et al*.1975, Sherouse 1983). Such home visits are, of course, a matter of common practice amongst social workers. However, voluntary workers in some councils on alcohol are becoming much more office orientated, with home visits an exception rather than the rule; sometimes rather complex procedures are involved in order to obtain "permission" for home visits. Clearly in the case of older people there is a need to facilitate visits as easily and as readily as possible.

4. Empathy is as important in working with older problem drinkers as in counselling any other clients.

5. As a worker one may be thought of, and responded to, in relation to previous helping contacts which the elderly person has had in their life which may or may not have been positive. The worker may represent grandchild, child, parent, and peer at various points in the helping relationship, even in the same interview at the same time.

6.	There is a need to use all possible resources on the client's behalf, helping to establish an involvement or reinvolvement in various community groups, contacts or activities, if that is the elderly person's wish.

Overall, the task of the worker in intervening with the elderly problem drinker can be summed up as:–

> *"To assist them in rediscovering strengths, getting involved with people and discovering life is worth living at whatever age."*
> (Sherouse 1983 : 122)

Families and Elderly People with Drink Problems

Many elderly people with drink problems live with their families. Here again the social worker will have transferable knowledge of family interaction and skills in working with families (Fanti 1990). However, it should be noted that some studies have indicated that the use of alcohol by elderly people can be encouraged by family members "in the belief that it was somehow socially and psychologically therapeutic for alcohol intake to increase in the later years" (Hubbard *et al.* 1979 : 170). Those taking on the role of encourager/facilitator of drinking have been described as "enablers" by Wegscheider who has made extensive studies of families with a drink-abusing member (Wegscheider 1981). As noted in an earlier chapter on adolescents the enabler supports the alcohol misuser and lets them function as freely as possible, while avoiding the consequences of drinking. The enabler helps to delay any crisis that may threaten the problem drinker or threaten the stability of the family and regularly "covers up" for the drinker's behaviour, plus taking on responsibility for maintaining the family (Fanti 1990).

In situations of problem drinking by an elderly person the enabler may be either the partner or the parent. For problem drinkers aged over 80 there may rarely be a partner and the drinker may well be living with an adult child, a brother or a sister, or another relative (or may well be living in a hostel, in sheltered accommodation, or an elderly persons' home). As drink problems progress and continue, the people surrounding the elderly problem drinker are inevitably affected.

In addition, there are other elderly people who do not actually have drinking problems themselves but suffer as a result of interacting with those who do. In these situations the elderly people "were essentially trapped; unable to be totally independent, they relied on the most logical form of support, family and friends. Although they recognised that they were being abused, these clients saw the alternative as non-support and eventual institutionalisation" (Hubbard *et al.* 1979:169). Verbal, economic and sometimes physical abuse is directed from drinking husbands towards elderly wives, from drinking in-laws to elderly relatives and from drinking friends or neighbours to elderly friends and neighbours.

Work with Adult Children or Others

In some instances elderly people with drink problems may be living with adult children. The child or children acting as carer(s) may have mixed emotions and strong feelings, varying between love and affection, resentment and annoyance, genuine care, and carrying out tasks because of a sense of duty or obligation (Froggatt 1990). It is possible that the elderly person's behaviour may become bizarre as problem drinking continues. The person may become unkempt, use abusive language and steal money to buy drink; there may be accidents and falls. One of the more difficult aspects for social workers is to know how to put the immediate difficulty into context (Fanti 1990). As Fanti inquires (1990 : 133):–

> *"Is the presenting problem new to the family? How threatening is it to their stability? Is the problem a part of a chaotic alcohol focussed life-style? How and when should social workers respond in a way that helps the family eliminate its focus on alcohol?"*

As noted in Chapter 5 Fanti goes on to adopt Steinglass's (1980) model, with its emphasis on the three c's – calm, chaos, and crisis. The latter stage of crisis is the family state which results from a new problem that endangers the entire stability of the family. A family experiencing a crisis, such as an elderly member attacking someone following a drinking bout or seriously injuring themselves, is much more likely to be interested in major structural change, because they believe things just cannot return to the way they were (Fanti 1990). The structural change can free-up efforts to eliminate problem alcohol use rather than examining "presenting" problems such as financial difficulties. The social worker can get trapped into the role of family enabler and try to clear up and clean up the "messes" presented by the elderly person who is abusing alcohol and the worker can start to believe that only he or she can save the family from real disruption. Therefore an alcohol-related crisis may be prevented and the family continues to be doomed to long term failure in dealing with drink problems (Fanti 1990). A crisis can destabilise the whole family system and open it up to new ways of functioning. A crisis related to problem-atic alcohol use in an elderly parent is an opportunity for change in the use of alcohol within the family – a major possibility for alterations in family dynamics and to bring into prominence previous drinking difficulties. Such crises can be used by social workers, as noted earlier, to help families more effectively promote change (O'Hagan 1986).

Work with Partners

In working with partners of elderly problem drinkers various factors, according to Sherouse (1983), will influence the partners' thinking and feelings about entering into the helping process:–

1. The extent of the difficulties presented by the elderly problem drinker and how the drinker has responded to helping endeavours in the past.

2. Whether the partner believes his or her own involvement will make a difference and the extent to which he or she recognises the partner's problems or tries to minimise them.

3. Whether the partner of the elderly problem drinker also abuses alcohol.

4. The health and functional capacity of the partner.

5. The strength of the partnership; its stability and ability to meet mutual needs.

Some of the emotional difficulties, stress, and possible physical abuse suffered by elderly partners of problem drinkers may be such as to make them feel unwilling to be involved in any helping process (Gayford 1978, Orford *et al.* 1976, Byles 1978). Alternatively, further attempts or a "last try" effort may be possible. Whatever the case, social work involvement with an elderly partner is essential at initial contact and assessment stages; hopefully, it will be possible during continued intervention. In working with the partner of an older problem drinker on an individual basis the worker may find that the partner is not expecting any help. The worker may need to assist the partner to become engaged and involved in the helping process. Practical and emotional support should be given, helping the partner to relieve feelings of confusion, anger, shame, guilt, or anxiety – if such feelings are evident – and they may well be. The partner may benefit from receiving information about alcohol and its effects, if they are not already in possession of such knowledge. If the partner wishes to do so, the worker can assist him or her to move away from what might be a socially withdrawn position and help in the re-establishment of social interests and relationships. Or in the taking up of new interests and relationships, in order to empower the partner to meet their own needs more effectively, thus avoiding preoccupation with the needs of the problem drinking partner.

Coping tactics can be discussed with the partner – that is, strategies for helping them to deal with difficulties presented by the drinker. These could include a refusal on the partner's part to ignore problem drinking, an approach which does not condone the drinking but encourages contemplation and action about its problems. Drunkenness and drunken behaviour should not be rewarded by providing a steady stream of positive reinforcement after such incidents; rather, the partner should be encouraged to respect the drinker as a person, but help them face up to their responsibilities, the costs and consequences of their actions, such as when sustaining injuries after falls when drunk or spending too much money on a "binge".

The worker may need to make decisions about seeing the elderly problem drinker and their partner for regular, joint interviews depending on how they see their relationship, its strengths and its problems (James & Wilson 1986). There can be many benefits in such joint interviews. Usually, if the partnership has lasted for many years into "old age" it is likely that it will continue, either destructively or constructively. Joint interviews can open up communication, clarify mutual needs, encourage mutual understanding, the continuation and development of positive behaviours, and, hopefully, the reduction or extinction of negative behaviours between the partners. At a minimum, the time, opportunity, and space for mutual discussion can be most valuable and, if interviews are sometimes stormy, they are unlikely to be very different from day-to-day communication experienced by the partners.

General Survival Tips
It is also helpful for the social worker to be aware of some "general survival tips" in working with family members when they are living with an elderly person's drinking. Adopted from suggestions by Fanti (1990), these include:–

1. Encouraging and suggesting that discussions, debates, and arguments during periods of actual drinking should be avoided and the best times to discuss and work on difficulties are when the older problem drinker is sober or free of alcohol.

2. Responsibility for continuing drinking or stopping drinking rests with the elderly person. Family members should be encouraged to allow the person doing the drinking to take on responsibility for continuing or stopping by not hiding difficulties, or "covering up" problems and negative consequences, but allowing the elderly person to experience consequences directly and to learn from them.

3. Family members should be encouraged to see themselves as important in their own right, with their own particular needs which should be expressed honestly and asserted, without endangering anyone's safety,

even if this could mean short term problems or arguments with the older person who is drinking.

4.   Adult children in the family living with an elderly problem drinker should be encouraged to consider carefully the needs of other family members, such as their own young children. Equal consideration should be given to all who are suffering.

5.   The family member who is looking for help with an elderly problem drinker should be encouraged to find someone close to them, a relative or friend, who is readily available, with whom they can share their thoughts and feelings over a longer period if required.

Alcohol Anonymous also offers support and advice for family members, as do some councils on alcohol and, where available, these opportunities for support should be used as required.

6.   The family member should be helped to make decisions, to follow them through and take action about family difficulties. Support should be offered to them in these decisions and actions, bearing in mind that they should not cause harm to others.

Conclusion

As we have noted earlier, our knowledge of, and work with, elderly people experiencing drink problems is a much neglected area. Only limited information and research are available on this topic. However, once again, we do have transferable, generic, social work knowledge and skills and some specific knowledge and skills in work with older problem drinkers which are particularly useful in our interventive efforts. Also we have knowledge and understanding of what it may mean to be an elderly person because of some of the common themes that are experienced at that life stage. Yet, as in work with other clients/users of social work services, we should remind ourselves of the individuality and uniqueness of each elderly person who is experiencing problems with drink. Their individuality will be based upon a whole range of factors noted earlier, including personal history and their class, "race", and gender.

Interventions with elderly people experiencing drink problems can take place at individual, partner, family, and, less frequently, group levels. There is also a key role in liaising with other professionals, para-professionals, and volunteers who may be involved, as well as attempting to influence agency policies in these matters.

We should not be hypervigilant or overreact to problem drinking amongst elderly people. We should be alert to work in such situations with skill, sensitivity, awareness, calmness, and thoughtfulness built upon as sound a knowledge base as possible, with our interventions being permeated with core social work values. As Simpson *et al.* (1994 : 586) so aptly put it, working with elderly people experiencing drinking problems reflects "a pressing need to develop interventions which are ethically sound and sensitive as well as effective and preventive".

Chapter 7
Black Communities and Alcohol

Research Evidence

Very little research evidence is available on the topic of alcohol misuse and black people. Even in the United States, as recently as the mid-1970s, a survey of 16,000 articles on alcohol revealed that only 77 had included discussion on alcohol use by black people and only 11 of those dealt primarily with a black population, while not one empirical study had been written about alcohol and black women. Up to 1983, only three books had been published on the use of alcohol by black people (Harper, 1983). The situation in Great Britain has been more gloomy, with even fewer articles and books available on this topic. Thus there is little information available about black people's patterns of consumption and alcohol-related harm, their use of available services, and the effectiveness of various helping endeavours that are offered. Therefore, we are at an early stage in our thinking about black people and their use of alcohol and, in view of the lack of empirical research evidence, only tentative comments can be made about these matters.

For black males in the United States there appears to be graver, more serious consequences following alcohol misuse compared with white alcohol misuse, with higher incidences of physical illness, accidents, assaults, arrests, imprisonment, and homicides following drinking episodes (McGroy & Shorkey, 1985). As a result, alcohol is seen as a major health problem for black people in the United States with cirrhosis of the liver, heart disease, and hypertension more common amongst black alcohol abusers (McGroy & Shorkey, 1985).

Most American writers on black people and alcohol draw attention to the long history of prejudice and discrimination suffered by black people (King, 1983; Watts & Wright, 1983; Bell & Evans,1983; McGroy & Shorkey, 1985). Some writers emphasise the central issue of racism (Beverley, 1985), while King is quite unequivocal:–

> *"Consideration must be given to racism, poverty, unequal access to health care [and] cultural barriers . . . [as] . . . research [on alcohol problems] does not reflect direct concerns with the issues of racism and poverty"* (King, 1983 : 51).

Furthermore, it is stated that alcohol is used by

> *"many black men as self medication for countering the frustration and depression which result from the prejudice . . . that many have experienced".* (McGroy & Shorkey, 1983 : 204)

In turn, drinking is seen as a recreation and social activity,

> *"to escape unpleasant experience of racial discrimination".* (McGroy & Shorkey, 1985:204).

Black People, Prejudice, Discrimination, and Racism

Hence in our consideration of black people's drinking we should be clear about terms such as black, prejudice, discrimination, and racism. These have been defined as follows:–

Black: In accordance with other writers (Ahmad 1990, D 'Ardenne & Mahtani 1989, Vaughan & Badger 1995) black is used in the *political* sense to describe all non-white groups who could experience racism and share experiences of being discriminated against. It could be correctly argued that racism goes well beyond issues of black and white and involves other ethnic groups such as, for example, Chinese, Greek Cypriot, Jewish, Polish, Italian, and Irish people, (Dominelli, 1988). However, in this chapter the concentration will be upon those of Asian, African, and Caribbean descent who are visibly different, as "the groups . . . subjected to the most vicious and intractable expressions of racism in Britain are black people" (Dominelli, 1988: 7).

Prejudice is "an opinion or judgment without considering the relevant facts or arguments; a biased or intolerant attitude towards particular people or social groups; *an opinion or attitude* which is rigidly and irrationally maintained even in the face of strong contradictory evidence or in the persistent absence of supportive evidence" (Thompson, 1993 : 32). Prejudice usually carries negative connotations, often involves unfavourable *thoughts, beliefs or feelings* and tends to reinforce myths and stereotypes about groups of people. Stereotyping is a simplified, generalised labelling of particular groups of people. Stereotypes have negative repercussions when people use them to make dogmatic predictions about others without appropriate information, thus leading to self-fulfilling prophecies (Ridley 1995). An example here could be the erroneous view that "Muslims do not have drinking problems because their religion and their families would not allow it". In reality, despite the fact that the vast majority of Muslims do not drink, evidence available indicates that a small proportion of older Muslims do have problems with heavy drinking and dependency (Cochran & Bal 1990; Ghosh 1984).

Some members of the "general public" and some professionals are racist and hold negative and stereotyped views about those from minority ethnic groups. A similar comment could be made about problem drinkers who can be labelled "alcoholics" and therefore perceived as quarrelsome, argumentative, aggressive, troublesome, unkempt, dirty, and unreliable (Collins *et al*.1988). Hence a male problem drinker from a black minority is likely to suffer from double jeopardy because the person is black and a problem drinker. In the case of a black female problem drinker then triple jeopardy is likely to occur. A complex interaction is likely to follow because "black women have to confront a form of sexism and sexual abuse" (Bryan *et al*. 1985 : 212) to which is added stereotyping and labelling surrounding racism *and* problem drinking as well.

Discrimination is seen as "unfair or unequal treatment of individuals or groups [and involves] *acting* against the interests of those people who characteristically tend to belong to relatively powerless groups [such as] women and ethnic minorities" (Thompson 1993: 31). Therefore, discrimination tends to involve *decisions or actions* which lead to particular groups being treated differently. Also it can be evident that discrimination occurs in an unconscious or unthinking way when the person concerned is not aware that they are behaving badly or being unfair.

Discrimination can occur when a black problem drinker may have only limited access to services because, for example, information about what help is available is not well publicised or literature may be available only in English when, for example, some Sikhs and Hindus may require information in their native languages.

Racism is seen as "the belief in the inherent superiority of one race over all others and thereby the right to dominance " (Lorde (1984) in Dominelli 1988: 192) or "a set of beliefs or way of thinking within which groups identified on the basis of real or imagined biological characteristics (skin colour for example) are thought necessarily to possess other characteristics that are viewed in a negative light. . . . Racism is rooted in the belief that certain groups . . . races . . . ethnic minorities share characteristics such as attitudes or abilities [and]. . . behaviour. The assumption is made that every person . . . classified as belonging to such a group is possessed of all these characteristics" (Chakrabarti1990: 15). Racism always involves harmful behaviour, the acting out and carrying out of negative beliefs and assumptions. It "systematically denies access to opportunities or privileges to members of one racial group while perpetuating access to opportunities and privileges to members of another racial group" (Ridley 1995 : 28). Racism exists at both individual and institutional levels. In the latter instance it "is built in to the structure of society and its dominant institutions" (Thompson 1993: 61). For instance, most white people are likely to have internalised a form of racism which is linked to Britain's colonial past. Within the colonial system white male power, language, and culture were dominant and imposed upon the "native" people. Those of "European" origin constituted the ruling class and made laws and policies that were imposed upon others.

The management of social services departments, probation services, and voluntary alcohol agencies has been, and is, dominated by white males. Hence policies emerge from a dominant, white male culture that are insensitive to the needs of black people and a colour blind approach may be evident that neglects the needs of those who stand outside the "mainstream" (Nyak 1985). This negative approach by agencies has been most pungently expressed by Westermeyer as,

"Take it or leave it: we are here for people of all backgrounds and if they [black people] do not utilise our resources it is not our responsibility."
(Westermayer 1984: 16 in Thompson 1993: 74)

When discussing work with black people experiencing drink problems it is also important to note that approaches to, and models of, problem drinking are essentially Eurocentric. That is, the models used in both assessing and intervening are based in Western culture. Ridley describes this quite succinctly, stating: "Professional paradigms and models often categorise people, favouring persons whose behaviours are consistent with traditional Western values. These paradigms may very well contribute to unintentional racist outcomes. Hence counsellors [with problem drinkers] are socialised and trained to behave as racists without even knowing it" (Ridley 1995: 33 and 39).

Education and training for work with problem drinkers will have been based on theories and practices which have either central European or North American origins and emphases. Therefore, such methods "are . . . culturally encapsulated within a white western view of the world and are consequently insensitive and inappropriate in their unthinking application to all [problem drinking] situations" (Lago & Thompson 1989: 208). Workers with problem drinkers will "tend to see cultural differences as deviations from norms which are perceived as global and differences can be perceived as intrinsic to clients and problematic, rather than a reflection of cultural contrast" (D 'Ardenne & Mahtani, 1989: preface). There are parallels here to the situation in psychiatry, where the dominance of western models has been well documented by several authors (Littlewood & Lipsedge 1989, Fernando 1988, 1991). In psychiatry, models based upon the majority, dominant, western, culture alienate people who do not belong to it and these models lack an appropriate frame of reference for assessing the behaviour and standards of people from other cultures. Also, similarly, in the counselling field dominant models again tend to incorporate western cultural values and

> *"approaches to counselling such as rational emotive therapy, gestalt therapy, reality therapy, transactional analysis and assertiveness training . . . were developed by white practitioners enmeshed in Western cultural values. The application of these theories to multi-cultural populations . . . is questionable".* (Katz 1985: 619)

It is not surprising that the hegemony of these Eurocentric models in psychiatry and counselling is duplicated in the field of working with problem drinkers. As a result the needs of problem drinkers from ethnic groups are less likely to be explored and known about by the majority culture. Indeed, this is reflected in the comparatively small amount of research and literature which considers the needs of problem drinkers from ethnic groups in Britain.

Attitudes and Behaviours of Individual Helpers to Black People with Drinking Problems

There are perhaps two particularly important elements to consider here.
The first relates to anti-racist practice, while the second relates to the place of ethnically sensitive, transcultural and bicultural practice.

For the white worker helping a black person experiencing difficulties with drink, there are many issues to consider. Bell and Evans (1983) have identified five white counselling styles when interacting with a black client who has drinking problems. These are:–

1. *Overt racism and hostility.*

2. *Covert (hidden) prejudice.* Here the worker attempts to hide their feelings such as possible dislike or fear of black people.

3. *Cultural ignorance.* Here the worker has had limited experience of engaging with black clients and has little knowledge of black culture. The worker may experience fear or an inability to relate to the client.

4. *Colour blind.* The worker denies the reality of cultural difference and the importance of race and culture, which are vital in helping black people and integral to the black client's personality and life history.

5. *Culturally liberated.* Here the worker does not fear social or cultural differences, is aware of his or her attitudes and chooses to be actively

involved in solutions to any racial problems. The worker is aware of cross-cultural counselling dynamics and can express both positive regard and confrontation. The worker encourages the black client to express his or her feelings about being black and this is used as a shared learning experience.

When considering power issues the combination of a white worker with a black client experiencing drink problems carries potential dangers. For example, the white worker has considerable power, derived from various sources including agency obligations and resources, knowledge and skills, and, possibly, legal sanctions. In particular, there is a "potential danger, namely a perpetuation of the notion of white superiority" (Lago & Thompson 1989) and of the black client experiencing, yet again, the powerful and controlling elements of social work rather than the caring elements, especially when referrals involve legal requirements such as probation orders with conditions of receiving help or treatment for drink problems.

Anti-racist Practice
There are likely to be problem drinkers from many different minority ethnic groups who present themselves to helping agencies, but all are likely to have shared the experience of racism. Racism is a central issue in work with black clients who are experiencing problems with drink. Roys has described this clearly:–

"The difficulties faced by the black population are the result not only of migration and differences in culture but also of living in a society which is hostile to black people . . . and [this] can expose them to enormous material and psychological pressure. The clients . . . present with not only linguistic and cultural complexities but also with the profound effects of racism" (Roys 1988: 221).

Racism may well "drive people to drink", although, at the present time, there is insufficient research evidence available to support this statement. In the mental health field there has been considerable concern expressed about the high incidence of schizophrenia amongst Afro-Caribbean people born in Britain (Littlewood & Lipsedge 1989). Debates rage about the causes of these high-prevalence rates. Some argue around misdiagnosis of symptoms, while many others contend that individual racist attitudes and behaviour and institutional racism may well push Afro-Caribbean people into experiencing mental health problems. In the alcohol field some writers are clear and unequivocal that psychological causes should not be over-emphasised, seeing black drinking behaviour as;

"A means of escape from the rejection caused by individual and institutional racism." (McGroy & Shorkey 1985 : 207)

Already we have defined racism, but it is important to consider how this may affect the individual white worker interacting with a black problem drinker. Most white workers interacting with those experiencing drink problems would not identify themselves as racist and most likely would perceive racism as associated with racial attacks and racial abuse. They would most probably accept that there is evidence of institutional racism in the courts, in the criminal justice system and in some psychiatric assessment and practices (Voakes & Fowler 1986, Whitehouse 1986, NACRO 1986, Barnes & Maple 1990, Ahmad 1990, Cope 1989). They might find it harder to accept the "more pervasive and culturally supported form of racism that is present in British society which it is likely that all white people will have internalised to some degree . . . [derived from Britain's recent] colonial past" (Vaughan & Badger 1995: 68). However, if as a result of this imperialist inheritance workers can accept elements of personal racism both in themselves, and in their practice then movement can be made towards anti-racist practice in working with problem drinkers. Indeed, even within this chapter on black people and alcohol and in this book as a whole the reader may well discover evidence of racist assumptions. Thompson (1993) outlines some steps towards anti-racist practice which can readily be adapted to work with problem drinkers; these include:-

- Acknowledging the structural and cultural influences on our behaviour and attitudes and recognising our own racism.

- Encouraging and committing oneself to tackling and eradicating these difficulties.

- Avoiding negative stereotypes and operating upon a foundation of cultural difference and not deficit.

- Helping black clients with drink problems develop a positive black identity.

- Recognising the accumulation of disadvantage suffered by black people with drink problems as a consequence of racism and putting together policies and practices to overcome these difficulties.

- Challenging racist comments, actions or attitudes in other workers or clients with drink problems.

- Creating anti-racist alliances through collectives to tackle racist structures and practices that exist in social services and services for problem drinkers.

It is through such approaches that "the institutionalisation of anti racism" can be established in the provision of services for problem drinkers (Williams, 1989 : 107). Without recognition of the fact that racism permeates both individual and institutional forms, and should be fought at every opportunity, ethnically sensitive practice and multicultural approaches can have only a limited effect. Hence anti-racism is the foundation stone upon which good practice with problem drinkers must be built. Ethnically sensitive work should always be preceded by a recognition of the centrality of racism and the importance of anti-racist practice.

Ethnically Sensitive and Transcultural Work
Ethnically sensitive practice can help "to avoid the problems of devaluing minority cultures or seeing them as inferior to white culture and thereby alienating the people who share those cultures " (Thompson 1993 : 70). Ethnically sensitive social work "involves developing at least a basic understanding of local ethnic minority communities and cultures" while at the same time recognising that there is no single black culture, because "black cultures are many and varied and to ignore this is to operate at a stereotypical level, to oversimplify a complex picture" (Thompson 1993 : 68). The study of Asian problem drinkers by Cochran & Bal (1990) and that of attitudes of Asians to problem drinking by Nyak (1985) and Malseed (1990) indicate there are very distinct views and attitudes between Muslims, Hindus, and Sikhs and variations within each of these groups based upon age, class, and gender. Hence there are no easy answers when we start to consider the significance of cultural awareness for social workers in work with black people who are experiencing drink problems.

General sensitivity to language issues is important in work with any client/user group including black people experiencing drink problems. For instance, clients from ethnic groups whose first language is not English are doubly disadvantaged in communication. They may not be able to communicate easily outside their own community, while at the same time racism leads to limited opportunities to learn the conventions and rules surrounding the English language (D 'Ardenne & Mahtani 1989).

It is easy for monoglot "standard" English-speaking workers to devalue those speakers who may use another form of English. For example, Sue (1981) quotes an instance of a black adolescent in New York whose street talk is misunderstood by his counsellor, while Thomas & Sillen (1972) quote work which challenged stereotypes about the language used by underprivileged black children in the United States. Their language and abstract thinking were fully developed *in their own form of English* but they had to contend with other English speakers who did not comprehend their form of English and judged it to be inferior to their own. It is clear that the culturally sensitive worker must appreciate that "standard" English is not spoken by all. This can impose additional barriers to effective communications with black people using "non-standard" English. Therefore, the worker should be aware that many black clients with alcohol problems, speaking an alternative form of English, will be often disadvantaged by, and suffer, prejudice about being black, about their culture *and* about their language (D'Ardenne and Mahtani 1989). Language involves power and when a "non-standard" English speaker approaches an agency such as a council on alcohol, a social services or probation department they have to communicate on the terms of that agency. The worker is an authority figure, who rarely takes responsibility for learning the client's language, finding a common language, or trying to learn about the problems experienced by the client in communicating in another language. The worker is part of the dominant discourse (Rojek *et al.* 1988). The black person whose first language is not English, or who speaks a form of language other than "standard" English, is placed in a situation of even greater stress – stress which is imposed in addition to that experienced by having to admit some difficulties with alcohol and a need for help with drinking problems.

If interpreters are used care must be taken to ensure that the client/user has "the right to be understood" (Shackman 1985). The dangers of using unofficial interpreters are listed by Shackman as follows:–

- "Inaccurate translation by unofficial interpreters

- bias and distortion introduced by these interpreters

- lack of confidentiality for the client

- unofficial interpreters not understanding their role in the counselling process

- unofficial interpreters not explaining cultural differences between the counsellor and the client

- personal unsuitability of these interpreters in the counselling process

- exploitation of clients by unofficial interpreters

- unofficial interpreters, over identification with the counsellors agency leading to bias."

Shackman (1985) in D'Ardenne & Mahtani (1989: 69)

Shackman also points out that the worker is seen by both the interpreter and the client as powerful; the responsibility for conduct of the interview lies with the worker to ensure clarity and continuity. The following checklist for workers using official interpreters is provided by Shackman:–

- Check that both the interpreter and client do speak the same language or dialect
- Discuss beforehand with the interpreter the content of the interview and way of working together
- Encourage the interpreter to interrupt and intervene when necessary
- Use plain and straightforward language
- Actively listen to both interpreter and client observing body language and maintaining eye contact
- Allow extra time for the interview
- Constantly check the client's understanding of what has been said
- Have a post interview discussion with the interpreter about communication during the interview."

Shackman (1985) in D'Ardenne and Mahtani (1989: 69 and 70)

The white worker needs to gain awareness of their own culture, cultural style and racial origins so that they know where they are coming from, both historically and, in behavioural terms in the present, because most relationships between black and white have been founded upon traditions of imperialism, exploitation, and oppression (Katz 1978). Many white people do not find it easy to cope with black people's pain or hurt – and anger. White workers need to acknowledge and learn that "I think white". They need to respond with empathy and, where relevant, to try to enter black people's experiences of hate and resentment and communicate that understanding – when this is a vibrant part of their reality of racism and discrimination. Thus white workers need to be aware of beliefs and feelings that may be triggered when interacting with a black problem-drinker. They need to have the opportunity to discuss these feelings with a supervisor or consultant. The work of Shaw *et al.* (1978), Cartwright (1986), and Lightfoot and Orford (1986) has highlighted the need for informed, competent support and supervision to assist those working with problem drinkers to feel confident and secure in their role in order to provide high quality services. This would seem to be particularly the case when a white worker is helping a black problem-drinker.

The white worker also should accept and understand – and work to gain knowledge of – the black client's culture, history, beliefs and racial origins (D'Ardenne & Mahtani 1989). The white worker should develop an approach which reflects the cultural needs of the black client, acknowledge and stress the importance and value of difference, potential, positives, strengths, and skills as well as problems experienced with drinking (Triseliotis 1986, Sue 1981, Pedersen 1985, 1988).

Transcultural Counselling

Institutionalised racism has meant that cultural issues are rarely given importance and, as in other fields of helping such as counselling and psychiatry, their significance is often underestimated in work with problem drinkers. Workers have a tendency to match and fit their clients with existing resources, rather than develop particular and flexible skills in response to each client's cultural needs, thus providing a more effective service to problem drinkers across cultures. There is only limited research and literature available to guide readers through some complex issues and it is suggested that a transcultural approach does not have standardised rules for specific cultures. It "is not about being an expert on any given culture . . . rather it is a way of thinking about clients [with drinking problems] where culture is acknowledged and valued" (D'Ardenne & Mahtani, 1989: x).

There are many definitions of culture but that provided by D'Ardenne & Mahtani (1989 : 4) will be used,

> *"Culture means the shared history, practices, beliefs and values of a racial, regional or religious group of people."*

A transcultural worker will be responsible for working across, through or beyond cultural differences in an active and reciprocal way. This includes the following, according to D'Ardenne and Mahtani,

"● counsellors sensitivity to the cultural variations and bias of their own approach

● counsellors grasp of the cultural knowledge of their clients [experiencing problems with drink]

- counsellors ability and commitment to develop an approach that reflects the cultural needs of their . . . clients [who have drink problems]

- counsellors ability to face increased complexity in working across cultures".

(D'Ardenne & Mahtani 1989: 6)

While empathy is a key ingredient in helping individuals with drink problems (Valle 1981, Miller 1983, Cartwright 1986) and one of the "necessary and sufficient " core conditions in counselling according to Rogers (1978, 1980), this may not be "sufficient" in transcultural counselling with those experiencing drink problems (Smith 1985). All helpers hold historically based "attitudes and expectations about their own culture which are biased [and this bias becomes the foundation of prejudice when counselling a client transculturally" (D'Ardenne & Mahtani 1989: 36). If the worker's attitudes and *expectations* are prejudiced, the black client may find it hard to raise this matter on account of power differences. Furthermore, the white worker may have low expectations of the black client's successful involvement in helping and feel pessimistic about the outcome. On the one hand, the white worker may stereotype the black problem-drinker as "a wounded soldier", a pathological victim of racism, place excessive emphasis on this and see drinking as an understandable response to racism – the irreversible "mark of oppression" described by Thomas and Sillen (1972). Or, on the other hand, the worker can be "colour blind", set excessively high expectations, and minimise the outcomes of racial oppression, interacting with the black client as a "white man [woman] in a black skin" (Thomas & Sillen 1972: 65 in D'Ardenne & Mahtani: 37), neglecting to understand that the helping offered is so white and western as to constitute cultural bias and prejudice.

Issues of prejudice and racism may need to be explicitly acknowledged and explored by the white worker who should feel sufficiently knowledgeable and comfortable to undertake this task from the early stages of counselling the black problem-drinker. Paradoxically, the white worker is a part of the oppression the client may be challenging and, at the same time, part of the help that is being sought. White workers are from the majority culture (Ridley 1995). They may be identified with white racist society and can be seen as a continuation of earlier encounters with other white professionals, helpers or voluntary workers which may not have been either productive or helpful. This may have led to feelings of hostility or resentment. Either way it may not be easy to establish a trusting relationship with a black person experiencing drinking problems, who may have suffered from racism, prejudice, and limited opportunities in health, education, and housing over long periods and even for a lifetime (Sue 1981).

Alternatively, some black problem-drinkers may not be concerned about "race differences between themselves and the alcohol counsellor. If race is not a major issue for the client, [alcohol] counsellors should not harp on it but move on to other issues. Other [black] clients are deeply troubled by race differences. . . . If [alcohol] counsellors sense that racial dynamics are affecting the client, they should explore these issues in depth [as] . . . failure to explore [them] can block progress" (Ridley 1995 : 107).

Bicultural Counselling

Bicultural aspects also need to be considered. Most ethnic groups encounter the conflicting values and demands of two worlds: their own communities and that of the dominant white society. There are numerous transactions across cultures and one of the important goals for most ethnic groups is to function in both the "majority" culture and society (Ridley 1995) and the ethnic community and culture (Phinney *et al.* 1990, De Anda 1984). Beverley has expressed matters thus in relation to the helping process with black problem drinkers:–

> *"Black clients must be able to navigate, orchestrate and negotiate life in two worlds – one black and one white – and that success depends on one's ability to function in both. [Black] people have been forced to assess their social reality according to their primary point of reference – the black community and broader reference European-American culture. The two cultures rarely, if ever, merge; thus the competing and often contradictory imperatives of the two cultures create the need for dual consciousness. For the practitioner, dual consciousness means that all communications must be delivered and received at two levels – the inner reality of being black and the outer reality of living in a society in which being black interferes with opportunities for creative develop-ment, transcendence and redemption." (Beverly 1989 : 374.)*

Beverley argues that counselling with black problem drinkers should be bicul-tural because:–

(1) This gives a clear perspective on the meaning of the black experience.

(2) It helps to clarify the behavioural components among black people that have fostered their survival.

(3)   It highlights the implications of counselling and helping in a racist society.

In Beverley's words:–

"Bicultural counselling has to do with assisting black clients to negotiate for themselves, their families and their communities in a known hostile [white] environment while at the same time not negating the positiveness, support and identification associated with maintaining ... ties to the black community."

Beverly (1975: 174-5)

Black families with a member experiencing alcohol problems, will experience society differently largely because of racism and be differentiated further by variations in lifestyle according to class (Ziter 1987).   In other words the worker needs to consider the "black world", the "interracial world" and the "white world", with a particular emphasis on the strengths of positive involvement with the "black world" (Ziter 1987).   Such ideas may not have the same meaning for every black family or black person because, for example, not every black British person is deeply Afrocentric and not every white British person is   deeply Eurocentric.   Nonetheless, most black Britons and other ethnic groups regularly confront Eurocentric values in order to survive. Similar pressure is not placed on white people to negotiate ethnic cultures in order to survive. Hence, biculturalism and a dual perspective stimulate thought about interracial relationships.   Ethnic clients clearly differ considerably in their biculturality and each client will need to decide if changes are needed and, if so, what changes should be made and how (Ridley 1995).

Drinking Patterns Amongst Black Communities in Britain

In moving on to consider drinking patterns and help for problem drinkers amongst black communities in Britain we have to acknowledge two important points. First, to reiterate that there is little research evidence in this area on which to base policy decisions to determine the most effective means of help that might be made available. Second, to acknowledge the enormous diversity and differences that exist within black communities because we need to bear in mind a whole range of black groups, alongside gender, religious, and class issues, and the different needs of younger people and older people within black communities. Hence we are discussing a complex topic that is constantly in flux and change. For example, Patel's (1993) work in Bradford indicated that the predominantly local Asian population "comprised several different cultural groups, between them speaking nine different languages, belonging to three main religious groups, and coming from three different generations" (Harrison 1996 : 235).

The small amount of research that has examined problem drinking amongst black people in Britain has tended to be of a quantitative nature, based on survey questionnaires administered in small geographical areas. These have provided statistical information, but have tended to give only vague impressions of qualitative aspects such as people's needs and feelings (Mather & Marjot 1989, Cochran & Bal 1990, Ghosh 1984, Burke 1984). Hardly any empirical work appears to have been undertaken actually looking at the needs of problem drinkers from black communities, their views of helping agencies and the quality of services offered to them (Cochran & Bal 1990, Nyak 1985, Malseed 1990). So, what do we know about problem drinking among black groups in Britain?

Indirect Estimates

Indirect estimates of levels of alcohol-related problems have been made from surveys of alcohol consumption, such as those obtained by using questions contained within the General Household Survey. Data from 1978 was analysed by country of birth by Balarjan and Yuen (1986). They found male drinking ratios of 103 for men born in England and 131 for men born in Northern Ireland and the Irish Republic. The drinking ratio for West Indian males was only 52 and 45 for sub-continental Indian males, thus indicating much lower consumption levels than the UK average.

However, there are numerous reasons for believing these figures to be an underestimate of alcohol consumption levels amongst black people. First, the data is 20 years old. Second, country of birth is not synonymous with ethnic origin. The data only referred to first generation migrants, although over 40% of Britain's present black population is "black British" and born in the UK (Bhat *et al*. 1988). Third, the General Household Survey excludes those living in insecure accommodation and "it is amongst such groups that the highest levels of problems are found in every community" (Harrison *et al*. 1996: 225). Fourth, explorations of, and questions about, amounts of alcohol consumed each week may not be readily understood by those whose second language is English, which could include members of Asian communities who moved to Britain in more recent years. Fifth, there may be a reluctance to discuss sensitive information to yet another faceless white official and uncertainty about how such information might be used in the future.

Direct Estimates

One early study of psychiatric hospital admissions "for alcoholism" over a 15-year period up to 1971 noted a very low incidence of alcoholism amongst males and females who had migrated from Pakistan, the West Indies, and India, compared with large percentages of people from Scotland, Northern Ireland, and the Irish Republic (Cochran *et al.* 1977). Twenty-five times as many men from Northern Ireland were admitted to hospital diagnosed as "alcoholics" as there were from the Caribbean; 25% of male psychiatric patients from Northern Ireland were having treatment for drinking problems compared with only 3% of West Indian men (Littlewood & Lipsedge 1989). Littlewood and Lipsedge were unable to provide reasons for these figures, especially as the rates of admission to psychiatric hospital for alcoholism in the Caribbean islands themselves were high – for example, one in five on the island of Antigua as compared with one in 33 admissions for West Indians in England (Littlewood & Lipsedge 1989).

A community study by Burke (1984) in Birmingham had confirmed these findings, noting that the "migrant" West Indians in his study "drank frequently, became intoxicated, but did not have symptoms of alcoholism" (Burke 1984: 200). Overall, then, it seems that West Indians who migrated to Britain had better levels of mental health as regards "alcoholism", in contrast to their considerable over-representation amongst those diagnosed schizophrenic (Littlewood & Lipsedge 1989). As far as is known this is the only specific community survey data on drinking problems amongst Afro-Caribbean people in Britain.

A survey by Cochrane and Bal of mental hospital admissions for "alcoholism" between 1971 and 1981 had revealed significant changes from the previous years and a surprisingly high prevalence rate of alcohol-related disorders among men born in India but living in England (Cochran & Bal 1989). Their rate of admission to mental hospitals with alcohol-related diagnoses (75 per 100,000) was considerably higher than that of the native-born population (49 per 100,000). The survey also revealed, compared with the previous decade, an increase in the rate of admissions to mental hospital for the same group of men, of 121% when compared with the native English rate of increase of 75%. Admission rates to mental hospitals for Caribbean-born men with alcohol-related disorders increased by 75% over this same 10 year period (1971 – 1981). Also, the admission rate for Afro-Caribbean men of 27 per 100,000 population in 1981 was considerably more than the 4 per 100,000 reported in the West Indies (Cochran & Bal 1989, Burke 1984). Furthermore, Harrison (1996) examined cirrhosis mortality rates amongst those born in Ireland, in the Caribbean and

India, noting that up to 80% of all cirrhosis mortality is the consequence of heavy alcohol consumption. Cirrhosis rates for the minority groups were elevated and "in contrast to the 1970's, those born in the Caribbean no longer appear to be in an advantageous position: there are now more deaths from cirrhosis than would be expected" (Harrison 1996: 231). Therefore, there is clear evidence that alcohol-related problems are increasing more rapidly in some ethnic groups than in the general population.

A point to note again about these data is that clearly and obviously mental hospital admissions for "alcoholism" and deaths as a result of cirrhosis are by no means the only index of drinking problems, although *per capita* consumption levels are strongly correlated with alcohol admission rates (Poikallainen 1983). It is clear that "the latter [i.e. those admitted to hospital for 'alcoholism'] will obviously only represent a very small proportion of all those with alcohol related problems" (Cochran & Bal, 1990: 759). Hence, "most of the studies based on hospital or general medical populations cannot be used to estimate prevalence levels in the community" (Harrison *et al.* 1996 : 228).

Studies by Ghosh (1984) of south Asian people in north-west England and studies by Mather and Marjot (1989) in Southall, revealed further concerns about Hindu, Sikh, and Muslim drinkers. Mather and Marjot examined admission rates at one psychiatric hospital in Southall for alcohol-related diagnoses between 1980 and 1987. They discovered that the incidence amongst Asian men was markedly higher than in Caucasian men (126 out of 186) and the incidence amongst Asian women was markedly lower than Caucasian women. Most of the Asian males were Sikhs and Hindus from the Punjab, aged between 30 and 44. Mather and Marjot confirmed the earlier view of Merrill and Owens that "alcoholism in the male Sikh community is a rapidly escalating problem" and " alcoholism is increasingly prevalent within the local [i.e. Southall] Asian community" (Mather and Marjot, 1989 : 329). Ghosh (1984) interviewed a group of Asian men and women from general practitioner lists in Liverpool and Manchester. It was discovered that 10% of the men were either drinking at high risk levels or were alcohol dependent.

Cochran and Bal's (1990) community study in the west Midlands revealed that men born in India but living in Britain have higher-than-expected prevalence rates of alcohol-related disorders. "Sikhs were most likely to be heavy drinkers . . . [while] the very few Muslim men who drank consumed the most alcohol on average. In both these groups older men reported consuming more alcohol than did young men" (Cochran & Bal 1990: 759).

In Cochran and Bal's (1990) study large numbers of Asian men were in social classes III, IV, and V, while second generation Asian men born in Britain or who migrated before the age of 11 consumed fewer units of alcohol than first generation Asian men. Men aged between 40 and 50 had the highest alcohol problem scores. More than a quarter of Sikhs drank above 21 units of alcohol per week, the threshold at which alcohol-related problems begin to appear (Royal College of Psychiatrists 1986); 30% of the Sikhs said that they had so much to drink on occasions that they could not remember what they had been doing the night before. Two possible explanations have been put forward for the higher rates of alcohol problems amongst Sikh men. Firstly, alcohol may be viewed as a "fortifying" drink by Sikh male factory workers which enables them to work harder and longer. Secondly, alcohol use is very much part of Sikh culture in the Punjab, where socialising, recreation, and alcohol use apparently are synonymous (Cochran and Bal 1990).

When asked generally about what sources of help for alcohol problems they might recommend the Asian men said they were more likely to cite the family doctor or hospital than white men and were less likely to mention voluntary agencies such as AA than were white men. Therefore, Asian men may be more likely to use GPs or hospitals for help with drinking problems than other sources such as voluntary and statutory agencies. This is a cause for concern in view of considerable evidence that general practitioners and general hospital staff have received little basic or on going training or education in identifying, intervening, and working with drink problems (Anderson 1985, Flaherty & Flaherty 1989, Glass 1989).

Qualitative Studies
One of the few qualitative studies of black people's alcohol consumption and attitudes was undertaken by Malseed (1990). This focused upon black people in their 20s and early 30s in north-west England, mainly Muslim, Hindu, and Sikh. She noted that "attitudes towards and experiences of alcohol consumption were extremely varied both across and within different ethnic groups participating in the study" (Malseed 1990: 8). They reflected complex pressures such as religious beliefs, community acceptability, family and peer pressures, and the influences of "white British culture".

None of the Muslims in Malseed's study drank alcohol, while all the Hindus and Sikhs did so. Alcohol seemed to be more acceptable among Sikhs than the other groups in the study. For Muslims, rejection of alcohol is based upon religious law, as is seen in the following comments:–

"Alcohol in Islam is not a grey area. You can't and that's it" (Muslim man)

"Drinking is an evil act" (Muslim man)

"In our religion we're not allowed to drink fullstop. It's like one of the ten commandments, if you like to put it that way" (Muslim woman).

(Malseed 1990: 10)

In turn this was reinforced by pressures from the Muslim family,peers, culture, and community which again made it difficult for Muslims to drink and to purchase drink in their localities because:–

"There is a religious and community feeling against alcohol" (Muslim man)

and

"If they did [drink] it would be 200 miles away from their house" (Muslim man).

(Malseed, 1990 : 12)

Therefore, Muslims in this study had not absorbed the general "white" acceptance of alcohol and the widespread consumption of alcohol in Britain. Two male respondents commented:–

"British culture is a constant source of threat to our values, religion and culture. Muslims feel inhibited to drink because of advertisements on the television and in magazines"

and

"I try to fight British culture".

(Malseed 1990 : 21)

One woman noted:–

"There is a conflict between Muslim beliefs and British cultural influences. You are kind of brought up with certain values and even if you do not stick to them there are certain things a Muslim just does not do."

(Malseed 1990 : 22)

The Muslim respondents questioned whether drinking alcohol and socialising with white people would result in acceptance by whites and reduce racism. One male respondent noted:–

"I don't think drinking is a great influence to acceptance . . . [or] gets rid of the inherent racism amongst white people."
(Malseed 1990 : 22)

The rejection by Muslims of alcohol also was seen as a positive thing because alcohol was associated with family problems,violence towards partners, and chaotic behaviour. It was not perceived that alcohol might be consumed in moderation but rather as addictive and likely to be drunk to excess and be destructive.

Hence it can be seen that Muslims involved with problem drinking would be subject to considerable censure by their family, peers, culture, and community and it would be hard to seek help from within their own community. This has important implications as both Ghosh's (1984) study and the work of Cochran & Bal (1990) indicate that a small minority of their samples of Muslims *did* have problems with heavy or dependent drinking. This could result in Muslim problem drinkers being very reluctant to seek help on account of feelings of shame and guilt or, alternatively, they may be more willing to use general practitioners, hospital facilities, statutory agencies, or voluntary alcohol advice agencies, knowing that little help or understanding would be available from their own community groups.

For the Sikhs in Malseed's study there were no significant restrictions on the use of alcohol within the home and peer group pressure encouraged alcohol consumption. As one Sikh male commented:–

"There is always pressure. . . somebody will say 'Have a drink' and carry on asking you . . . until you relent or move away." (Malseed 1990: 19)

Yet some Sikh men found that drinking in pubs could be accompanied by racism and racist violence; they tended to feel safer when drinking with other Sikhs where they were less at risk for such incidents.

As regards female drinking generally amongst black people, in Malseed's study this was seen to be less socially acceptable as a result of family and community pressures. Most first, and some second, generation women tended not to drink or go to bars while younger women, especially Hindus and Sikhs, appeared to be breaking away from these traditional patterns. The implications of such changes are not clear at the present (Malseed 1990).

In Malseed's study all the participants were aware of health problems caused by heavy drinking, such as cirrhosis and heart disease. Only Muslims stressed the negative social effects of alcohol use, as noted earlier, and perceived it as a threat to family life and social order. Muslims seemed to know less about sensible limits for alcohol consumption (Royal College of Psychiatrists 1986), probably due to their avoidance of alcohol. Knowledge amongst other groups was patchy. Few knew about the sensible drinking limits for men and women and there was a lot of confusion about translating drinking "units" into the drink measurements used in pubs, i.e. pints and glasses of spirits and wine. Similar findings emerged from Nyak's (1985) study of Asian people drinking in Coventry.

Awareness and Use of Helping Agencies
Knowledge of helping agencies was scanty (Nyak 1985, Malseed1990). Many respondents in Malseed's study commented on the considerable publicity given to HIV/AIDS issues compared with the poor amount dedicated to alcohol problems and the relevant and appropriate helping organisations. Some mentioned AA but were unsure how to approach such groups. There was poor knowledge of local advisory services, most regarding their general practitioner as the major source of help. Women in many ethnic groups found it difficult to seek help from within their communities, and outside agencies might provide more valuable support if services were appropriately designed and available (Malseed 1990).

As Russell *et al.* (1993) have pointed out, it is not unusual for alcohol agencies to see very few black clients – male or female – and 40% of agencies surveyed for the London Alcohol Forum in 1990 had no Afro-Caribbean service users. Also a study undertaken by Patel (1993) in Bradford examined the low take-up of alcohol services provided by the Bridge Project in an area with numerous potential Asian clients. Only 1% of the agency clients were black compared with 20% of the local population. Again, many potential users were unaware of the agency's existence. Those who knew about it tended not to use it because it was seen as a white-run agency for white clients, as were other health and social care agencies in the area.

Help for Black People with Drink Problems
If we have some information about drinking patterns and drinking problems amongst black people, and the under use of helping agencies, what improve-ments can be made to existing services? These can be considered by examining the overall responsiveness of agencies and the needs of black workers.

Overall Responsiveness of Agencies and the Needs of Black Workers
As Harrison (1996: 232) has pointed out, "there are two principal strategies available to service providers: the creation of specialist Black agencies and the enhancement of existing services".

Arguments are made for and against the provision of separate agencies run by and for black people. Those in favour include "the fact that in a Black agency the responsibility for organising black people is undertaken by black people and . . . offers validation to black people in that they can be seen to be dealing with their own problems themselves" (Harrison 1996 :233). Separate organisations can speak with a distinctive voice, spelling out the needs of black problem-drinkers and making explicit demands for them. Separate organisations also can provide the possibilities for research, conducted by black people from a black perspective, from the black community and closely identified with their interests thus enabling culturally sensitive and anti-racist approaches to be developed (Harrison 1993). Therefore, centres for black people with alcohol problems can provide a genuine choice for those of different ethnic and cultural backgrounds.

In fact, *Choices*, established in 1993 in Brixton, south London, was the first advisory centre in the UK specifically for black people with alcohol-related problems (Cohen 1994). A strong motivating factor behind the establishment of *Choices*, which is part of the Alcohol Recovery Project and is funded by Alcohol Concern and South East London Health Authority, is the fact that black drinkers are reluctant to use mainstream services. A team of several black workers attracts clients of Caribbean, African, and Asian origin with black women drinkers constituting nearly half the total number of clients. These are sometimes self-referrals or are passed on from voluntary groups, hospital detoxification units, and probation and social services. Initial impressions suggest that the black clients have a number of undiagnosed mental health problems alongside diagnosed mental health problems, where alcohol-related problems have not been recognised. Now joint work is undertaken with the Afro Caribbean Mental Health Association on these difficulties.

Choices, funding from the local health authority is on a time-limited basis. Plans to develop further areas of work and employ more staff are dependent on future funding decisions. This is one of the arguments put forward against providing separate services for black people with drinking problems – the difficulties of obtaining "permanent" funding. Black agencies tend to be small and their organisers may find it difficult to get access to organisational networks, possibly lacking friends in high places to get policy workers to do the work which is essential for development and resource acquisition. In addition, black people have an obvious right to access to mainstream services. It is possible that mainstream providers might well use the existence of alternative black provision as a reason for not appropriately developing their own services for black people. Finally, some argue that separate black services are a form of apartheid which plays into the hands of racists who argue that multiracial services will not work (Harrison 1996).

The answer to these arguments is clearly the point that both separate black provision and more appropriate mainstream services are equally valid and required to co-exist in order to provide overall high quality provision at all levels for black people with drinking problems.

Already, in the Introduction, we have noted that most organisations which offer help to those with drinking problems are dominated by white, middle class males who *ipso facto* are liable to produce services oriented to white, middle class males. Changes can be achieved in such organisations by encouraging and increasing employment opportunities for black people, both males and females, at both management and grass roots levels. It is then that the needs of black people can be more readily detected, and responded to, and trust established in an appropriate and sensitive manner. Power is a key concept here and empowerment a key answer. Services should be influenced, and provided, by black people whenever possible. This is equally important in areas where there are high proportions of black people in the local population – for example, in cities such as London, Birmingham, Bradford, Glasgow, Leeds, Liverpool, Manchester, as well as in areas where there are few black people. Local organisations representing black people should be approached to ascertain their needs, their views on existing services and on developing services that will more appropriately meet the needs of black people who are problem drinkers. Local black radio programmes and black newspapers should be used to publicise available resources for those with alcohol problems. The literature available on existing services should be culturally sensitive and produced in a range of languages especially to communicate appropriately with older, first generation black people. More choice should be available to those from the black community. For example, some might be satisfied with the idea of receiving help from a white, monolingual worker, while others, such as some first generation members of a community, might prefer to receive help from individuals from their own ethnic group who they perceived would understand their culture and speak their language.

We should now consider the question of "matching" black workers to black clients with drink problems and whether a white worker can help a black person with such a problem. It seems many clients from black groups perceive black workers positively. It is thought black people would generally welcome the opportunity of interfacing with a black worker because of positive identification with someone who may have gone through possibly similar experiences to their own (Lago & Thompson 1989). In other words, black workers themselves will have struggled to cope with prejudice and racism and will have acquired a variety of skills to cope with alien and hostile environments. They may have also suffered economic hardship and deprivation, received racist taunts, jibes and insults. In addition, it may be that the black worker experiences strong identification with, and less distancing from, a black client and, in turn, is less strongly identified with white racist society. Brisbane and Womble (1985: 259) in considering black "alcoholics" are very clear:–

> *"Black professionals in predominantly white agencies must not be socialised away from considering [being] black as an important dimension [in helping]. Not to recognise the importance of [being black] is to become disconnected from black people, black pride and social consciousness."*

Brisbane and Womble are equally clear that black workers are generally better able to help black people with drink problems than are people from other racial groups, noting that the black helper should be secure in his or her racial identity in order to carefully consider the racial identity of black problem drinkers (Brisbane & Womble 1985). Similarly Westermayer (1984) is clear in his consideration of the role of ethnicity in substance abuse that substance misusers are more attracted to facilities that have ethnic peers. This situation is associated with better opportunities to establish trusting relationships, better identification of clients with workers, and better communication between the two. However, a black worker could over-identify with the black client experiencing drink problems precisely because they have both faced and shared the challenges posed by racism, discrimination, and prejudice (Lago & Thompson 1989). The danger here is that there could be excessive discussion of issues surrounding rage and anger about racism with some clients and, as a result, clients having extensive difficulties with drink . . .

> *"will tend to see his or her alcohol abuse as related to racism and will tend not to take personal responsibility for that behaviour. A positive outcome with this client is in part determined by the counsellor's ability to legitimise the realities of racism and oppression but not at the expense of holding the client accountable for his or her inappropriate alcohol abusing behaviour".*

(Bell and Evans 1983: 106)

At the same time there are dangers in "dumping" upon black workers the label of "expert" and responsibilities for providing services to other black people. All organisations providing help to problem drinkers have a responsibility to provide an effective service that is based upon the appropriate preparation and commitment of all workers to ethnically sensitive practice and to anti-racism. The burden of transforming the racist workplace should be, as Dominelli points out, "spread across a number of shoulders, making it easier for each individual to maintain energy and enthusiasm for the work" (Dominelli 1988: 145). The dangers of black workers with problem drinkers being "bombed out" should be acknowledged. The stress of having to carry out major responsibility for developing anti-racist services for problem drinkers – perhaps being the only black worker in the organisation and the possible victim of overt or subtle racism – imposes considerable pressure (Collins 1995). The establishment of support groups for black workers helping those with drink problems could assist in coping with the stress imposed by excessive demands and by possible feelings of isolation. It is essential to establish and develop a forum where strengths can be reinforced and mutual problems addressed, because energy and creativity can be maintained with the support of other black workers. Collective support is an essential element in the struggle to combat the stress imposed by racism which black workers may encounter in their work with problem drinkers.

Therefore, it is a particular responsibility of managers in probation and social services and in voluntary agencies that provide help for problem drinkers to ensure that appropriate support and help are available for black workers. The small number of black workers in these agencies may mean other, white, workers have myths, stereotypes, and fantasies about working with black people. Managers of black workers need to develop their sensitivity, knowledge and awareness of racism through their experiences and through training, to enable them to be more aware of the stress, pain, and anger caused by racism. In addition, middle and top managers in helping agencies for problem drinkers need to recognise themselves how dehumanising racism can be and to act upon this. Action which requires a readiness to examine – and a readiness to continue to examine – and challenge one's understanding of racism in favour of those who live with it and survive it. Furthermore, appropriate organisational policies and priorities need not only to be established but to be backed up by day to day implementation. The appointment of more black workers at grass roots and managerial levels in agencies that work with problem drinkers is likely to provide positive role models and to lead to more understanding, support, and opportunities for black workers.

While equal opportunities policies provoke thought about anti-racist approaches it seems such policies may have made only limited impact. Organisations designed to provide help for problem drinkers need to pursue equal opportunity policies both enthusiastically and energetically, setting appropriate targets, undertaking rigorous monitoring, and publishing details of progress that has been made (Collins 1995). A much firmer and stronger legislative base is needed to develop compulsory monitoring and attain contract compliance. The slow-moving, piecemeal and uneven development of equal opportunities in helping agencies for problem drinkers has delayed chances for black people to take up appointments at senior levels. This has undermined the establishment of an appropriate organisational ethos and the implementation of required strategies. If people from ethnic minorities have better promotion opportunities in alcohol agencies, and a more powerful say in decision making, then the self-esteem, confidence, and aspirations of other black workers would be encouraged.

Conclusion

There are some key concepts that need to be stressed as we conclude our discussions on work with black people who are problem drinkers. These are drawn from Fernando's work on mental health, race, and culture but have equal relevance to this chapter. Firstly, "racist conceptions" of cultural forms and habits must be challenged" (Fernando 1991: 197). A non-racist view of cultural, medical, and helping practices linked with problem drinking should be developed – ranging from ways of thinking and perceptions of family systems to religious beliefs – which should lead to anti-racist practice.

Models of assessment and intervention in working with problem drinkers are part of western culture and do not exist independently outside the culture in which they are located. Furthermore, careful attention should be given to black people's spiritual needs, social experiences, economic situation, and the cultural and political context in which they live. Black people's experiences of, and response to, problem drinking are fashioned by these factors.

White workers with problem drinkers should "accept the fact that the majority of the world is neither culturally Western nor racially white, [they should recognise] the validity of the black experience in a white dominated world . . . [and] should acknowledge the importance of concepts about human life from Asia and Africa" (Fernando 1991: 198). Workers should maintain vital fluidity of thought about black people's problem drinking, an approach that is flexible, culture sensitive, free of racism, and actively anti-racist at both individual and institutional levels. At the same time, culture should be an integral part of the way problem drinking is defined; models of problem drinking will vary with the culture and each model should incorporate culture into its fabric. All explanatory models should be embedded in their own cultures and not bound within one culture, hence all cultures would be seen as equally valid and important (Fernando 1991). There is a need to select interventions that are suited to the unique needs and problems of the client. Sue (1977) was perhaps the first to challenge the idea of using the same interventions with white and black clients, arguing that "equal" treatment in counselling and helping might mean discriminatory treatment. Alternatively, "*differential* treatment does not necessarily imply discriminatory treatment . . . because equal access and equal opportunity for all clients is the real issue, Sue favours the use of differential techniques that are not discriminatory" (Ridley 1995 : 96). Similar ideas have been developed by Solomon (1976), Ziter (1987), and Beverley (1989).

It is important also to bear in mind "the need to understand the personal meaning held by the [individual] as a particular person not simply as a representative of certain groups" (Ridley 1995 : 83). Therefore, the individuality of each black person experiencing drinking problems is obviously very important. The question of how to help the black problem-drinker is a naïve and simplistic one. "Knowing that a [client] is black fails to inform adequately about his[her] views of [helping], about his [her] personality and psychological conflict, about his[her] aspirations and goals in helping, let alone about educational level, social background or environmental context. There is enormous variability. The question is not how to treat *the* black [problem] drinker, but how to treat *this* black [problem] drinker" (Jones 1985 in Ridley 1995 : 84).

Chapter 8
Working with Adult Offenders

Drink and Offending

Drink and offending are often linked and there is a substantial literature on this topic (Collins 1982). In fact, alcohol and offending may be related in a variety of ways (Prins 1980, Purser 1987, Baldwin 1990, McMurran 1996).

(1)   Offences committed where alcohol is specifically mentioned, such as drunk and disorderly or driving a vehicle while under the influence of drink.

(2)   Offences committed when under the influence of alcohol, when a person is disinhibited or their judgement may have been affected, such as becoming involved in a crime after drinking, having used drink as a possible preparation for offending or, in having used drink, lost control and then become involved, for example, in an argument or an assault.

(3)   Offences taking place not while the person is intoxicated but as a result of a need to steal alcohol or to obtain money to buy alcohol, or as a result of overspending on alcohol.

(4)   Drinking context and situations providing opportunities for offences, such as meeting criminally inclined friends in a pub and then going on to commit an offence.

However, while direct links do exist between the cause and effect of some offences such as drunk and disorderly or drunk driving, in other cases the relationship between alcohol and offending is both unclear and complex and has been highlighted by several commentators (Baldwin 1990, Collins & Tate 1988, McMurran 1993). While many offenders and prisoners see a direct relationship between their drinking and offending, as well as the perceived effects of alcohol itself, the social context for drinking is equally important because "meeting and drinking with friends was often given as the beginning of a train of social exchanges culminating in offending" (McMurran & Hollin 1993: 8). Indeed, one study of young offenders by McMurran and Hollin indicated that drinking was a *consequence* rather than an antecedent of delinquency. In other words, a number of young offenders said they drank *after* an offence either to celebrate or to relieve feelings of anxiety and guilt (McMurran & Hollin 1989). Finally, while a substantial number of young offenders in the study said that they were heavy drinkers, their drinking was *not* connected to, or with, their criminal activities. Hence we should be very wary of *always* assuming that alcohol "causes" crime. Murdoch *et al*. have expressed this quite succinctly:–

> *"Evidence does not establish that people who drink commit crimes, nor does it prove that those who commit violent crimes drink to excess. It does reveal how often one is intoxicated when caught in the act of committing a crime. This is problematic if the very act of being intoxicated increases the probability of being apprehended."* (Murdoch *et al*. 1990: 107)

Furthermore, many of the research studies undertaken into alcohol and offending have been with small sample sizes and without adequate control groups. In addition there have been difficulties with use of terminology in that definitions of "problem" and "heavy" drinking have been used inconsistently, which has restricted valid comparisons between studies and limited the generalisability of the findings. (Baldwin 1990.)

Despite these caveats, "the existence of an *association* between [alcohol] and crime is now well established" (McMurran 1996 : 211) For example, studies have been undertaken of drunkenness, various samples of offences, offenders and prisoners, which give some indication of the size of the problem. Recorded offences for public drunkenness in England and Wales reveal that around 60,000 people were found guilty or cautioned in 1993. Those aged 18 - 20 represented 12% of the total; those aged 21 - 29 constituted 34% and those aged 30 - 59 47% of the total. As in previous years, the peak age for such offences was around 19 and 20 for both men and women. Of these offenders 91% were men (Home Office 1993).

In addition, alcohol has been strongly linked with other types of criminal behaviour such as murder, rape, assaults, partner/child assaults, and especially violent crime by males in general (Miller & Welte 1986, Baldwin 1990, Cookson 1992). A review by Collins about the relationship between problem drinking and offending concluded that "problem drinking is associated with criminal behaviour, especially violent criminal behaviour in the young adult years" (Collins 1986 : 111). In a study undertaken in a south coast resort in England by Jeffs and Saunders, 64% of all persons arrested by the police had been drinking in the four hours previous to their arrest. Between 10.00 p.m. and 2.00 a.m. 93% of all arrested persons were intoxicated and alcohol was involved in 78% of assault charges, 80% of breach of peace charges, and 88% of criminal damage arrests (Jeffs & Saunders 1983). In Scotland, persons were believed to be under the influence of drink in half of the prosecutions for breach of the peace, a third of the prosecutions for assault, a quarter of the prosecutions for causing death by dangerous driving, and in almost a fifth of the convictions for culpable homicide (Rix *et al.* 1976).

Overall, studies of prisoners have suggested that between one-half and two-thirds of incarcerated offenders perceive a relationship between alcohol intake and subsequent offending behaviour (Baldwin 1990). In England 68% of a sample of prisoners claimed to have been drinking prior to offending, while 63% of prisoners in a Scottish young offenders institution, claimed they were intoxicated during offending (Edwards *et al.* 1976, Heather 1981). The overall prison population in England and Wales exceeds 50,000 and it has been estimated by some writers that 38% to 46% of this population have been involved in drink-related offending (Cookson 1986, Hollin 1983, Welte & Miller 1987). In a Home Office survey of prisoners in south-east England one-quarter of the sample had a recorded drink problem (Bruun 1982). These difficulties, i.e. drink problems, had been particularly prevalent among short term prisoners, where 40% of a sample had previous convictions for drunkenness (Purser 1987). Also, a study of persistent petty offenders in Pentonville Prison which examined men serving fewer than 12 months, with five or more previous convictions, found that no fewer than two-thirds were "habitual heavy drinkers" (Fairhead 1981).

Therefore, there is strong evidence to suggest that alcohol and crime are associated. "Offenders are likely to be heavy drinkers and people who use alcohol . . . heavily are more likely to be involved in criminal activities." (McMurran 1996: 214.) Also, alcohol use at the time of the offence occurs in a large number of cases and many alcohol-using offenders report a relationship between their drinking and crime.

The Courts and Offenders with Drink Problems
Research studies in magistrates courts have also indicated links between alcohol and offending. For example, work in Hereford and Worcester showed that for 28% of male offenders and 22% of female offenders, offences were alcohol related (Hereford & Worcester Probation Service 1982). Magistrates and justices clerks have expressed considerable concern about this situation, as seen in the following comments from the Justices Clerks Society:–

> *"We are concerned deeply . . . as we see the effect of alcohol consumption on our daily court lists. There can be few, if any, Courts which do not see as a daily occurrence the effect of excessive consumption of alcohol manifesting itself in drunkenness, drunken driving and all those offences connected with public disorder, assault and criminal damage. Many offences of dishonesty including burglary and theft are committed while in drink."* (Justices Clerks Society in Menary 1990: 33)

For offenders convicted of breach of the peace, and drunk and disorderly viola-
tions, options available to courts have been limited by legislative restrictions and
restraints on available disposals (Moody 1976). Such persons are overwhelm-
ingly dealt with by fines, yet:–

> *"It is clear that these offenders present the Court with a problem of*
> *magnitude. Fining and imprisonment seem quite ineffective."*
> (Prins 1980 : 274)

When fines are not paid, short prison sentences eventually follow. Some
attempts have been made to replace traditional methods by diversionary ones
which use "an amalgamation of the law enforcement, health and social
services" (Carr 1983 : 155). Alternatives have been introduced to apply to the
offender who has committed an offence other than one where alcohol is specifically mentioned, such as when there is a charge other than drunk and
disorderly, drunk and incapable or drunk driving, where alcohol has been
involved as a significant "background" factor in the present offence and
perhaps in previous offences.

Diversion has been seen as "a loose term substituting a whole array of means of
dealing with offenders other than by custody" (Sheppard 1980 : 53) and
involves three elements – primary, secondary, and tertiary.

(1)　Primary diversion – takes place before, or instead of, a charge being
　　　made against a person arrested. Examples of primary diversion include
　　　the provision of detoxification centres, to divert those involved in petty
　　　drunkenness incidents from court. Also the increased use of cautions in
　　　some areas, following drunken incidents, occasionally accompanied by
　　　an opportunity to take up voluntary counselling for alcohol problems.

(2)　Secondary diversion – takes place after a charge has been made, but
　　　before the accused appears in court. This decision is taken by a variety of
　　　organisations such as the police, the prosecution, the court, probation or
　　　social services departments.

(3)　Tertiary diversion – involves a degree of coercion and occurs after a
　　　finding of guilt has been established. The decision to divert lies with the
　　　judiciary. In regard to alcohol-related offenders, schemes involving the
　　　use of probation orders for drunk drivers with a rehabilitation course
　　　condition or, for other offenders, probation orders with an alcohol
　　　education programme could be seen as an example of tertiary diversion.
　　　There are many examples of these projects which will be described later.
　　　Also deferred sentences with the offender receiving individual and group

counselling for alcohol problems from a voluntary agency is another example of tertiary diversion, as is the Fine Alternative Alcohol Project Scheme in Lothian Region, Scotland (Dickie 1985, Collins & Tate 1988).

Two important points need to be made here. The first is that when an individual appears before a court, it needs information and evidence that an alcohol problem exists. This may emerge from the previous record of convictions, from accounts of the circumstances surrounding the offence, from background information provided by a legal representative, from a pre-sentence report prepared by the Probation Service, or from a report from a drugs agency or from other sources. In some instances there may be unmistakable evidence of alcohol problems, but in others the evidence may be much less clear and an offender with a drink problem may "slip through the net". It is important to distinguish between situations where so-called "habitually drunk" offenders may present themselves on several occasions for minor drunkenness offences, and others where a transgressor may appear as a result of a very rare occurrence of intoxication or as a result of persistent, regular heavy drinking or alcohol dependence. It is identification and assessment which are vital in these instances. A great deal depends on the presence and use of skilled and knowledgeable assessment in the "less obvious" cases of problem drinking that are presented to the court. It is here that informed probation officers or workers from voluntary organisations, such as the service provided by Aquarius staff to Birmingham courts, can provide the required details and suggest guidance towards appropriate help, if it is required.

Secondly, a great deal depends on the attitudes of sentencers. While some are only too well aware of a requirement for action and appropriate facilities, such as some sheriffs in Scotland (Baldwin 1990) and the magistrate quoted by McLoughlin (1988 : 40) who commented on the "crying need to do something . . . [and] . . . anything is better than what we have", other sentencers make less effective use of services available for problem drinkers. Baldwin (1990) has pointed out some of the barriers presented by court officials to alcohol education courses in magistrates courts in England and Wales and district courts in Scotland. The low rate of referrals of offenders with drink problems to alcohol education courses seems to have been a result of various factors including:–

● pressure to give custodial sentences in a "law and order" climate to avoid "soft options".

● inconsistency of attitudes of court officials.

- public opinion about appropriate sentencing.
- limited knowledge of sentencing procedures and legal tariffs.
- uncertain consequences for an offender upon completion of an AEC.
- uncertain consequences for an offender upon non-completion of an AEC.
- negative climate for referrals to "controlled drinking" programmes.
- doubts about the establishment of "experimental" programmes.

This suggests that active canvassing of magistrates and magistrates' clerks is vital to obtain good rates of referral of offenders with drink problems to alcohol education courses (Menary 1986).

The Probation Service and Problem Drinkers

It is interesting to note that the origins of the Probation Service are to be found in the work of the police court missionaries in the late nineteenth century which had "evolved in a time of rising concern at the level of [so called] moral degeneration of a particular section of the population, namely working class habitual petty offenders whose patterns of offending were thought to be linked with their drinking habits " (May 1991 : 4). This led the Church of England Temperance Society to appoint the first Police Court Missionary in 1876. The task was to interview drunken people, decide upon those who were likely to respond to help, and suggest a plan to the court to put the offender on the "straight and narrow". Then in 1907 the Probation of Offenders Act gave the Probation Service its first statutory duty to supervise drunken offenders. Hence, from the above, it can be seen that the "establishment of Probation Services in England and Wales was inextricably linked with work undertaken with offenders in trouble through drink" (Singer 1991: 613).

Almost a century later, probation officers continue to be concerned about drink-related offending as seen in the following comments from a probation officer:–

> *"A lot [of probation officers] avoid taking . . . the drinkers on board.*
> *In general they disregard the alcohol – disregard the person. They see*
> *themselves as unable to help. (They think) 'let's get him off the patch*
> *for a bit'. . . Problem drinkers are time consuming . . . they . . . take up*
> *a lot of your energy . . . and officers soon become disillusioned"*
> (Smith 1988 : 349)

Within the Humberside Probation Service, a study concluded that one-third of all offenders were problem drinkers, while about half of that number could be categorised as dependent drinkers. About one-fifth of all male offenders in this study drank more than 50 units per week and 13% of all female offenders drank more than 35 units per week – well in excess of the "sensible" limit of 21 units per week for men and 14 units per week for women. (Taylor 1985 in Purser 1987). A more recent survey of over 3,000 probation officer members by the National Association of Probation Officers (NAPO 1994) revealed that 30% of their caseloads had "severe" problems with alcohol and that for over 7 in 10 of this group alcohol was directly related to their last offence.

In examining court reports, prepared in Lothian region, Scotland, during a six-month period in 1983 at least 50% of offences were thought to be alcohol-related, with the offender having previous alcohol-related problems (Dickie 1985). In the mid 1980s a study of court reports in Somerset of over 1,200 offenders indicated that drink-related offending was a problem in 29% of the cases (Singer 1991). In another study of Scottish court reports alcohol was considered to be an important factor in 17% of the sample studied (Curran & Chambers 1982). Indeed, this figure could well be an underestimate, as one British study of court reports has suggested that only limited attention was given to drinking habits when preparing a report, "even in cases where large amounts of alcohol had been consumed prior to commission of an offence" (Coope 1979 : 23). Almost a quarter of the sample of offenders, when interviewed in prison at a later stage, saw themselves as having alcohol-related problems although such problems were not noted in the actual court report.

A study of offenders seen by the Lothian Region Social Work Department in Scotland suggested that one-third of the clients of the Central Offenders Unit defined alcohol as a problem for themselves (Dickie 1985). In a study of male probation clients undertaken by Knapman (1993) in Northamptonshire around one-half were seen to have a drink problem, but almost half of those had not been recognised or identified as such by their probation officers. The staff concerned disliked working with these clients and had a lower level of contact with them than their caseload in general and, in the pre-national standards days, they were twice as likely to be seen less frequently. Moreover, those in the sample studied were drinking twice the national norm and averaged 50 units per week. Also the majority – almost three–quarters – were unemployed, so drinking was making considerable inroads into their financial resources. The overall sample were four times more likely to get drunk than the general population and nine times more likely to be classified as having a drink problem (Knapman 1982).

If some pieces of past research have indicated uncertainties about probation officers' knowledge and skills in identifying, assessing, and intervening effectively with offenders experiencing drinking problems there is evidence to suggest that they do compare favourably with social workers. Clement's (1987) work in Salford indicated that probation officers were far less likely to view problem drinkers negatively than social workers and were more likely to see their managers assigning such work as "high priority". This confirmed earlier findings by Cartwright *et al.* (1975), suggesting that probation officers fared better than social workers in their ability to identify alcohol problems. Also Smith (1988) has pointed out that drinking difficulties feature much more often as an overt, "presenting" problem by probation clients/offenders and they are clearly seen as relevant to the central aims and objectives of the agency.

Helping Problem Drinkers Within a Probation Context
The impact of various pieces of research and concern about the large numbers of offenders with drink problems in contact with the Probation Service received further impetus from other developments in the 1990s. Firstly, a thematic inspection on drugs work by the probation inspectorate (Her Majesty's Inspectorate of Probation 1993). This recommended that each service should create harm-reduction policies, have a drug strategy and a senior manager responsible for it, should establish an information system so that managers could identify the number of drug users on probation officers' caseloads, with an increase in training opportunities for officers, and local partnerships developed to plan appropriate services. Secondly, the latter was reinforced by a requirement that each probation area should spend at least 5% of their budget on funding in partnership with the independent sector and substance abuse was one of the four priority areas cited in the Home Office guidance (Home Office 1993). Thirdly, the 1991 Criminal Justice Act included a specific sentencing option aimed at alcohol and drug offenders – a condition of non-residential, day service treatment could be inserted in a probation order as an equally valid treatment option to residential provision at a rehabilitation centre. Furthermore, treatment could be provided by a "suitably qualified or experienced person" who might be a drugs worker or a probation officer.

The partnership arrangements that have been made under the Home Office directive have varied a great deal according to local need (Hart & Webster 1994). Several probation areas have staff seconded to work in drug and alcohol agencies (e.g. North Wales), others funded voluntary projects to work with alcohol-related offenders, often involving one post. Outside of partnership arrangements some services appointed specialist alcohol workers (e.g. north-east London and Suffolk) while others emphasised good quality training for all probation staff (e.g. Devon, Somerset, and Leicestershire). Only one probation area (South Glamorgan) was thought to have its alcohol and drugs work focused into a specialist team, mainly because its population is concentrated into one large centre – Cardiff.

Workers from alcohol and drugs agencies have been involved with probation areas at a number of levels, for instance, via intensive bail support and information schemes or in providing a comprehensive programme for clients on probation orders with conditions of treatment. Some alcohol agencies provide services based on probation premises and operate individual or group-based help. Many alcohol agencies who have become involved in providing a service under the condition of treatment for drug or alcohol use in a probation order have built upon pre-existing arrangements. The 1993 Home Office guidance tended to put many well-established partnerships on a more formal footing (Hart & Webster 1994). In order "to be effective, partnership initiatives . . . need to be underpinned by common values, clarity of purpose, open dialogue and the willingness of each partner to contribute their best. Effective partnerships require that probation services commit sufficient resources to this work" (Home Office 1993 : 23).

The adoption of written formal partnership agreements has been found helpful in order to start, sustain, review, and monitor arrangements. Under partnership arrangements some probation officers have felt anxious about the possibilities of part of their counselling work being "taken over" and may have had an initial reluctance to refer to voluntary agencies, with a danger of workers stereotyping each other, with different interpretations being made about some issues in particular, such as confidentiality. Clarification has been needed about the provision of Pre-Sentence Reports (PSRs) and assessment work by an alcohol agency. A PSR prepared by the probation officer includes:–

- Discussion of the offence, facts surrounding it, its seriousness and the defendant's attitude to it.

- Information about the offender that relates to the reasons for committing the offence, e.g. previous offences, patterns of offending, problems connected to offending.

- Conclusion and proposal for sentence.

An alcohol workers report includes:–

- History and pattern of alcohol use.

- Current alcohol use and links with the offence(s) or offending.

- Current and previous contact with alcohol agencies.

- Motivation of the offender to work on alcohol problems.

- Assessment of whether the alcohol agency provides an appropriate service for this particular client or if another agency would be more appropriate.

(Adapted from Hart & Webster 1994: 28).

If a probation order follows and is made with a condition of treatment, or if an alcohol agency is to undertake voluntary ongoing work whilst the client is on probation, then there is an obvious need to clarify who will do what. For instance, clear responsibility for supervising the order and any possible breach action rests with the Probation Service.

As noted earlier, forms of partnership will vary. In some areas there may be no formal partnerships with alcohol agencies. Whatever forms partnerships may, or may not take, probation officers will find themselves regularly encountering offenders with alcohol-related problems when they themselves will be required to assess or intervene in that situation. Therefore it is vital that officers continue to obtain, develop, and expand their knowledge and skills in the area of alcohol-related offending. The following are some guidelines for such work.

Matching Offenders to Interventions

There is no one approach that is equally effective in working with offenders experiencing drink problems, but the matching of individuals with appropriate interventions is more likely to lead to a successful outcome. As noted in Chapters 1 & 2, a model based upon the following can be helpful:–

1. Intoxication.

2. Regular, heavy drinking.

3. Dependence.

1. Some younger offenders may be occasionally intoxicated and commit offences while thus. However, drinking may not be a "serious " problem for them and they may get drunk only very occasionally, but become involved in some offences as a result.

2. Other offenders may be regular heavy drinkers, "binge" a lot, and frequently get drunk, often becoming involved in offences as a result, with alcohol thus playing a significant part in committing crime.

3. A small number of offenders, often aged over 25 and probably over 40, may be dependent drinkers – those who are often labelled "alcoholics". They may have been involved in numerous alcohol-related offences. They may be isolated, have received or require help from alcohol treatment units, have received or require detoxification and longer-term support with accommodation (Robinson 1979). They may find an abstinence goal and the services of Alcoholics Anonymous to be of particular relevance although, of course, much help can be given by probation officers, social workers, and other voluntary agencies.

It can be argued that there is a further group of *"emotionally distressed"* offenders who abuse both drink and drugs, exhibiting high levels of dependency on both, who are "emotionally unstable" and reveal high levels of associated problems. For these offenders, there may be a need to stabilise emotional problems before effective help with drink and drug problems can commence (Lightfoot & Hodgins 1993).

However, in general, it is argued that offending with associated drink problems exists on a continuum. The patterns of alcohol abuse noted above do not necessarily exist separately: there may well be overlap and movement between the three drinking patterns. Nevertheless, different degrees of harm require different kinds of responses and offenders may well be at different stages in their willingness to change drinking behaviour. (Adapted from Prochaska & DiClemente 1986, Barrie 1990, McMurran & Hollin 1993.)

STAGE	FEATURES	FOCUS OF INTERVENTION
Pre-contemplation	Lack of concern about offending and drinking. Benefits of drinking and offending outweigh costs.	Harm reduction. Increase commitment to change. Inform and educate about healthy, and consequences of unhealthy drinking. Encourage making links between drinking and offending.
Contemplation	Considering stopping or reducing offending and drinking. Wanting information. Some awareness of drinking linked with offending.	Increase consciousness of problem and commitment to change behaviour by information giving, motivational interviewing, assessment and self-monitoring of drinking.
Action	Making active, committed efforts to stop or cut down drinking and offending. Wanting to use help. Seeing costs of drinking and offending outweigh benefits.	Behavioural self-control, monitoring of drinking, setting goals, modifying life-styles, social skills training, using problem-solving methods, changing behaviour.
Maintenance	Maintain behaviour change, reduced drinking, or no drinking, no offending.	Continue commitment to new behaviours, new life-style. Vigilance to risky situations. Relapse prevention and management.

As McMurran & Hollin (1993) have pointed out, this model suggests the types of intervention appropriate at any one of the change stages, but it does not suggest appropriate goals for intervention, the style and intensity of intervention.

Goals - Level of Alcohol Consumption
Goals for change in the level of alcohol consumption will vary. Some offenders with drink problems, especially those aged over 25 and, in particular, those aged over 40 with many convictions for drunkenness and many years of alcohol dependence, may well need to aim for total abstinence, especially in those situations where physical health is at risk, when there has been a history of repeated attempts to try to reduce consumption which have failed.

Other offenders with drink problems may wish to control or reduce their alcohol intake. These would tend to be younger offenders, aged about 18 to 25, who have fewer alcohol-related problems and whose problems have been of shorter duration (Miller 1983, McMurran & Hollin 1993).

Styles of Intervention
These can vary from individual work to family and group work, depending on, for instance, the knowledge and skills of the worker, demands on time and resources, agency policies, accessibility of clients, and the nature of the geo-graphical area, be it urban, semi-rural or rural. Group work can have advantages but requires careful planning, appropriate aims, and sound selection criteria. For example, members should be of comparable intellectual ability, be able to engage in discussion and exercises, and be at roughly similar stages in their willingness to change – such as at the contemplation and action stages. It would be inappropriate to have members who might primarily experience only occasional problems of intoxication combined with those whose difficulties surround their inability to refrain from drinking heavily. Thus a young offender whose occasional violation related to being drunk, would not be appropriately helped in a group composed of regular, heavy, or dependent middle-aged drinkers who persistently offended and experienced withdrawal symptoms and vice versa (Barrie 1990).

Intensity of Intervention
This can vary from short term, brief advice giving to much more protracted intervention. Short term advice giving can be sufficient for some problem drinkers (Edwards *et al.* 1977, Miller & Sovereign 1989). It may be adequate for early stage offenders who encounter problems as a result of drink on one or two occasions. However, most will no doubt require to move on to more-extended programmes, involving behavioural self-control training, social skills

training, and relapse prevention work of varying degrees of intensity at an individual level or in groups.

Individual Interventions

During individual intervention with an offender who has a drink problem the worker can draw upon transferable knowledge and skills which are developed on all social work courses and have been described earlier (also see Chapters 4, 5 & 6). However, there may be particular knowledge and skills which are useful in working with an individual offender. These will be outlined in the following section and link in with material described in Chapter 4, where the importance of motivational interviewing is described. Readers are also referred to a tried and tested pack such as *Targets for Change* (Marshall & Weaver 1991), which offers a range of issue-focused one-to-one material for work with offenders, including alcohol problems.

Assessment Skills

These are clearly important when working with an offender who has a drink problem. There are several aspects that workers might want to consider, including the following:–

The relationship between alcohol and offending

As noted earlier, offences related to drink can be explored in an assessment interview, either by using forms with Likert-type scoring scales, e.g. 1 - 7, or in more open-ended discussion (McMurran & Hollin 1993). These could include consideration of

- Drinking *as my crime*, such as drunk and disorderly, drinking and driving.

- Drinking *changes my behaviour*, disinhibits me, gives me courage to get involved with crime.

- Drinking *causes me financial problems* , causes me to spend too much money, to need more money, and get involved with crime.

- *The places* where I drink are where crimes are planned or where crime occurs.

- Committing crimes to *make it easier to drink* and stealing money to buy alcohol or steal alcohol itself.

Alcohol consumption - a simple drinker's diary

Alcohol consumption levels also can be clarified by, for example, considering drinking patterns over a week, looking at what is drunk and how much is drunk, with whom, during each day, each morning, afternoon, and evening.

The 5-WH Situational Analysis
A technique recommended by McGuire and Priestley (1985). This involves an offender undertaking a situational analysis of one or more alcohol-related offences. The five 'w' questions to be asked are:–

- *Who*?   Who were you with when the offence occurred?
- *What*?   What were you drinking? What else was happening?
- *When*?   When did the offence occur?
- *Where*?   Where were you when the offence occurred?
- *Why*?   Why do you think the offence occurred?

The "How?" question is aimed at change, in terms of how can drinking and offending be avoided in future by, for example, drawing up sensible drinking guidelines, avoiding particular drinkers and crime-prone friends, or pubs that are known as "trouble spots" at particular times, leaving home later, taking less money, leaving the pub earlier, and so on. This will be explored in more detail later.

The ABC – Functional Analysis
In this model, factors both internal and external to the individual can be examined:–

- Antecedents – The wider background and the specific context for drinking.
- Behaviour – The actual drinking behaviour.
- Consequences – The consequences of drinking behaviour.

Antecedents can include the cultural, familial, social, cognitive, and emotional aspects of an alcohol-related offence, located both against a broad, historical background and in the narrow specific terms of the recent offence. Behaviour is the actual drinking. Consequences include positive reinforcement such as social rewards and enlivened mood, while negative reinforcement could result in an avoidance of boredom and possible relief of withdrawal symptoms. On the other hand, positive punishment could include hangovers and committing the crime. Negative punishment could include continued difficulties with employment and problems in relationships.

McMurran and Hollin (1993) present a vivid example of a young man, B, with a history of offences of fraud and theft.

Antecedents
His *antecedents* included a disturbed early life, characterised by the departure of his mother when he was young, as a result of violent attacks from his father

and B himself was subject to similar violence. B played truant from school a lot. He started drinking with older boys. Drinking became more and more important to him. By the age of 19 he could not keep a job and could not retain close friendships with males or females.

Behaviour
B's drinking was reported at 180 units of alcohol per week, compared with an average consumption of 21 units among men of his age. He scored 35 on the Short Alcohol Dependence Data Questionnaire, well in excess of the average score of 8 for young male offenders.

He started drinking upon waking, drinking two cans of lager to stop "the shakes". Most of his day was spent drinking at the home or in the pub. He suffered memory lapses, had bouts of depression, and several additional problems, including suffering from impotence. However, B sees drinking as making him happy, cheerful and funny, helping along his social interaction with others. Alcohol helps to conceal his inner hurt. Nevertheless, he recognises that drinking has caused him physical problems, he is worried about his lack of close relationships, has insight into his lost educational and employment opportunities and his involvement in offending and prison sentences.

Consequences
Drinking is positively reinforced because it brings happiness and social contact. If he didn't drink he would suffer "the shakes" in the morning. Drinking continues to cause problems as he becomes less competitive in a highly competitive job market. He spends much money on drink and commits crimes to get money for drinking.

Possible targets for change here could involve controlled drinking goals, skills training, and relationship-enhancement skills (McMurran & Hollin 1993).

Helping Intervention Skills
A whole range of interventions are possible in helping offenders with alcohol-related problems. What follows is a selection of techniques that might be used productively with offenders experiencing problems with drink.

Behavioural Self-Control Training
Behavioural self-control involves "the process of teaching people the skills and strategies required to control their own behaviour" (McMurran & Hollin 1993: 95). It is often used when attempting to achieve moderate drinking goals. Techniques involved include self-monitoring, setting goals, altering the antecedents to drinking, and making changes in drinking styles. The use of these techniques is seen as the responsibility of the client, with the worker

providing guidance. Behavioural self-control approaches can be used with groups as well as with individuals. Some clients also can use self-help manuals as effectively as worker-directed endeavours (Miller & Baca 1983, Heather *et al.* 1986). There are a number of manuals available such as *That's the Limit* (Health Education Council 1985) and *Let's Drink to your Health* (Robertson & Heather 1986). For those offenders with drink problems who are contemplating change and ready to move into Prochaska & DiClemente's (1986) action stage this readiness should be met with techniques for action and BSCT is appropriate. Hester and Miller (1987) state that those who are likely to benefit from BSCT are at the lower end of the continuum of those experiencing problems with drink, i.e. those who have had shorter drinking careers, less-severe alcohol problems, and lower levels of dependence. Many offenders can be obviously helped by such approaches but not necessarily all, especially those who have had longer-term problems and those who may have been seen as dependent drinkers with severe stressors in their emotional and social situations. Clearly one should be very wary of labelling or categorising offenders in this way, but matching individuals to appropriate interventions is an important aspect of working with offenders with drink problems.

There is evidence for the effectiveness of BSCT in work with young offenders (McMurran & Whitman 1990). This study of 51 young male offenders who had reduced their alcohol consumption discovered three major strategies that were useful to these offenders/drinkers.

1. *Social Change* Involved finding alternative activities, avoiding friends who were heavy drinkers, avoiding situations where heavy drinking occurred such as some town or city centre pubs. In brief, avoiding previous heavy drinking patterns, linked with developing new activities or renewing previously enjoyed activities to fill the time previously used for drinking.

2. *Setting Limits* Involved restricting the days of the week and the times of the day when drinking occurred, by setting limits on the amount of money to be spent on alcohol and by limiting the amount of alcohol that would be consumed in any drinking session.

3. *Rate Control* Involved restricting the amount of alcohol intake in any drinking session. This included eating a meal before drinking, drinking slowly, and switching from drinks with a high alcohol content to those containing less alcohol.

Self-monitoring is important in using BSCT approaches to gain information about *antecedents* to drinking, *behaviour* during drinking, and *consequences* of drinking. Self-monitoring identifies targets for situational and environmental change in order to reduce the likelihood of drinking or offending after drinking (McMurran & Hollin 1993). Drinking diaries are particularly useful in this respect, in highlighting dangerous or risky situations, such as particular pubs and friends, dangerous or risky times of the week or day, the mood the offender was in before drinking began, and the amount of money they had available (Hester & Miller 1987).

After monitoring for a week or more, the diary can be examined and goals set – reducing alcohol consumption and stopping offending behaviour. In cutting down alcohol intake, limits can be set on:

- times when drinking is allowed
- the amount of money to be spent on drink
- the quantity of alcohol to be drunk in any one session.

Short and simple records can be kept on reminder cards.

Changing Antecedents
Offending is often the culmination of a chain of events, each setting off the next. As noted earlier, week-end evenings are often part of this chain of events. There is preparation for the event – getting washed, dressing up in particular leisure clothes, going out, meeting friends, going to a particular pub or pubs, moving on to a town or city centre pub or club, leaving the pub or club, getting fish and chips, kebabs or pizza, arguing and perhaps getting into a fight. As McMurran and Hollin (1993) note, the easiest way to stop the fight is to break the chain of events. For example, not to visit the town or city centre, to avoid particular friends, or leave the pub early. Hence antecedents are altered to prevent unwanted behaviour by making decisions or setting rules for oneself (Kanfer & Gaelick 1986). Again, the decisions or rules can be recorded on cards.

Changing Drinking Behaviour
Strategies will need to be devised to help control the rate of alcohol intake over a period of time during a drinking session (Kanfer & Gaelick 1986). These could include:–

- eating a meal before drinking so that alcohol is absorbed into the blood less quickly
- not eating salty crisps and peanuts, which increase thirst and encourage drinking
- switching to lower alcohol drinks away from high alcohol content lagers such as Pils and Carlsberg "Special"

- drinking half-pints instead of pints

- not mixing drinks, e.g. beer and spirits, snakebites (cider and lager or beer)

- drinking slowly

- avoid involvement in buying rounds with large numbers of people

- avoid pub crawls.

Changing Consequences

The use of *self-reward* differentiates between problem drinkers who succeed in cutting down their alcohol consumption and those who do not (Perri 1985). Self-reward is often used by young offenders who manage to control their problem drinking (McMurran & Whitman 1990). Varied, realistic, individualised, early rewards can be material goods such as buying clothes, a tape, or a CD; there can be involvement in a special activity such as going to a gig or the cinema or positive self-statements, when the person acknowledges his or her achievements that they have kept to their limits.

Social Skills Training

Social skills training involves verbal and non-verbal communication. The latter includes bodily contact, gesture and posture, and facial expressions. Social behaviour involves perception, translation, and response (Trower *et al.* 1978). "Abnormal" social behaviour can involve breakdown in any of those three stages. Social skills training tends to focus on assessment and skills training methods. The most frequently used training methods include modelling, rehearsal, feedback, and reinforcement.

Not all offenders with drink problems will experience social skills problems, but some are likely to do so. For example, there is a long-standing association between social ability, social competence, and "alcoholism" (Levine & Zeigler 1973). Adolescent problem drinkers have been found to be aggressive, lacking in personal control, and too impulsive (Braucht *et al.* 1973). Also, heavy drinkers are likely to form relationships with others who are heavy drinkers, which can lead to other problems as a result of being part of a "drinking culture" and being labelled "anti-social". Alcohol can be expected to make it easier for adults to cope with social encounters, often in those situations which require assertive behaviour and the "combination of a negative emotional state plus the inability to express oneself effectively can lead to an increase in alcohol consumption" (Monti *et al.* 1986 : 117).

In fact, there are several typical goals in social skills training with problem drinkers such as

- managing situations that require assertive behaviour, which can produce frustration and anger

- coping with negative feelings such as loneliness and boredom, and

- managing situations in which there is social pressure to drink.

(McMurran & Hollin 1993)

Through the learning of appropriate non-verbal and verbal communication skills an offender with drink problems can improve assertiveness and conversational skills, drink-refusal skills, and skills in coping with negative feelings. The aim of these programmes is "to help [the offender] achieve social goals without the need for heavy drinking" (McMurran & Hollin 1993 : 125).

Relapse Prevention

As noted earlier in this book in any interventive attempts with offenders who are problem drinkers, the likelihood of a lapse or a relapse is extremely high (Allsop & Saunders 1987). A lapse has been defined as an initial, single, violation of an individual's goals to stop or reduce drinking. A relapse has been defined as binge drinking, a return to uncontrolled drinking, to previous levels of consumption, or an abandonment of attempts to change drinking patterns (Marlatt 1990). In fact, lapse or relapse is "normal" for offenders who have drink problems. It should not be seen as a failure or as being "back to square one", because relapse is an active part of the process of change. Individuals at this stage of change use a range of strategies which seem to be a combination of those used in the contemplation and action stages (Barrie 1990:163). Therefore, it is valuable to build-in some relapse prevention strategies when implementing any helping interventions rather as one might prepare for a possible fire by having fire-drills. For example, to teach problem-solving skills which can be applied to managing a wide range of difficult or risky situations (D'Zurilla & Goldfried 1971). These difficult situations can be separated into two main categories: intrapersonal and interpersonal (Marlatt 1985).

Intrapersonal determinants include:–

- Unpleasant emotions, such as experiencing frustration, anxiety, anger, loneliness, boredom, and other bad emotional states following, for example, failure to get a job or arguments with Social Security.

- Physical discomfort, such as pain, illness, or tiredness.

- Pleasant emotions, such as feeling happy, excited, and pleased and other good emotional states.

- Testing personal control, by engaging in moderate drinking to see what happens.

- Urges and temptations, such as unexpectedly finding oneself in drinking situations, meeting a heavy-drinking friend (or friends), or finding oneself close to a favourite pub.

Interpersonal determinants include:–

- Conflict, such as having disagreements with partners or family, arguments or fights with other people.

- Social pressures, such as being urged to drink by friends or seeing people drinking and feeling the need to join in.

- Pleasant times with others, such as drinking to improve good times such as sexual situations, an evening out, or celebration of a birthday.

Annis (1990) has identified two relapse profiles – the high negative profile and the high positive profile. People with a high negative profile are more likely to drink in response to situations which involve unpleasant emotions or conflict with others, to drink alone, to be highly dependent on alcohol, and to be female. On the other hand, those with more-positive profiles are more likely to drink in situations involving positive emotions, to drink with others, to respond to social pressures to drink, to have low levels of alcohol dependence, and to be male.

This kind of information can help in assessment of an offender's risky situations for drinking. When the risks are identified, coping skills can be developed for relapse prevention, but a person also needs to *believe* that they can apply the coping skills to the situation, so that when they apply them they will work. It is suggested that cue exposure, modelling skills, rehearsal and real life experience of coping with high risk situations, such as those encountered in pubs, are very important for offenders with drink problems (Hodgson 1989, McMurran 1991).

High risk situations can be identified by accounts of past relapses, drinking diaries, and relapse fantasies. Coping skills can be identified by knowing what strategies to use and believing that one can use them effectively. Preparation can be made to help the offender understand that they can expect to feel a desire to drink from time to time. This should not come as a surprise. The desire to drink will depend on particular internal or situational cues. They will be time limited and pass by (Marlatt & George 1984). Positive self-statements can help here, noting that the desire doesn't need to be acted on and will end. The offender also can review their reasons, their decision to cut down drinking, consider the benefits gained, which outweigh the costs of heavy drinking in the short term and the long term. The offender can be encouraged to consider the PIG – the *Problems of Immediate Gratification* – which is the tendency to concentrate on the initial effects at the expense of long term health and well–being (Marlatt 1985).

Marlatt (1985) also urges that SIDs should be considered – the *Seemingly Irrelevant Decisions*. These are choices which appear to be distractions from the desire to drink, but place the offender in a situation of even stronger temptation. For example, visiting a friend when the friend strongly and enthusiastically offers a lot of drink to visitors. Also to do shopping in a supermarket where the drinks section is prominently located.

Furthermore Marlatt (1985) stresses that it is important to cope with any setbacks that do occur by avoiding the GVE (the Goal Violation Effect) or the AVE (the Abstinence Violation Effect). A lapse can lead to a full-blown relapse when offenders attribute their lapses to themselves, to internal states or causes. They are less likely to regain control and may feel powerless to do so. The offender can be encouraged to attribute the cause of the lapse to external and changeable factors associated with a high-risk situation. In other words, it is the situation presented rather than the person, which is problematic. It is then less likely that offenders will see themselves as "having no will power", as a "lost cause", or a "hopeless case" who has failed again. Plans can be made for coping with similar situations in the future. Lapse should be seen as a single event, occurring at a specific point and place in time, not as an inevitable part of a process of decline leading to protracted and wholesale drinking. This involves "cognitive reframing", seeing the event not as a failure but as a learning experience, helping to develop awareness of the high-risk situations to which they might be vulnerable (Marlatt 1985). Sometimes reminder cards can help the offender extricate themselves from the "one drink, one drunk" syndrome and help them stop after one or two drinks and leave the high-risk situation.

In conclusion, therefore, lapse and relapse prevention is an important aspect of helping offenders with drink problems to identify situations of high risk and to develop management skills and strategies for coping with them. This requires some knowledge of learning theory, cognitive behavioural approaches, and skills in applying them, which are included usually in most social work courses. If a worker has not had the opportunity to learn about such approaches, then these would need to be acquired by reading relevant literature and/or by attending appropriate post-qualification courses and by receiving supervision or consultation from an experienced worker. In some instances relapse prevention work might be inappropriate with offenders where there is clear evidence of physical damage as a result of dependent drinking and prolonged alcohol abuse, while offenders going through or emerging from psychotic episodes, with a fragile hold on reality, would be unlikely to benefit from this approach. Abstinence is the preferred focus on these occasions.

Alcohol Education Groups/Courses
Another main way of helping offenders with alcohol-related problems has been through the use of alcohol education courses. They began in the late 1970s and early 1980s and were mainly developed by probation services, or rather probation officers and social workers with an especial interest in alcohol and offending. Those located in Corby, Coventry, Oxford, Clacton, and Reading and Dundee and Forfar in Scotland were amongst the pioneering courses. The first published account seems to have been a study of the Corby Alcohol Therapy Group (Northamptonshire Probation Service 1982), a "rehabilitative" option for clients involved in alcohol related offending. Another early published report was a further probation service initiative, an alcohol education course in Coventry, which had developed from the earlier Corby Model (Bailey & Purser 1982). Also significant was the development of rehabilitation courses for drivers impaired by alcohol which first commenced in 1983 (Cook 1993).

Most alcohol education courses are based on groups coming together over a six to eight-week period, meeting once a week, sometimes with individual introductory and follow up sessions. Usually offenders attend as a condition of a probation order or, less often, during a deferred sentence. A survey of UK alcohol education initiatives, based on data from 20 agencies revealed that the average course length was 12 hours. The main aim of half the courses was to provide education, while about one-third of the courses looked for behaviour change (Baldwin & Heather 1987). All courses included group discussions. Almost all used drink diaries and health education materials. The 1987 review indicated that since 1981 about 250 courses had been completed with around 2,000 people taking part in them (Baldwin & Heather 1987). An update of the review confirmed many of the findings and extended the study (Cochran *et al.* 1989). Several trends were confirmed:–

1. Alcohol education courses were directed mainly at offenders aged between 17 and 29.

2. Courses generally had not been available for female offenders.

3.   There was a trend towards shorter courses (a reduction of 25% in average length).

4.   The emphasis had continued on education and information provision rather than on the acquisition of skills.

5.   Around seven offenders continued to complete each alcohol education course.

6.   There was more use of deferred sentences by the courts.

7.   Use of controlled evaluations to investigate the effectiveness of courses remained minimal.

(Baldwin 1990)

It is now suggested that certain ingredients are more likely to lead to successful outcomes in alcohol education courses for offenders (Baldwin *et al.*1988, 1990; McMurran 1993). These include:–

1.   Action-based strategies for the specific client group, i.e. offenders who are problem drinkers.

2.   The need to produce materials specifically for problem behaviours related to offending and excessive drinking.

3.   The provision of skills teaching/learning in order to modify specific problem behaviours and not just provide information (McGuire & Priestley 1985, Heather & Robertson 1983, Robertson & Heather 1982).

4.   The need to use self-monitoring and self-recording methods (Stumphauser 1986).

5.   The need to use behavioural contracts involving responsibilities, privileges, sanctions, and bonuses (Stuart 1971).

In particular, behavioural alcohol education courses are seen as preferable to discussion, or talk-based AECs (Baldwin *et al.* 1988). Discussion-based AECs have used non-directive counselling and rely on verbal methods. Specific goals are not set. It is expected that change will occur as a result of a generally positive, encouraging climate developed by the course leader than by explicit suggestions or guidance. Behavioural alcohol education courses set more specific behavioural goals negotiated with individual members and require them to be achieved. It is expected that those undertaking the course will acquire specific skills to assist them in reducing drinking (or achieving abstinence) and, in particular, in avoiding offending. Behavioural AECs have few "drop-outs", achieve better outcomes, and obtain more-favourable ratings from group members especially because of the structure and problem-specific content (Baldwin *et al.* 1988, Baldwin 1990). Some studies suggest that younger offenders/problem drinkers, aged 17 to 20, are more likely to improve on their behaviour involving offending and drinking, while those with chronic offending and drinking patterns do not necessarily do less well following an AEC (Baldwin 1990).

Evaluation of subsequent offending rates following AECs has been rare. Singer (1983) provided the first, a 12-month follow-up evaluation of an alcohol study group in Berkshire. Those who completed the course had a much lower reconviction rate than those who had dropped out, while measured improvements included increased knowledge of alcohol, increased awareness of "risky" drinking situations, and reduced alcohol intake. A study in Devon in the mid-1980s (Godfrey & Leahy 1986) revealed almost all participants had developed significant increases in alcohol knowledge, a third had cut down their drinking to a level within their personal targets, and a third had reduced their overall consumption, with "a slightly lower reconviction rate for compulsory attenders" (Godfrey & Leahy 1986: 2). A three-year evaluation study of 152 offenders on alcohol education courses in Somerset (Singer 1991) again revealed significant increases in alcohol knowledge. A drink-profile questionnaire was used to test drinking attitudes and drinking behaviour, a crucial element in measuring the effectiveness of AECs. Almost three-quarters of the participants reduced drinking to a medium or low level of risk. When information was obtained from drink diaries it was discovered that there was a shift from high to moderate drinking levels for males, i.e. from 40 to 32 units each week. After a 12-month follow-up it was discovered that 63% of the sample were not recorded as having committed further offences. Therefore, almost two out of three participants had kept away from further trouble through drink. As one participant observed:–

> *"Yeah, drinking's always got me into trouble in the past, I mean now I've thought about it, I've thought what a stupid idiot I'd be, so you know if it wasn't for the course, then I probably would have gone and done it again ... without a second thought."*

(Singer 1991 :623)

The above findings seemed particularly important when compared with Phillpotts and Lanuchi's findings that 53% of *all* male offenders with over five preconvictions were reconvicted within a year, while members of the AEC group had an average of seven convictions before undertaking the course (Phillpotts & Lanuchi 1979 :24).

Alcohol Education Groups – Some Issues

However, there are several issues surrounding the use of AECs. One concerns the low referral rate of female offenders, when female offenders might form up to 15% of those eligible. Referrals of females for AEC assessment have been, and are, rare (Baldwin 1990). "When referred to AECs they are likely to be older than the average male referral and have a shorter criminal career" (Brown 1990: 99). Moreover, women offenders may prefer to be involved with an exclusively female group, led by women; 76% of agencies in the UK provide AEC courses for males and females and 16% provide courses exclusively for females (Gamba *et al.* 1989). There may be a bias against female offenders related to discrimination in other parts of the criminal justice system, such as police behaviour, behaviour at arrest, and sentencing procedures (Inglehart & Stein 1985). Institutionalised sexism may account for the low rate of referrals to AECs with the perception of female offending behaviour as requiring "psychiatric type" help and assistance and not being perceived as a social, interpersonal or "law and order" problem (McLoughlin 1985). Furthermore, male-dominated models of offending and drinking behaviour lead to the construction of AEC programmes that may not be either designed or have appropriate content for female offenders with drink problems. This is yet a further example of the fact that "theory building in the alcohol world is fundamentally a male preserve" (Ettorre 1992 : 33), while a female offender with a drink problem is likely to suffer triple jeopardy and stigma – because she is a woman, is seen as an offender, and as a "drunk" or an "alcoholic". Therefore it is clear that if women offenders with drink problems are characterised by poly-stereotypes they are likely to be defined as having poly-problems such as being promiscuous, a "bad mother", uncaring for her children, and an irresponsible wife, not considering her husband's needs (Ettorre 1992). Clearly, it is thus evident that female offenders with drink problems will experience greater stigma – "a stigma that is more distressing and more destructive than that suffered by men" (Ettorre 1992:38. Alcohol education courses need to take these matters into account and become more sensitive to the needs of different groups of women of varying ages, social class, sexual orientation, and ethnic origins.

A further issue encompasses controversy about compulsion and voluntarism in work on AEC courses. The 1982 and 1991 Criminal Justice Acts enabled AEC groups to be made a statutory condition within a probation order. Some have expressed reservations about such conditions, arguing against compulsion and associating it with bad group-work practice (McLoone *et al.* 1987). It has been suggested that careful assessment and well-thought-out goals, allied to enthusiastic and soundly planned interventions, are more important than the special conditions of attendance at AECs as attendance can be achieved within the general conditions of a probation order. Also, imposing a special condition clause might lead to a higher tariff sentence if the person commits further offences.

Others suggest compulsion increases credibility with sentencers, and otherwise reluctant clients will attend and can be motivated and helped to overcome their mixed feelings about being involved with a group, ultimately finding it to be a valuable experience. It has been argued that the clear additional conditions spelt out in the probation order ensure the court, the offender, and the Probation Service are more accountable and better able to concentrate on the alcohol problem (Purser 1987). It is argued that offenders with alcohol problems might well want to avoid a situation that is challenging, may not usually, at first, make links between their drinking and offending, and, initially, may not see alcohol education courses as valuable or beneficial (Menary 1990). Compulsion can be seen as a positive aid to motivation. In addition, the introduction and establishment of national standards in probation, whilst they may have some drawbacks, have reduced local variation in implementation of policies involving compulsory attendance and led to the development of more consistency in breach proceedings.

The reluctance, fantasies, and uncertainties about what an AEC might involve are seen in the following comments of participants:–

> *"At first I didn't like it, then after a while I enjoyed it."*

> *"My probation officer was telling me about it . . . but I didn't think it would be like it was."*

> *"I wasn't looking forward to going at all. I thought it was going to be like walking into a room with loads of people who were . . . alcoholics . . . I didn't know what the people would be like."*

> *"I thought it would be really strict and put you against drinking [but it was] totally different."*

> *"It was completely different from what I thought it was going to be."*

(Menary 1990: 41)

These comments indicate that "resistance" and ambivalence are natural, but can be overcome, even if the initial impetus comes from compulsion. Compulsion can make available helping opportunities which might otherwise have been denigrated, avoided, and put aside. Indications are that people can be assisted to move from precontemplation to contemplation and action by the process of a court appearance, referral for assessment, and the actual undertaking of an education course. Furthermore, available research evidence suggests similar outcomes, with both voluntary and compulsory referrals achieving equal reductions in alcohol intake after completing their programmes, but compulsory referrals reveal higher rates of actual completion of the course (Vogler *et al*. 1976, Hoffmann *et al*. 1987, Stitzer & McCaul 1987, Watson *et al*. 1988).

An issue surrounds those who drop out of courses or do not reduce their drinking or offending. For example, Singer (1991) has noted that a quarter of those referred to the Berkshire Alcohol Study Group and the Somerset Alcohol Education Course still had alcohol levels of 61 units per week reported at the end of the programme – a very high level, at which liver damage may occur. Also 63% of the Berkshire sample who dropped out of the course reoffended. Hence, alternatives need to be sought for these "failures" and lessons need to be learnt from them.

The issue of the staffing of AECs also requires attention. In England and Wales 78% of AECs have been provided by probation officers or social workers. AECs do represent a cost effective use of resources in times of financial restraints and cut-backs. Group-based interventions are, and should remain, a high priority for probation services. Some have argued that there are dangers in services establishing alcohol specialists who are seen as "experts" in AECs, when all probation officers have the ability to run such groups, given enough time (Goodman 1987). Menary (1990), however, has argued strongly that ongoing AECs require considerable preparation, planning, commitment, maintenance and updating, as well as high priority in a probation officer's workload. In a few areas, for example in Somerset, a team was set up to establish and develop alcohol interventions and to facilitate full probation staff ownership and involvement in the AEC project. Under the leadership of an assistant chief probation officer, probation officers from various field teams were appointed to the specialist team. A high level of referrals was obtained for AEC courses. Over a half of the probation officers in the local Somerset service were involved in the running of groups. In addition, the service eventually made appropriate financial resourcing, acknowledging the time involved and making proper workload allowances. Staff development and training were available so that staff became more aware of group processes, developed their own knowledge of alcohol, and became accustomed to the active, skills-based approach of the groups. A leaders handbook was prepared for the Somerset staff to provide alcohol knowledge, give details of the exercises on the course, and provide general guidance on the course structure and teaching approaches.

Subsequently, a standardised behavioural AEC course has been produced by Baldwin *et al.* (1988) in the form of a teaching pack, with videos, acetates, diaries, and self-recording cards, to be used in non-institutional settings with offenders experiencing drink problems.

Therefore, to summarise, we have covered several issues relating to alcohol education courses, including the limited provision for women, the place of compulsion issues surrounding resources and staffing, and offenders who do not succeed on the courses. It is clear that, while alcohol education groups are not a panacea, they do offer a positive way forward for assisting many offenders with alcohol-related problems.

Conclusion

In this chapter we have noted the complexities of the association between alcohol and offending. Alcohol does not "cause" crime, but it is often linked with it, as part of an interaction between alcohol, the personality of the offender, the environment, and the context in which drinking occurs. It is known that a high percentage of offenders have experienced, and do experience, problems with drink to varying degrees. Courts have only a limited range of sentences available to them but a number of alternative approaches and schemes have been developed to help the offender who has a drink problem. A great deal can depend on the attitude of sentencers in the actual use of such schemes.

We have considered the role of the Probation Service in working with problem drinkers and the development of partnerships with independent agencies. There are important skills and knowledge in working with offenders experiencing drink problems and in matching such offenders to appropriate interventions. In working with individual offenders we have noted the importance of cognitive behavioural and social skills approaches and in working with situations of lapse and relapse. Also we have noted that, in working with groups, the role of alcohol education courses has been particularly important. Their development, the increasing emphasis on behavioural-based courses, the evaluation of offenders' experiences, and the organisational issues associated with them, are all of considerable significance for the future.

Once more, as we have stated in the previous chapters, the individuality and uniqueness of users of services, in this case offenders, must never be neglected. Only then can available knowledge and skills be used to maximum advantage by workers from organisations committed to providing appropriately resourced and supported services. Organisations which, in turn, must receive appropriate financial backing from central government policies.

Bibliography

Abel, P. (1983) *Alcohol Related Problems in Current Social Work Cases*. Avon. Avon Social Services Dept.

Ahmad, B. (1990) *Black Perspectives in Social Work*. Birmingham. Venture Press.

Aitken P. (1978) *Ten-Fourteen Year Olds & Alcohol: A Development Study in the Central Region of Scotland* (Vol.3). Edinburgh. HMSO.

Aitken, P. & Leathar, D. (1981) *Adults Attitudes Towards Drinking and Smoking Among Young People in Scotland* Vol. IV. Edinburgh. HMSO.

Alaszewski, A. & Harrison, L. (1992) "Alcohol and Social Work : A. Literature Review" *British Journal of Social Work* 22(3). 331-43.

Alcohol Concern (1987) *Alcohol Services – The Future*. London. Alcohol Concern.

Alcohol Concern (1988) *The Drinking Revolution*. Cambridge. Woodhead Faulkner.

Alcohol Concern (1996) *Acquire* 13. Winter 1995/96. London. Alcohol Concern.

Alcoholics Anonymous (1976) *The Big Book* Alcoholics Anonymous. World Services Inc.

Alcoholics Anonymous (1982 & 1986) *Survey of AA in Great Britain* General Service Board of Alcoholics Anonymous Ltd.

Allsop, S. & Saunders, W. (1987) "Relapse : A Psychological Perspective" *British Journal of Addiction*. 82(4). 417-29.

Allsop, S. & Saunders, W. (1989) "Relapse and Alcohol Problems" in Gossop, M. (ed) *Relapse and Addictive Behaviour*. London. Routledge.

American Medical Association (1977) *Manual on alcoholism* 3rd edition. Chicago. American Medical Association.

Anderson, D. (1981) *The Minnesota Experience*. Minnesota. Haselden Foundation.

Anderson, G. (1980) "*Alcoholism and the Ageing America*" 20 April 1980. 143. 139-42.

Anderson, P. (1985) "Managing Alcohol Problems in General Practice" *British Medical Journal* 290. 1873-5.

Annis, H. (1990) "Relapse to substance abuse : Empirical findings within a cognitive-social learning approach" *Journal of Psychoactive Drugs* 22. 117-24.

Atkinson, R. (1984) "Substance use and abuse in later life" in Atkinson, R. (ed) *Alcohol and drug use in Old Age.* Washington. American Psychiatric Press.

Atkinson, R. & Kofed, L. (1982) "Alcohol and Drug Use in Old Age: A Clinical Perspective," in *Substance and Alcohol Actions/Misuse* 353-68.

Babor, T. F., Dolinsky, Z., Rounsaville, B. & Jaffe, J. (1988) "Unitary versus multidimensional models of alcoholism treatment outcome : An empirical study" *Journal of Social Studies* 49. 167-77.

Babor, T. F., Ritson, E. & Hodgson, R. (1986) "Alcohol Related Problems in the Primary Health Care Setting : A Review of Early Intervention Strategies" *British Journal of Addiction* 81(1). 23-46.

Bagnall, G. (1991) "Alcohol and Drug Use in a Scottish Cohort : Ten Years On" *British Journal of Addiction* 86, 895-904.

Bailey, H. & Purser, B. (1982) *Coventry Alcohol Education Group.* Unpublished paper. Coventry Alcohol Information Centre.

Balarjan, R. & Yuen, R. (1986) "British smoking and drinking habits: variations by country of birth" *Community medicine* 8 (3): 237-9.

Baldwin S. (1990) "Helping Problem Drinkers : Some new developments" in Collins, S. (ed) *Alcohol, Social Work and Helping.* London. Routledge.

Baldwin, S. (1990) *Alcohol Education and Offenders.* London. Batsford.

Baldwin, S. & Heather, N. (1987) "Alcohol Education Courses for Offenders : A Survey of British Agencies" *Alcohol and Alcoholism* 22.1. 79-82.

Baldwin, S., Wilson, M., Lancaster, A. & Allsop, D. (1988) *Ending Offending* Glasgow. Scottish Council on Alcohol.

Bandura, A. (1977) *Social Learning Theory.* New York. Englewood Cliffs.

Barber, J. (1995) *Social Work with Addictions.* London. Macmillan.

Barnes, G. (1979) "Alcohol use among older persons : Findings from a Western New York State general population survey" *Journal of American Geriatricians Society* 27, 244-50.

Barnes, G. & Windle, M. (1987) "Family Factors in Adolescent Alcohol and Drug Use" *Paediatrician* 14. 13-18.

Barnes, M. & Maple, N. (1990) *Women & Mental Health : Challenging the Stereotypes*. Birmingham. Venture Press.

Barrie, K. (1988) *The Impact of Alcohol on Social Work in Scotland*. Paisley. Alcohol Studies Centre, Paisley College.

Barrie, K. (1990) "Helping in Groups" in Collins, S. (ed) *Alcohol, Social Work and Helping*. London. Routledge.

Bebbington, J. (1976) "The Efficiency of AA : The elusiveness of Hard Data" *British Journal of Psychiatry* 128. 527.

Beck, A. T. (1989) *Cognitive Therapy and the Emotional Disorders*. International Universities Press Inc.

Bell, P. & Evans, J. (1983) "Counselling the Black Alcoholic Client" in Watts, T. & Wright, R. (eds) *Black Alcoholism: Towards a Comprehensive Understanding* Springfield Ill : Charles C. Thomas.

Bensley, L. & Wu, R. (1991) "The Role of Psychological Reactance in Drinking following Alcohol Prevention Messages" *Journal of Applied Social Psychology* 24, 1111-24.

Bergin, A. & Garfield, S. (eds) (1978) *Psychotherapy and behaviour change*. New York. Wiley.

Beverley, C, (1975) "Towards a Model for Counselling Black Alcoholics" *Journal of Non White Concerns* 3. 169-76.

Beverley, C. (1989) "Treatment Issues for black alcoholic clients" *Social Casework* 706: 370-4.

Bhat, A. Carr-Hill, R.. & Ohri, S. (eds) (1988) *Britain's Black Population*. Aldershot. Gower.

Billings, A. & Moos, R. (1983) "Psychosocial processes of recovery among alcoholics and their families : Implications for clinicians and program evaluators" *Addictive Behaviour* 8. 205-18.

Black, C. (1981) I*t will never happen to me! Children of Alcoholics : As Youngsters, Adolescents, Adults*. Denver Co. Medical Administration Corp.

Black, D. (1990) "Changing Patterns and Consequences of Alcohol Abuse in Old Age" *Geriatric Medicine* (January): 19-20.

Blackmon, B. (1985) "Networking Community Services for Elderly Clients with Alcohol Problems" in Freeman, E. (ed) *Social Work Practice with Clients who have Alcohol Problems.* Springfield. Charles C. Thomas.

Blose, I. (1978) "The relationship of alcoholism to ageing and the elderly" *Alcoholism : Clinical and Experimental Research* 2(1), 17-21.

Bolles, R. C. (1979) *Learning Theory.* New York. Holt, Rinehart & Winston.

Botvin, G. & Tortu, S. (1988) "Peer relationships, social competences and substance abuse prevention : Implications for the family" in Coombes, R. H. (ed) *The Family Context of Adolescent Drug Use.* New York. Haworth Press.

Bratter, T. (1989) "Group Psychotherapy with Alcohol and Drug Addicted Adolescents : Special Clinical Concerns and Challenges" in Cramer-Azima, F. & Richmond, L. (eds) *Adolescent Group Psychotherapy.* Madison. International Universities.

Braucht, G., Brackasch, D., Folungstad, D. & Berry, K. (1973) "Deviant Drug Use in Adolescence" *Psychological Bulletin* 79. 92-106.

Bridgwater, R., Lee, S., James, O., & Patter, J. (1987) "Alcohol consumption and dependence in elderly patients in an urban community" *British Medical Journal* 295. 884-5.

Brisbane, F. & Womble, M. (1985) *Treatment of Black Alcoholics.* New York. Haworth press.

Bristow, M. & Clare, A. (1992) "Prevalence and characteristics of at risk drinkers among elderly acute medical in-patients" *British Journal of Addiction* 87(2). 291-4.

British Association of Social Workers (1989) *Alcohol Policy Guidelines.* Birmingham. BASW.

British Association of Social Workers (1989) *Dealing with Alcohol Problems : Practice Guidelines.* Birmingham. BASW.

British Medical Association (1986) *Young People and Alcohol* London. British Medical Association.

British Psychological Society (1987) *Psychological Aspects of Alcohol : Report of Parliamentary Group of the Standing Committee on Communications.* London. British Psychological Society.

Brown, A. (1990) "Alcohol Group Education: A model for practice" in Baldwin, S. (ed) *Alcohol Education and Offenders*. London. Batsford.

Brown, R. & Lewinson, P. (1984) "A Psycho-educational approach to the treatment of Depression: Comparison of group, individual and minimal contact procedures" *Journal of Consulting and Clinical Psychology* 55. 516-23.

Brown, S. A., Goldman, M. A. & Christiansen, B. A. (1985) "Do Alcohol Expectancies Mediate Drinking Patterns of Adults?" *Journal of Consulting and Clinical Psychology* 53. 419-26.

Bruun, K. (1982) *Alcohol Policies in the U.K.* Stockholm. University of Stockholm.

Bryan, B., Dadzie, S. & Scafe, S. (1985) *The Heart of Race*. London. Virago.

Burke, A. (1984) "Cultural aspects of Drinking Behaviour amongst Migrant West Indians and related groups" in Krasner, N., Madden, J. & Walker, R.. (eds) *Alcohol Related Problems*. New York: John Wiley & Sons.

Butler, R. & Lewis, M. (1977) *Ageing and Mental Health*. St. Louis.

Byles, J. (1978) "Violence, alcohol problems and other problems in disintegrating families" *Journal of Studies on Alcohol* 39(3). 551-3.

Bytheway, W. & Johnson, J. (1990) "On Defining Ageism" *Critical Social Policy* 29. 41-56.

Cahalan, D. & Room, R. (1974) *Problem Drinking Among American Men*. New York. Rutgers Centre of Alcohol Studies.

Carr, A. (1983) "Problems and Issues and the study and treatment of alcoholic offenders" in Lishman, J. (ed) *Social Work with Adult Offenders - Research Highlights 5*. London. Kogan Page.

Carruth, B. (1973) *Lifestyles, Drinking Practices and Drinking Problems of Older Alcoholics*. New Brunswick, New Jersey. Rutgers Centre of Alcohol Studies.

Carruth, B., Williams, E., Mysack, P., Boudreaux, L., Hyman, M., Maxwell, M., Jones, C. & Roth, B. (1974) *Alcoholism and problem drinking amongst older persons - Report to Administration on Ageing*. US Department of Health, Education and Welfare.

Carter, E. & McGoldrick, M. (1980) "The Family Life Cycle and Family Therapy : An overview" in Carter, E. & McGoldrick, M. (eds) in *The Family Life Cycle : A Framework for Family Therapy*. New York. Gardner.

Cartwright, A. (1980) "The attitudes of helping agents towards the alcoholic client : the influence of experience, support, training and self esteem" *British Journal of Addiction* 75. 413-31.

Cartwright, A. (1986) "Is treatment an effective way of helping clients resolve difficulties associated with alcohol?" in Heather, N., Roberston, I. & Davies, P. (eds) *The Misuse of Alcohol.* London. Croom Helm.

Cartwright, A., Shaw, S. & Spratley, T. (1975) "Designing a Comprehensive Community Response to Problems of Alcohol Abuse" Unpublished report by the Maudsley Alcoholism Pilot Project to DHSS.

Cartwright, A, & Smith, C. (1988) *Elderly People, Their Medicines and Their Doctors.* London. Routledge.

Catania, C. & Harnad, S. (eds) (1988) *The Selection of Behaviour* Cambridge. Cambridge University Press.

Cavaiola, A. & Schiff, M. (1989) "Self Esteem in Abused Chemically Dependent Adolescents" *Child Abuse and Neglect* 13, 327-34.

Central Council for Education and Training in Social Work (1992) *Substance Misuse: Guidance Notes for the Diploma in Social Work.* London. CCETSW.

Central Council for Education and Training in Social Work (1995) *Alcohol Interventions Education and Training for CCETSW's Post Qualifying and Advanced Awards.* London. CCETSW.

Chakrabarti, M. (1990) Racial Prejudice, Open University Workbook 6, Part 1 of K254 *Working with Children and Young People.* Buckingham Open University Press.

Chick, J. (1985) "Counselling Problem Drinkers in Medical Wards : A Controlled Study" in *British Medical Journal* 290. 965-7.

Chick, J. & Cantwell, R. (1994) "Dependence : Concepts and Definitions" in Chick, J. & Cantwell, R. (eds) *Seminars in Alcohol and Drug Misuse.* London. Gaskell.

Clark, W. B. (1976) "Loss of Control, heavy drinking and drinking problems in a longitudinal study" *Journal of Studies on Alcohol* 37, 1256-90.

Clement, S. (1987) "The Salford Experiment : An Account of the Community Alcohol Team Approach" in Stockwell, T. & Clement, S. (eds) *Helping the Problem Drinker: New Initiatives in Community Care.* London. Croom Helm.

Bibliography

Cochran, R., Hashimi, F. & Stopes-Row, M. (1977) "Measuring Psychological Disturbance in Asian Immigrants to Britain" *Social Science and Medicine* 11. 157-64.

Cochran, R. & Bal, S. (1989) "Mental hospital admission rates of immigrants to England : A comparison of 1971 and 1981" *Social Psychiatry and Psychiatric Epidemiology* 24. 2-12.

Cochran, R. & Bal, S. (1990) "The drinking habits of Sikh, Hindu, Muslim & White men in the West Midlands : A community survey" *British Journal of Addiction* 85 (6). 759-69.

Cochran, S., Baldwin, S., Greer, C. & McLuskey, S. (1989) "Alcohol Education Courses and Offenders : An update on U.K. services" *Alcohol and Alcoholics*.

Coggans, N. & Mckellar, S. (1995) *Alcohol, Aggression & Adolescence.* London. Cassell.

Cohen, P. (1985) "Drink Up . . ." *Community Care* 14-20 Sept. 16-17.

Cohen, P. (1994) "The Right Diagnosis" *Community Care* 30 June - 6 July. p15.

Cohen, S. (ed) (1971) *Images of Deviance.* Harmondsworth. Penguin.

Cole, P. & Weissberg, R. (1994) "Substance Use Among Urban Adolescents" in Gullotta, T., Adams, G. & Montemayor, R. (eds) *Substance Misuse in Adolescence.* London. Sage.

Collins, J (1982) *Drinking and Crime.* London. Tavistock.

Collins, J. (1986) "The relationship of problem drinking to individual offending sequences" in Blumstein, A., Cohen, J., Roth, J. & C., & Visher, C. (eds) *Criminal Careers and Career Criminals* Vol. 2. Washington. National Academy Press.

Collins, S., Ottley, G. & Wilson M. (1988) "Counselling Problem Drinkers and Social Work Education in Scotland" *Social Work Education* 7(3): 17-24.

Collins, S. & Tate, D. (1988) "Alcohol-related offenders and a voluntary organisation in a Scottish community" *The Howard Journal of Criminal Justice* 27(1). 44-57.

Collins, S., Ottley, G. & Wilson, M. (1990) "Historical Perspectives and the Development of Community Services" in Collins, S. (ed) (1990) *Alcohol, Social Work and Helping.* London. Routledge.

Collins, S. (1995) "Stress and Social Work Lecturers" *Social Work Education* 14.4. 11-37.

Cook, C. (1988) "The Minnesota Model in the Management of Drug and Alcohol Dependency Part 1, Philosophy and Programme" *British Journal of Addiction* 83, 625 "Part 2, Guidance and Conclusions" *British Journal of Addiction* 83, 735.

Cook, C. (1993) "The Evaluation of Rehabilitation Courses for Drivers Impaired by Alcohol in the U.K." in Black, J. (ed) *Drinking and Driving: A decade of development*. Winchester. Waterside Press.

Cookson, H. (1986) *Type of offence and alcohol consumption in young offenders*. Unpublished paper. London. Home Office, Directorate of Psychological Services.

Cookson, H. (1992) "Alcohol use and offence type in young offenders" *British Journal of Criminology* 32. 352-60.

Coons, P., Bowman, E., Fellow, T. and Shneider, P. (1989) "Post traumatic aspects of the treatment of victims of sexual abuse and incest" *Psychiatric Clinics of North America* 12(2) 325-35.

Coope, G. (1979) *The Probation Service and drink related offenders in prison*. Unpublished manuscript.

Cope, R. (1989) "The compulsory detention of Afro Caribbeans under the Mental Health Act" *New Community* 15(3). 343-56.

Creighton, S. (1984) *Trends in Child Abuse : Fourth Report on the Children Placed on the NSPCC Special Unit Registers*. London. NSPCC.

Crome, P. (1991) "What about the elderly?" in Glass, I. (ed) *The International Handbook of Addiction Behaviour*. London. Routledge.

Curran, J. & Chambers, G. (1982) *Social Enquiry Reports in Scotland*. Edinburgh. HMSO.

Davidson, G. (1992) *Problem Drinking as a Factor in Cases of Child Mistreatment – Comments and Observations*. Cardiff. Alcohol Concern Wales. (Unpublished Report).

Davidson, R., Rollnick, S. and McEwan, I. (1991) *Counselling Problem Drinkers*. London. Routledge

Davies, J. & Stacey, B. (1972) *Teenagers and Alcohol : A Developmental Study in Glasgow*. London. HMSO.

Davis, A. (1989) *Pssst . . . A Really Useful Guide to Alcohol*. London. Pan.

D'Ardenne, P. & Mahtani, A. (1989) *Transcultural Counselling in Action* London. Sage.

DeAnda D. (1984) "Bicultural Socialisation : Factors affecting the minority experience" *Social Work* 29 (2) 101-7.

De Lint, A. (1969) "The status of alcoholism as a disease: a brief comment" *British Journal of Addiction* 66, 108-9.

Denzin, N. K. (1986) *The Recovering Alcoholic*. California. Sage Publications.

Denzin, N. K. (1987a) *Treating Alcoholism: An Alcoholics Anonymous Approach* California. Sage Human Services Guides 46.

Denzin, N. K. (1987b) *The Alcoholic Self*. California. Sage Publications.

Department of Health (1992) *Community Care in the Next Decade and Beyond, Policy Guidelines*. London. Department of Health.

Department of Health (1993) *The Health of the Nation*. London. HMSO.

Department of Health (1993b) *Alcohol and Drug Services and Community Care*. LAC(93)2 London. Department of Health.de Sauza, V. (1991) *Home Help Questionnaire: Analysis of questionnaire* unpublished.

Department of Health and Social Security (1973) *Community Services for Alcoholics* Circular 21/73. London. DHSS.

Department of Health and Social Security (1975) *Better Services for the Mentally Ill* Cm. 6233. London. HMSO.

Department of Health and Social Security and the Welsh Office (1977) *Prevention: Report of the Advisory Committee on Alcoholism*. London. DHSS.

Department of Health and Social Security and the Welsh Office (1978) *The Pattern and Range of Services for Problem Drinkers*. London. HMSO.

Department of Health and Social Security and the Welsh Office (1979) *Education and Training for Professional Staff and Voluntary Workers in the Field*. London. DHSS.

de Sauza, V. (1991) *Home Help Questionnaire: Analysis of questionnaire* Unpublished paper.

Dickie, D. (1985) *Central Offenders Unit Fines Alternative Alcohol Project.* Edinburgh, Lothian Region Social Work Department.

Dielman, T., Shope, J., Butchart, A. & Campanelli, P. (1986) "Prevention of Adolescent Alcohol Misuse: An Elementary School Programme". *Journal of Paediatric Psychology* 11, 259-81.

Dominelli, L. (1988) *Anti-Racist Social Work.* London. Macmillan.

Donovan, D. M. & Marlatt, G. A. (1980) "Assessment of expectancies and behaviours associated with alcohol consumption: A cognitive behavioural approach" *Journal of Studies on Alcohol* 41, 1156-85.

Dorn, N. (1983) *Alcohol, Youth and the State.* London. Croom Helm.

Drew, L. (1968) "Alcoholism as a self-limiting disease" *Quarterly Journal of Studies on Alcohol* (December) 956 - 967.

Duffy, T. (1993) "Alcohol and Drug Training for Social Work Managers in Scotland" in *Proceedings of the 36th International Congress on Alcohol and Drug Dependence.* Lausanne. ICAA.

Dunne, D. & Schipperheijn, J. (1989) "Alcohol and the elderly" *British Medical Journal* 298. 1660-61.

D'Zurilla, T. & Goldfried, M. (1971) "Problem solving and behaviour modification" *Journal of Abnormal Psychology* 78. 107-26.

Edwards, G. & Grant, M. (eds) (1977) *Alcoholism.* Oxford. Oxford University Press.

Edwards, G. & Gross, M. (1976) "Alcohol dependence : Provisional description of a clinical syndrome" *British Medical Journal* 1. 1058-61.

Edwards, G., Grattoni, F., Hensman, C. & Peter, J. (1976) "Drinking Problems in Prison Populations" in Edwards, G. *et al.* (eds) *Alcohol Dependence and Smoking Behaviour.* New York. Saxton House.

Edwards, G., Orford, J., Egert, S., Guthrie, S., Hawker, A., Hensman, C., Micheson, M., Oppenheimer, E. & Taylor, C. (1977) "Alcoholism: A Controlled Trial of 'treatment' and 'advice'. *Journal of Studies on Alcohol* 38. 1004-31.

Edwards, G. (1986a) "The Alcohol Dependence Syndrome" *British Journal of Addiction* 81. 171.

Edwards, G. (1986b) "Normal drinking in a recovered alcohol addict" *British Journal of Addiction* 81, 127.

Edwards, G. (1988) "Long Term Outcome for Patients with Drinking Problems : The Search for Predictors" *British Journal of Addiction* 83, 917-27.

Edwards, G. (1989) "As the Years go Rolling By: Drinking Problems in the Time Dimension" *British Journal of Psychiatry* 154. 18-26.

Egan, G. (1990) *The Skilled Helper: A Systematic Approach to effective helping.* California. Brooks Cole.

Elkind, D. (1985) "Cognitive Development and Adolescent Disabilities" *Journal of Adolescent Health Care* 6. 84-89.

Ellis, A. (1962) *Reason and Emotion in Psychotherapy.* New York. Lyle Stuart.

Ellis, A. (1987) "The Evolution of Rationale-emotive therapy (RET) and Cognitive-behaviour therapy (CBT)" in Zeig, J. ed. *The Evolution of Psychotherapy.* New York. Brunner/Mazel.

Emrick, C. D. (1975) "A review of psychologically orientated treatment of alcoholism : II The relative effectiveness of treatment versus no treatment" *Journal of Studies on Alcohol* 36. 88-108.

Ettorre, E. (1992) *Women and Substance Abuse.* London. Macmillan.

Fairhead, S. (1981) *Persistent Petty Offenders.* Home Office Research Studies. London. HMSO.

Fanti, G. (1985), Personal communication on Home Help study quoted in Leckie, T. "Social Work and Alcohol" in Collins, S. (ed) *Alcohol, Social Work and Helping.* London. Routledge.

Fanti, G. (1990) "Helping the Family" in Collins, S. (ed) *Alcohol, Social Work and Helping* London. Routledge.

Fernando, S. (1988) *Race & Culture in Psychiatry.* London. Croom Helm.

Fernando, S. (1991) *Mental Health, Race & Culture.* Basingstoke. Macmillan.

Fillmore, K. (1988) *Alcohol Across the Life Course.* Toronto. Addiction Foundation.

Fingarette, H. (1988) *Heavy Drinking: The Myth of Alcoholism as a Disease* Berkeley. University of California Press.

Finlayson, R., Hurt, R., Davis, L. & Morse, R. (1988) "Alcoholism in elderly persons: A study of the psychiatric and social features of 216 in-patients" *Mayo Clinic Proceedings* 63. 761-8.

Flaherty, J. & Flaherty, E. (1989) "Medical Students Performance in Reporting Alcohol Related Problems" *Journal of Studies on Alcohol* 44(6). 1083-7.

Fleck, S. (1980) "Family Functioning and Family Pathology" *Psychiatric Annals* 10. 46-57.

Fossey, E. (1994) *Growing up with Alcohol*. London. Routledge.

Fossey, E., Loretto, W. & Plant, M. (1996) "Alcohol and Youth" in L. Harrison (ed) *Alcohol Problems in the Community*. London. Routledge.

Foxcroft, D. & Lowe, G. (1991) "Adolescent drinking behaviour and family socialisation factors : A meta analysis" *Journal of Addiction* 14, 255-73.

Frank, J. (1974) *Persuasion and Healing: A Comparative Study of Psychotherapy*. Baltimore. Johns Hopkins University Press.

Froggatt, A. (1990) *Family Work with Elderly People*. London. Macmillan.

Fuller, J. R. (1979) "Alcohol Abuse and the Treatment of Young Offenders" *Directorate of Psychological Services Report* 1.13, London. Home Office.

Gamba, S., Baldwin, S., Greer, C., & McLuskey, S. (1989) "Alcohol education courses and offenders : An update on UK services" in *Alcohol and Alcoholism*.

Gayford, J. (1978) "Wife battering: A preliminary survey of 100 cases" *British Medical Journal* 1. 194-7.

Ghodsian, M. & Power, C. (1987) "Alcohol consumption between the ages of 16 and 23 in Britain: A longitudinal study" *British Journal of Addiction* 82, 175-80.

Ghosh K. (1984) "Prevalence study of drinking alcohol and alcohol dependence in the Asian population in the U.K" in Krasner, N., Madden, J. & Walker, R. (eds) *Alcohol Related Problems*. New York: Wiley.

Glass I. (1989) "Undergraduate Training in Substance Abuse in the UK" *British Journal of Addiction* 84. 197-202.

Glatt, M. (1972) *The alcoholic and the help he needs*. London. Priory Press.

Glatt, M. (1974) *A Guide to Addiction and its Treatment*. Lancaster. Medical & Technical Publishing.

Goddard, E. (1991) *Drinking in England and Wales in the late 1980s*. London. HMSO.

Godfrey, R. & Leahy, N. (1986) "Education with the Probation Service" *Alcohol Concern* 2 March (8) 17-19.

Gomberg, E (1982) "Patterns of alcohol use and abuse among the elderly" in *Special Population Issues*. Alcohol and Health Monograph No. 4 Rockville NIAAA

Goodman, P. (1987) "Drink Drivers: Pause before Swallowing" *Probation Journal* June. 66-7.

Goodman, C. & Ward M (1989) A*lcohol Problems in Old Age*. London Staccato Books.

Goodstein, R. (1978) "Special Populations: The Elderly" in Kinney, J & Leaton, G. (eds) *Loosening the Grip*. St Louis. C. V. Mosby Co.

Googins, B (1984) "Avoidance of the Alcohol Client" *Social Work* 29. 161-6.

Gorman, D. M. (1993) "A theory-driven approach to the evaluation of professional training in alcohol abuse" *Addiction* 88 (2) 229-6.

Graham, K. (1986) "Identifying and measuring alcohol abuse among the elderly : Serious problems with existing instrumentation" *Quarterly Journal of Studies on Alcohol* 47. 322-326.

Graham, K. & Romaniec, J. (1986) "Case finding versus the right to privacy : a general dilemma emerging from a study of the elderly" *Journal of Drug Issues* 16, 391-5.

Haberman, P. (1970) "Denial of drinking in a household survey" *Quarterly Journal of Studies on Alcohol* 31. 710-17.

Harper, F. (1983) "Alcohol use and alcoholism among Black Americans : A Review" in Watts, J. & Wright, R. (eds) *Black Alcohol: Towards a Comprehensive Understanding*. Springfield Ill. Charles C. Thomas.

Harrison, L. (1992) *Substance Misuse: Guidance Notes for the Diploma in Social Work*. London. CCETSW.

Harrison L. (1992) "Substance misuse and social work qualifying training in the British Isles: a survey of CQSW courses" *British Journal of Addiction* 87,(4),635-42.

Harrison, L. (1993) *Alcohol Problems: A Resource Directory and Bibliography* London. CCETSW.

Harrison, L. (ed) (1996) *Alcohol Problems in the Community*. London. Routledge.

Harrison, L., Guy, P. & Sivyer, W. (1996) "Community Care Policy and the Future of Alcohol Services" in Harrison, L. (ed) *Alcohol Problems in the Community*. London. Routledge.

Harrison L., Manthorpe, J. & Carr-Hill, R. (1996) "Alcohol and the Care of Older People" in Harrison, L. (ed) *Alcohol Problems in the Community*. London. Routledge.

Harrison, M. (1993) "Substance problems: An anti-racist perspective" in Harrison, L. (ed) *Race, Culture and Substance Problems*. Hull. University of Hull.

Harrison, P., Edwall, G, Hoffman, N. & Worthen, M. (1990) "Correlates of sexual abuse among boys in treatment for chemical dependency" *Journal of Adolescent Chemical Dependency*. 1(4) 79 - 113.

Hart, D. & Webster, R. (1994) *Great Expectations: Drug Services and Probation: A Guide to Partnership*. Standing Conference on Drug Abuse. London.

Hartford, J. & Samoraishi, T. (eds) (1984) *Alcoholism in the Elderly: Social and Biomedical Issues*. New York. Raven Press.

Havassy, B., Hall, S. & Wassermam, D. (1991) "Social Support and Relapse : Commonalities among alcoholics, opiate users and cigarette smokers" *Addictive Behaviour*. 16. 235-46.

Hawker, A. (1978) *Adolescents and Alcohol*. London. Edsall.

Hawkins, J. (1976) "Lesbianism & Alcoholism" in Greenblatt, M. & Schukit, M. (eds.) *Alcoholism Problems in Women and Children*. New York. Grune & Stratton.

Health Education Council (1985) *That's the Limit*. London. Health Education Council.

Heather, N. (1981) "Relationship between delinquency and drunkenness among Scottish young offenders" *British Journal on Alcohol and Alcoholism* 16. 50-61.

Heather, N. & Robertson, I. (1981) *Controlled Drinking*. New York. Methuen.

Heather, N. & Robertson, I. (1983) "Why is abstinence necessary for the recovery of some problem drinkers" *British Journal of Addiction* 78. 139-144.

Heather, N., Whitton, B. & Robertson, I. (1986) "Evaluation of a self help manual for media recruited problem drinkers : Six month follow-up results" *British Journal of Clinical Psychology* 25. 19-34.

Heather, N. (1989) "Psychology and brief interventions" *British Journal of Addiction* 84 (4) 357-370.

Heather, N. & Robertson, I. (1989) *Problem Drinking*.Oxford. Oxford University Press.

Hereford & Worcester Probation Service (1982) *Report to Staff Conference*. Unpublished.

Hester, R. & Miller, W. (1987) "Self control training" in Blane, H. & Leonard, K. (eds) *Psychological Theories of Drinking and Alcoholism*. New York. Guildford Press.

Hester, R. & Miller, W. (1989) *Handbook of Alcoholism Treatment Approaches: Effective Approaches*. Oxford. Pergamon.

HM Inspectorate of Probation (1993) *Offenders who misuse drugs: the Probation Service Response*. London. Home Office.

HMSO (1996) *Living in Britain: Results from the 1994 General Household Survey*. London. HMSO.

Hodgman, C. (1983) "Current issues in adolescent psychiatry" *Hospital and Community Psychiatry* 34, 514-21.

Hodgson, R. (1976) "Modification of Compulsive Behaviour" in Eysenk, H,. (ed) *Case Histories in Behaviour Therapy*.

Hodgson, R. (1980) "The Alcohol Dependence Syndrome: A step in the wrong direction?" *British Journal of Addiction* 74. 255-63.

Hodgson, R. J. & Stockwell, T. R. (1977) "Does Alcohol Reduce Tension?" in *Alcoholism*. Edwards, G. (ed) Oxford. Oxford University Press.

Hodgson, R. (1989) "Resisting Temptation : A Psychological Analysis" *British Journal of Addiction* 84. 251-7.

Hodgson, R. (1994) "Treatment of alcohol problems; Section 5, Treatment" *Addiction* 89, 1529-34.

Hoffman, N., Ninouevo, F., Mozey, J. & Luzenberg, M. (1987) "Comparison of court referred DWI arrests with other outpatients in substance abuse treatment" *Journal of Studies on Alcohol* 48. 591-4.

Hollin, C. (1983) "Young Offenders and Alcohol: A survey of the drinking habits of a Borstal population". *Journal of Adolescence* 6, 161-74.

Home Office (1971) *Habitual Drunken Offenders: Report of the Working Party* London. HMSO.

Home Office (1990) *Tackling Drug Misuse: A Summary of Government's Strategy*. London. Home Office.

Home Office (1990) *Offences of Drunkenness, England and Wales 1989* Statistical Bulletin 40/90. London. Home Office.

Home Office (1993) *Partnership in Dealing with Offenders in the Community*. London. Home Office.

Home Office (1993) *Aspects of Crime: Drunkenness 1993* Research and Statistics Dept., London. Home Office.

Hope, J. (1985) "Drinking and Disorder in the Inner City" in *Implementing Crime Prevention Measures*. London. HMSO.

Hopkins, R., Mauss, A., Kearney, K. and Weisheit, R. (1988) "Comprehensive evaluation of a model alcohol education curriculum" *Journal of Studies on Alcohol* 49. 38-50.

Hubbard, R., Santos, J. & Santos, M. (1979) "Alcohol and Older Adults : Overt & Covert Influences" in *Social Casework* 60 (3). 166-70.

Huberty, D. & Huberty, C. (1984) "Helping the Parents to Survive: A family systems approach to adolescent alcoholism" in Kaufman E. (ed.) *Power to change: Family case studies in the treatment of alcoholism*. New York. Gardner.

Hunt, L. (1982) *Alcohol Related Problems*. London. Heinemann.

Hunt, L. & Harwin, J. (1979) "Social Work Theory and Practice" in Grant, M. & Gwynner, P. (eds). *Alcohol in Perspective*. London. Croom Helm.

Inglehart, A. & Stein, M. (1985) "The female offender: a forgotten client" *The Journal of Contemporary Social Work* March. 152-9.

Isaacs, I. & Moon, G. (1985) *Alcohol Problems – The Social Work Response*. Portsmouth. Portsmouth Social Services Research and Intelligence Unit.

Jahoda, G. & Crammond, J. (1972) *Children and Alcohol: A Developmental Study in Glasgow*. London. HMSO.

James, A. & Wilson, K. (1986) *Couples, Conflict and Change*. London. Routledge.

Jeffs, B. & Saunders, W. (1983) "Minimising alcohol related offences by enforcement of the existing licensing legislation" *British Journal of Addiction* 78. 67-77.

Jellinek, E. M. (1946) "Phases in the Drinking History of Alcoholics" *Quarterly Journal of Studies on Alcohol* 7. 1-88.

Jellinek, E. M. (1957) "Phases of Alcohol Addiction" *Quarterly Journal of Studies on Alcohol* 13, 673-7.

Jellinek, E. M. (1960) *The Disease Concept of Alcoholism*. New York. Hillhouse Press.

Johnson, L. & Goodrich, C. (1974) *Use of alcohol by persons 65 years and older*. Manhattan. Report to the National Institute on Alcohol Abuse and Alcoholism.

Jones, E. (1985) "Psychotherapy and counselling black clients" in Pedersen. P. (ed) *Handbook of cross cultural counselling and therapy*. Westport. Greenwood.

Jones, R. (1965) "Sectarian Characteristics of Alcoholics Anonymous" *Sociology* 4, 181-6.

Justices Clerks Society (1983) "Licensing law in the eighties".

Kanfer, F. & Gaelick, L. (1986) "Self Management Methods" in Kanfer, F. & Goldstein, A. (eds) *Helping People Change: A Textbook of Methods*. New York. Pergamon.

Karpman, S. (1968) "Script drama analysis" *Transactional Analysis Bulletin* 7, 39-43.

Katz, J. (1978) *White Awareness: Handbook for Anti-Racism Training* Norman & London. University of Oklahoma Press.

Keene, J, & Raynor, P. (1993) "Addiction as Soul Sickness: The Influence of Client and Therapist Beliefs" *Addiction Research* 1, 77-87.

Keene, J. (1994) *Alcohol Treatment: A Study of Therapists and Clients*. Aldershot. Avebury.

Kelly, G. (1955) *The Psychology of Personal Constructs.* New York. Norton.

Kent, R. (1990) "Focussing on Women" in Collins, S. (ed) *Alcohol, Social Work and Helping.* London. Routledge.

Kiner, B., Pape, N. & Walfish, S. (1980) "Drug and alcohol education programs : A review of outcome studies" *The International Journal of the Addictions.* 15. 1035-54.

Kiner, B., Pape, N. & Walfish, S. (1995) *Report of Medical Research Council workshop to discuss research issues and opportunities in the treatment of alcohol dependence.* Medical Research Council.

King, L. (1983) "Alcoholism : Studies regarding Black Americans" in Watts, T. D. & Wright, R. (eds) *Black Alcoholism: Towards a Comprehensive Understanding.* Springfield, Ill. Charles C. Thomas.

Knapman, E. (1993) "Hidden Problem Drinkers in Probation" in Broad, B. & Fletcher, C. (eds) *Practitioner Social Work Research in Action.* London. Whiting & Birch.

Kuhn, M, (1986) "Social Policy and Political Goals for an Ageing Society" in Phillipson, C., Bernard, M. & Strang, P. (eds) *Dependency and Inter Dependency in Later Life.* London. Croom Helm.

Kurtz, E. (nd.) *Not God: A History of Alcoholics Anonymous.* Minnesota. Hazelden Foundation.

Lago, C. & Thompson, J. (1989) "Counselling and Race" in Dryden. W. Charles-Edwards, D. & Woolfe, R. *Handbook of Counselling in Britain.* London. Routledge.

Laundergarden, M. A. (1982) *Easy Does It! Alcoholism Treatment Outcomes : Hazelden and the Minnesota Model.* Minnesota. Centre City.

Law, G., Peterson, J. & Lawson, A. (1983) *Alcoholism and the Family : A Guide to treatment and prevention.* Rockville, M. D. Aspen.

Lawson, A. (1994) "Identification of and Responses to Problem Drinking among Social Service Users" *British Journal of Social Work* 24. 325-42.

Leckie, T. (1990) "Social Work & Alcohol" in Collins, S. (ed) *Alcohol, Social Work and Helping.* London. Routledge.

LeFevre, R. (nd) *The Promise Handbook on Alcoholism, Addictions and Recovery.* Hazelden. Minnesota. Centre City.

Leigh, D. (1980) *Prevention work among the elderly: A workable model*. Paper presented at the Annual Forum of the National Council on Alcoholism.

Levine, J. & Ziegler, E. (1973) "The essential-reactive distinction in alcoholism: A developmental approach" *Journal of Abnormal Psychology* 81, 242-9.

Lightfoot, L. & Hodgins, D. (1993) "Characteristics of substance abusing offenders: implications for treatment programming" *International Journal of Offender Therapy and Comparative Criminology* 37, 239-50.

Lightfoot, P. & Orford, J. (1986)" Helping agents attitudes towards alcohol related problems: situations vacant ? A test and elaboration of a model" *British Journal of addition* 81. 749-56.

Lindstrom, L. (1992) M*anaging Alcoholism: Matching clients to treatments*. Oxford. Oxford University Press.

Lister Sharp, D. (1994) "Under age drinking in the United Kingdom since 1970: Public policy, the law and adolescent drinking behaviour" *Alcohol and Alcoholism* 29, 5-63.

Litman, A. (1977) *Once an Alcoholic, Always an Alcoholic: Controlled drinking as the goal of treatment*. Addiction Research Unit Paper.

Littlewood, R. & Lipsedge, M. (1989) *Aliens & Alienists: ethnic minorities & psychiatry*. London: Urwin Hyman.

Longman, A. (1985) Unpublished diploma dissertation.

Lorde. A. (1984) *Sister Outsider*. New York. The Crossing Press.

Loretto, W. (1994) *Alcohol and Alcoholism – Licit and Illicit Drug Use in Two Cultures : A Comparative Study of Adolescents in Scotland and Northern Ireland*. London. Harwood.

Luthringer, R (1973) "Outreach & Intervention: Problems & methods" in Newman (ed) *Alcohol & the Older Person*. Pittsburgh. University of Pittsburgh.

MacGregor, S., O'Gorman, A., Cattell, V., Flory, P., Savage, R. & Nelson, T. (1993) *Who Cares Now?* London. Goldsmith's College.

MacGregor, S., O'Gorman, A., Cattell, V., Flory, P., Savage, R. (1993) *Vulnerable Services for Vulnerable People*. London. Alcohol Concern and SCODA.

Malcolm, M. (1984) "Problem Drinking in the Elderly" in Krasner, N., Madden, J. & Walker, R. (eds) *Alcohol Related Problems*. Chichester. John Wiley & Sons.

Malseed, J. (1990) *Alcohol in Asian and Afro-Caribbean Communities.* Lancaster. University of Lancaster.

Mangion, D., Platt, J., & Syam, V. (1992) "Alcohol and acute medical admission of elderly people" *Age and Ageing* 21. 362-7.

Marlatt, G. A., Demming, B. & Reid, J. (1973) "Loss of control drinking in alcoholics: An experimental analogue" *Journal of Abnormal Psychology* 812. 223-241.

Marlatt, G. and Gordon, J. (1980) "Determinants of Relapse: Implications for the Maintenance of Behavioural Change" in Davidson, P. and Davidson, S. (eds) *Behavioural Medicine: Changing Health Lifestyles* New York. Bruner/Mazel.

Marlatt, G. & George, W. (1984) "Relapse Prevention: Introduction and overview of the model." *British Journal of Addiction* 79. 261-73.

Marlatt, G. (1985) "Relapse prevention : Theoretical rationale and overview of the model in Marlatt, G. & Gordon, J. (eds) *Relapse Prevention* New York. Guildford Press.

Marlatt G. & Gordon J.(eds) (1985) *Relapse Prevention.* New York. The Guildford Press.

Marlatt, G. A. (1988) "Matching Clients to Treatment: Treatment models and stages of change" in Donovan, D. M. and Marlatt, G. A. (eds.) *Assessment of Addictive Behaviours.* New York. Guildford Press.

Marlatt, G. (1990) "Cue exposure and relapse prevention in the treatment of addictive behaviours" *Addictive Behaviours* 15, 395-9.

Marsh, A., Dobbs, J. & White, A. (1986) *Adolescent Drinking.* London. HMSO.

Marshall, K. and Weaver, A. (1991) *Targets for Change* Nottingham. Nottinghamshire Probation Service.

Marshall, M. (1983) *Social Work with Old People.* London. Macmillan.

Marshall, M. (1989) "The Sound of Silence: Who cares about the quality of social work with older people?" in Rojek, C., Peacock, G. & Collins, S. (eds) *The Haunt of Misery.* London. Routledge.

Mather, B. (1988) *Child Mistreatment and the Misuse of Alcohol.* Devon. Devon County Council Social Services Dept.

Mather, H. and Marjot, D. (1989) "Alcohol Related Admissions to a Psychiatric Hospital: a comparison of Asians and Europeans" *British Journal of Addictions*. 84, 327-329.

May C. (1993) "Resistance to peer pressure: an inadequate basis for alcohol education" *Health Education Research*. 8,159-65.

May T. (1991) *Probation: Politics and Practice*. Buckingham. Open University Press

Maynard, A. (1989) "The costs of addiction and the costs of control" in Robinson, D., Maynard, A. & Chester, R. (eds) *Controlling Legal Addictions*. London. Macmillan.

McDonnell, R. & Maynard, A. (1985) "The costs of alcohol misuse. *British Journal of Addiction* 80 : 27-36.

McGarva, S. (1979) "The measurement of alcohol abuse in social workers caseloads" Unpublished Dissertation. Paisley. Paisley College Alcohol Studies Centre.

McGroy, R. and Sharkey, C. (1985) "Alcohol Use among Blacks" in Freeman, E. (ed) *Social Work Practice with Clients who have Alcohol Problems*. Springfield. Charles C. Thomas.

McGuire, J. & Priestley, P. (1985) *Offending Behaviour: Skills & Strategies for Going Straight*. London. Batsford.

McInnes, E., & Powell, J. (1994) "Drug and Alcohol Referrals: are elderly substance abuse diagnoses and referrals being missed?" *British Medical Journal* 306 (6926) 444-6.

McLoone, P., Olds, G. & Morris, P. (1987) "Alcohol Education Groups : Compulsion and Voluntarism" *Probation Journal* March 1987. 25-9.

McLoughlin, P. (1985) "Police Management of Drunkenness in Scotland" *British Journal of Criminology* 25(1) 344-64.

McLoughlin, P. (1988) *Managing Drunkenness in Scotland: Criminal Justice & Social Services*. Edinburgh. Scottish Office.

McMurran, M. (1981) "Young offenders and alcohol related crime" *British Journal of Criminology*. 29. 386-94.

McMurran, M. & Baldwin, S. (1989) "Services for Prisoners with alcohol related problems: A survey of UK Prisons" *British Journal of Addiction* 84. 1053-8.

McMurran, M. & Hollin, C. (1989) "Drinking and Delinquency: Another look at young offenders and their drinking" *British Journal of Criminology* 29, 386-94.

McMurran, M. & Hollin, C. (1993) *Young Offenders and Alcohol Related Crime*. Chichester. John Wiley.

McMurran, M and Whitman, J. (1990) "Strategies of self control in male young offenders who have reduced their alcohol consumption without formal intervention" *Journal of Adolescence* 13, 115-128.

McMurran, M. (1996) "Alcohol, Drugs and Criminal Behaviour" in Hollin, C. (ed.) *Working with Offenders*. Chichester. John Wiley.

Menary, R. (1986) *Alcohol Education for Offenders: Course Leaders Handbook*. Somerset Probation Service. Taunton. Somerset.

Menary, R. (1990) "Alcohol Education : A Local Approach" in Baldwin, S. (ed) *Alcohol Education & Offenders* London. Batsford.

Miller, B. & Welte, J. (1986) "Comparisons of incarcerated offenders according to use of alcohol and/or drugs prior to offence" *Criminal Justice and Behaviour*. 13. 366-92.

Miller, W. R. (1983) "Motivational Interviewing with Problem Drinkers" *Behavioural Psychotherapy* 11, 147-72.

Miller, W. R. (1983) "Controlled Drinking : A history and critical review" *Journal of Studies on Alcohol* 44, 68-83.

Miller, W. R. & Baca, L. (1983) "Two year follow-up of bibliotherapy and therapist directed controlled drinking for problem drinkers" *Behaviour Therapy* 14. 441-8.

Miller, W. R. & Hester, R. K. (1986) "The effectiveness of alcoholism treatment: What research reveals" in Miller, W. R. & Heather, N. (eds) *Treating Addictive Behaviours: processes of change*. New York. Plenum.

Miller, W. R., Sovereign, R. & Krege, B. (1988) "Motivational interviewing with problem drinkers II: The drinker's check-up as a preventive intervention" *Behavioural Psychotherapy* 16, 251-68.

Miller, W. R., Sovereign, R. (1989) "The Check Up: A model for early intervention in addictive behaviours" in Loberg, T., Miller, W., Nathan, P. & Marlatt, G. (eds.) *Addictive Behaviours: Prevention and Early Intervention*. Amsterdam. Swets & Zeitlinger.

Ministry of Health (1968) *Treatment of Alcoholism*. Memorandum HM(68)37. London. Ministry of Health.

Mishara, B. (1973) "Research in problem drinking in old age" in Newman, J. (ed) *Alcohol and the Older Person*. Pittsburgh. University of Pittsburgh Press.

Mishara, B., Kastenbaum, R., Baker, F. & Patterson, R. (1975) "Alcohol effects in old age: An experimental investigation" *Social Science Medicine* 9 (10) 535-47.

Mishara, B. & Kastenbaum, R. (1980) *Alcohol and Old Age*. New York. Grune & Stratton.

Monti, P., Abrams, D., Binkoff, J. & Zwick, W. (1986) "Social Skills Training and Substance Abuse" in Hollin, C. & Trower, P. (eds) *Handbook of Social Skills Training Vol 2 : Clinical Applications and New Directions*. Oxford. Pergamon.

Moody, S. (1976) *Drunkenness Offenders in Scotland: A review of the relevant literature*. Central Research Unit Papers. Edinburgh. Scottish Office.

Moos, R. H., Finney, J. W. & Cronkite, R. C. (1990) *Alcoholism Treatment, Context, Process and Outcome*. Oxford. Oxford University Press.

Morehouse, E. (1984) "Working with alcohol abusing children of alcoholics" *Alcohol Health and Research Work* 8(4), 14-9.

Morehouse, E. (1986) "Counselling adolescent children of alcoholics in groups" in R. J. Ackerman (ed) *Growing in the shadow: Children of Alcoholics*. Pompano Beach Fl. Health Communications.

Moss, M. & Beresford Davies, E. (1967) *Alcohol in an English County*. Cambridge. Geigy.

Muisener, P. (1994) *Understanding and Treating Adolescent Substance Abuse*. Thousand Oaks, California. Sage.

Murdoch, D., Pihl, R. & Ross, D. (1990) "Alcohol and Crimes of Violence : Present Issues" *The International Journal of Addictions* 25. 1065-81.

Murray, N. (1993) *Community Care* 21 Jan.

Myers, D. & Anderson, A. (1991) "Adolescent Addiction: Assessment and Identification" *Journal of Paediatric Health Care* 5(2) 86-93.

Myers, T. (1986) "An analysis of context and alcohol consumption in a group of criminal events" *Alcohol and Alcoholism* 21, 389-95.

NACRO (1986) *Black People and the Criminal Justice System: Summary of the Report of the NACRO Race Issue Advisory Committee.* London. NACRO.

Naik, P. & Jones, R. (1994) "Alcohol histories taken from elderly people on admission" *British Medical Journal* 308 (6923), 248.

National Association of Probation Officers (1994) *Substance Abuse, Mental Vulnerability and the Criminal Justice System.* NAPO. London.

National Health Service and Community Care Act (1990) London. HMSO.

Newcombe, R., Measham, F. & Parker, H. (1995) "A survey of drinking and deviant behaviour among 14/15 year olds in North West England" *Addiction Research* 2(4) 319-41.

Northamptonshire Probation Service (1982) *Corby Alcohol Therapy Group Report* (1979-1981.) Northampton. Northamptonshire Probation.

Nowinski, J. (1990) *Substance Abuse in adolescents and young adults: A guide to treatment.* New York. Newton.

Nyak. J. (1985) *Drinking and Drinking Problems in the Asian Community in Coventry. Alcohol Advisory Service.* Coventry & Warwickshire.

Office of Population Censuses and Surveys (1990) *Mortality Statistics, England and Wales (1988).* London. HMSO.

O'Hagan, K (1986) *Crisis Intervention in Social Services.* London. Macmillan.

Oliver, J. (1985) "Successive generations of child maltreatment : Social and medical disorders in the parents" *British Journal of Psychiatry* 147. 484-90.

Orford, J., Oppenheimer, E., Egert, S., Hensman, C. & Guthrie, S. (1976) "The cohesiveness of alcoholism - complicated marriages and their influence on treatment outcome" *British Journal of Psychiatry* 128. 318-39.

Orford, J. (1977) "Alcoholism and What Psychology Offers" in Edwards, G. & Grant, J. (eds) *Alcoholism.* Oxford. Oxford University Press.

Orford, J. & Edwards, G. (1977) *Alcoholism: A Comparison of Treatment and Advice with a Study of the Influence of Marriage.* Oxford. Oxford University Press.

Orford, J., Oppenheimer, E. & Edwards, G. (1979) "Abstinence or control : the outcome for excessive drinkers two years after consultation" *Behaviour Research and Therapy* 14. 409-18.

Orford, J. (1985) *Excessive Appetites: A Psychological View of the Addictions*. London. Wiley and Sons.

Osborn, A. & Leckie, T. (1980) "Alcohol Problems and Social Work Cases". Unpublished Paper. Edinburgh. Lothian.

Ostrov, E., & Howard, K. (1981) "The mental health professional's concept of the normal adolescent" *Archives of General Psychiatry* 38, 149-52.

Patel, K. (1993) "Ethnic minority access to services" in L. Harrison (ed) *Race, Culture and Substance Problems*. Hull. University of Hull.

Pederson, P. (1985) "Intercultural Criteria for Mental Health Training" in Pedersen, P. (ed) *Handbook of Cross Cultural Counselling and Therapy*. Westport. Greenwood.

Pederson, P. (1988) *A Handbook for Developing Multi Cultural Awareness*. Alexandria. American Association for Counselling and Development.

Perri, M. (1985) "Self change strategies for the control of smoking, obesity and problem drinking" in Schiffman, S. & Wills, T. (eds) *Coping and Substance Use*. London. Academic Press.

Phillipson, C. (1982) *Capitalism and the Construction of Old Age*. London. Macmillan.

Philpotts, G. & Lanuchi, L. (1979) *Previous Convictions, Sentence and Reconviction*. Home Office Research Study, 53. London. HMSO.

Phinney, J., Lochner, B. & Murphy, R. (1990) "Ethnic identity development and psychological adjustment in adolescence" in Stiffman, A. & Davis, E. (eds) *Ethnic issues in adolescent mental health*. Newbury Park. Sage.

Pincus, A & Minahan, A (1973) *Social Work Practice: Model & Method*. Itasca. Peacock

Pitt. B (1982) "Psychogeriatrics": *An Introduction to the Psychiatry of Old Age*. Edinburgh. Churchill Livingstone.

Plant, M., Peck, D. & Samuel, E. (1985) *Alcohol, Drugs and School Leavers*. London. Routledge.

Plant, M. (1985) *Women, Drinking and Pregnancy*. London. Tavistock.

Plant, M., Bagnall, G., Foster, J. & Sales, J. (1990) "Young People and Drinking : Results of an English national survey" *Alcohol and Alcoholism* 25, 685-90.

Plant, M. & Forster, J. (1991) "Teenagers and alcohol: results of a Scottish National Survey" *Drug and Alcohol Dependence* 28, 203-10.

Plant, M. & Plant, M. (1992) *Risk Takers, Alcohol, Drugs, Sex and Youth.* London. Routledge.

Plant, M. (1994) *Alcohol Education in Schools: A Users Guide.* London. Portman Group.

Poikallainen, L. (1983) "Increasing alcohol consumption correlated with hospital admission rates" *British Journal of Addiction* 78, 305-9

Preto, N. & Travis, N. (1985) "The adolescent phase of the family life cycle" in Mirkin, M. & Koman, S. (eds) *Handbook of adolescence and family therapy.* New York. Gardner.

Prins, H. (1980) *Offenders, Deviants or Patients.* London. Tavistock.

Prochaska, J. (1979) *Systems of Psychotherapy: A Transtheoretical Perspective.* Homewood, Ill. Dorsey Press.

Prochaska, J. & DiClemente, C. (1982) "Transtheoretical Therapy, Towards a more integrative model of Change". *Psychotherapy Theory, Research and Practice* 19 (3). 276-88.

Prochaska, J & DiClemente, C. (1983) "Stages and processes of self change of smoking : towards an integrative model of change." *Journal of Consulting & Clinical Psychology* 51.390-95

Prochaska J. & DiClemente C. (1986) "Towards a comprehensive model of change" in Heather, N & Miller, W. (eds) *Treating Addictive Behaviours : Process of change.* New York. Plenum press.

Prochaska, J. & DiClemente, C. (1994) *The transtheoretical approach: Crossing traditional boundaries of Therapy* New York. Irwin.

Project MATCH Research Group (1993) "Project MATCH : Rationale and methods for a multisite clinical trial matching patients to alcoholism treatment" *Alcoholism : Clinical and Experimental Research* 17 (6) Nov/Dec.

Pruzinsky, E. (1987) "Alcohol & the Elderly : An Overview of Problems in the Elderly & Implications for Social Work Practice" in *Journal of Gerontological Social Work* 11 (1-2) 81-93.

Purser, R. (1987) "Responding to the Drink/Drug Using Offender" in Harding, J. (ed) *Probation and Community*. London. Tavistock.

Quinn, M. & Johnstone, R. (1976) "Alcohol problems in acute male admissions" *Health Bulletin* 34. 253.

Ramsay, M. (1982) *City Centre Crime: The Scope for Situational Prevention*. London. HMSO.

Rathbone-McCuan, E., Lohn, H., Levenson, J. & Hsu, J. (1976) *Community Survey of Aged Alcoholics and Problem Drinkers*. Levindale Geriatric Research Centre, Baltimore. National Institute on Alcohol Abuse and Alcoholism.

Rathbone-McCuan, E. & Hashimi, I. (1982) *Isolated Elders*. Rockville. Aspen Systems Corporation.

Registrar General Scotland (1989) *Annual Report 1988*. Edinburgh HMSO.

Reilly, F., Leukefeld, C., Gao, J. & Allen, S. (1994) " Substance Abuse Among Rural Adolescents" in Gullotta, T., Adams, G. & Montemayor, R. (eds) *Substance Misuse in Adolescence*. London. Sage.

Rickel, A. & Becker-Lausen, E. (1994)" Treating the Adolescent Drug Misuser" in Gullotta, T., Adams, G. & Montemayor, R. (eds) *Substance Misuse in Adolescence*. London. Sage.

Ridley, C. (1995) *Overcoming Unintentional Racism in Counselling and Therapy*. London & Thousand Oaks. Sage.

Ritson, B. (1993) "Treatment and Evaluation of Alcohol- Dependent Children and Adolescents" in Jeanneret, E. (ed). *Child Health and Development* Vol. 2 Alcohol and Youth. London. Karger.

Ritson, B. (1994) "Epidemiology and primary prevention of alcohol misuse" in Chick, J. & Cantwell, C. (eds.) *Services in Alcohol and Drug Misuse*. London. Gaskell.

Rivinus, T. (ed) (1991) *Children of chemically dependant parents: multi perspectives from the cutting edge*. New York. Brunner/Mazel.

Rix, K., Buyers, M. & Fincham, D. (1976) "Alcoholism and the drunkenness offender in a Scottish burgh police court" *Medicine, Science & Law* 16. 188-92.

Robertson, I. & Heather, N. (1982) "An Alcohol Education Course for Young Offenders: A Preliminary Report" *British Journal on Alcohol and Alcoholism* 17(3). 102-5.

Robertson, I. & Heather, N. (1986) *Let's Drink to your Health*. Leicester. British Psychological Society.

Robinson, D. (1979) *Talking out of Alcoholism: The Self Help Processes of Alcoholics Anonymous*. London. Croom Helm.

Robinson, D. & Ettorre, B. (1980) "Special Units for common problems : Alcoholism Treatment Units in England and Wales" in Edwards, G. & Grant, M. (eds) *Alcoholism Treatment in Transition*. London. Croom Helm.

Robinson, D., Maynard, A. & Chester, R. (eds) (1989) *Controlling Legal Addictions*. London. Macmillan.

Robinson, D., Tether, P. & Teller, J. (eds) (1980) *Local Action on Alcohol Problems*. London. Routledge

Robinson, L. (1990) "In defence of parents" *Adolescent Psychiatry* 17, 36-50.

Rogers, C. (1978) *Carl Rogers on Personal Power*. London. Constable.

Rogers, C. (1980) *A Way of Being Boston*. Houghton-Mifflin.

Rojek, C., Peacock, G. & Collins, S. (1988) *Social Work and Received Ideas*. London. Tavistock.

Rollnick, S., Heather, N., Gold, R. & Hall, W. (1992) "Development of a short 'Readiness to Change' questionnaire for use in brief, opportunistic interventions with excessive drinkers" *British Journal of Addiction* 87, 743-54.

Room, R. (1984) "Sociology and the disease concept of alcoholism" in Gibbons, R. et al. (eds) *Research Advances in Drug and Alcohol Problems* 7. London. Plenum Press.

Rosin, A. & Glatt, M. (1971) "Alcohol Excess in the Elderly" *Quarterly Journal of Studies on Alcohol* 32. 53-9.

Rossi, J., Stach, A. & Bradley, N. (1963) "Effects of treatment of male alcoholics in a mental hospital" *Quarterly Journal on Alcohol* 24, 91-8.

Royal College of General Practitioners (1986) *Alcohol: A Balanced View*. London. Royal College of General Practitioners.

Royal College of Physicians (1987) *A Great and Growing Evil: The Medical Consequences of Alcohol Abuse*. London. Tavistock.

Royal College of Psychiatrists (1979) *Alcohol and Alcoholism*. London. Tavistock.

Royal College of Psychiatrists (1986) *Alcohol: Our Favourite Drug*. London. Tavistock.

Roys, P. (1988) "Social Services" in Bhat, A., Carr-Hill, R. & Ohri, S. (eds) *Britains Black Population: A New Perspective*. Aldershot. Gower.

Russell, J., Barker, P., Hinton, T. & Philo, J. (1993) *Survey of Alcohol Needs and Services in London*. London. London Research Centre.

Sanchez-Craig, M. (1986) "Is it useful to think of alcohol dependence as a continuum?" *British Journal of Addiction* 81, 188-90.

Sanchez-Craig, M. (1990) "Brief Didactic Treatment for Alcohol and Drug Related Problems : An Approach based on Client Choice" *British Journal of Addiction* 85, 169-77.

Sandmair, M. (1980) *The Invisible Alcoholics: Women and Alcohol Abuse in America* New York. McGraw Hill.

Saunders, B. (1994) "The cognitive behavioural approach to the management of addictive behaviours" in Chick, J. & Cantwell, R. (eds) *Seminars in Alcohol and Drug Misuse*. London. Gaskell.

Saunders, P. Copeland, J., Dewey, M., Davidson, I. McWilliam, C., Sharma, V., Sullivan, C & Voruganti L (1989). "Alcohol Use & Abuse in the Elderly: Findings from the Liverpool Study of Continuing Health in the Community." *International Journal of Geriatric Psychiatry* 4.103-8.

Schaefer, D. (1987) Choices and Consequences : What to do when a teenager uses alcohol/drugs Minneapolis. Johnson Institute.

Schmidt, M. (1991) "Problems of Child Abuse with Adults in Chemically Dependent Families" *Journal of Adolescent Chemical Dependency*. 1(4) 9-24.

Schmidt, W. (1977) "The epidemiology of cirrhosis of the liver: A statistical analysis of mortality data with specific reference to Canada" in Fisher, M. & Raskin, J. (eds) *Alcohol and the Liver*. New York. Plenum Press.

Schuckit, M. (1979) "Alcoholism & affective disorder : diagnostic confusion" in Goodwin E. & Erikson, C (eds) *Alcoholism & Affective disorders*. New York. Spectrum.

Schuckit, M & Pastor, P (1978) "The elderly as a unique population." *Alcoholism, Clinical & Experimental Research* 2 (1) 60-7.

Scottish Council on Alcohol (1990) *Helping Drinkers and Drug Users : A Pack for Social Work Educators and Trainers*. Glasgow. Scottish Council on Alcohol/Alcohol Studies Centre, Paisley College.

Scottish Council on Alcohol and Wilson, M. (1986) *Counsellor drop-out and retention - a research study into the relationship between voluntary counsellor retention, the quality of supervision and other factors*. Glasgow. Unpublished paper

Scottish Health Education Co-ordinating Committee (1985) *A Report on Health Education in the Prevention of Alcohol Related Problems*. Edinburgh. Scottish Health Education Group.

Scottish Home and Health Department (1981) *Statistics for 1981*. Edinburgh. HMSO.

Scrutton, S. (1989) *Counselling Older People*. London. Edward Arnold.

Shackman, J. (1985) *A Handbook on Working with, Employing and Training Interpreters*. Cambridge. N.E.C.

Shaw, S., Spratley, T., Cartwright A & Harwin J. (1978) *Responding to Drinking Problems*. London. Croom Helm.

Sheppard, A. (1995) "Alcohol and Drug Problems: Professional Controversies and Probation Control Strategies" in Williams, B. (ed) *Probation Values*. Birmingham. Venture Press.

Sheppard, B. (1980) Some Definitions of Diversion (*HORU* Bulletin 9) London. Home Office Research Unit.

Sherouse, D. (1983) *Professionals Handbook on Geriatric Alcoholism*. Springfield. Charles C. Thomas.

Shilts, L. (1991) "The relationship of early adolescent substance abuse to extra curricular activities, peer influences and personal attitudes" *Adolescence* 26. 613-617.

Simpson, M., Williams, B. & Kendrick, A. (1994) "Alcohol and Elderly People: An Overview of the Literature for Social Work". *Ageing and Society* 14, 575-87.

Singer, L. (1983) *Trouble Through Drink: An Evaluation of the Reading Alcohol Study Group*. Berkshire Probation Service. Reading.

Singer, L. (1990) "Evaluation of Alcohol Education Courses" in Baldwin, S. (ed.) *Alcohol Education and Offenders*. London. Batsford.

Singer, L. (1991) "A Non Punitive Paradigm of Probation Practice : Some Sobering Thoughts" British Journal of Social Work 21. 611-626.

Singer, M. & White, W. (1991) "Addressing substance abuse problems among psychiatrically hospitalised adolescents" *Journal of Chemical Dependency* 2(1), 13-27

Sleap, H. (1977) *Problem drinkers at Glen Parva : A survey of drinking habits and alcohol related problems of a delinquent male population* Unpublished manuscript HMYOI Glen Parva, Leicester.

Smith, D. (1988) "Social Work with Problem Drinkers: Some Issues of Practice" *Practice* 4. 346-57.

Smith, E. (1985) "Counselling Black Women" in Pedersen, P. (ed) *Handbook of Cross Cultural Counselling & Therapy.* Westport. Greenwood.

Smith, M. (1980) "Alcohol & elderly people" in Madden, I. (ed) *Aspects of Alcohol & Drug Dependence.* London. Pitman.

Social Services Inspectorate (1995) *Inspection of Social Services for People who Misuse Alcohol and Drugs.* London. Department of Health.

Social Work Services Group (1987) *Practice Guidance: Towards Effective Practice with Problem Drinkers.* Edinburgh. Scottish Office.

Solomon, B. (1976) *Black Empowerment.* New York. Columbia University Press.

Spicer, J. & Barnett, P. (1980) *Hospital Based Chemical Dependency Treatment: A Model for Outcome Evaluation.* London. Croom-Helm.

Steinglass, P. (1980) "A life history model of the alcohol family." *Family Process* 19(3). 211-26.

Steinglass, P. (1987) *The Alcoholic Family.* London. Hutchison.

Stitzer, M. & McAul, M. (1987) "Criminal Justice intervention with drug and alcohol abusers: the role of compulsory treatment" in Morris, E. & Braukmann, C. (eds.) *Behavioural Approaches to Crime and Delinquency: A Handbook of Application, Research and Concept*s. New York. Plenum.

Stuart, R. (1971) "Behavioural Contracting with the Families of Delinquents" *Journal of Behaviour Therapy and Experimental Psychiatry* 2. 1-11.

Stuart, R. (1974) "Teaching facts about Drugs: Pushing or Preventing"? *Journal of Educational Psychology* 66, 189-201.

Stumphauser, J. (1986) *Helping Delinquents Change.* New Jersey. Transaction Books.

Sue, D. (1977) "Counselling the Culturally Different: A Conceptual Analysis" *Personnel & Guidance Journal* 55(7) 422-25.

Sue, D. (1981) *Counselling the Culturally Different: Theory and Practice.* New York. John Wiley & Sons.

Sullivan, W. P., Wolk, J. L. & Hartman, D. J. (1992) "Case Management in alcohol and drug treatment : Improving client outcomes" *Families in Society* 73, 195-204.

Sullivan, W. P. & Hartman, D. J. (1994) "Implementing Case Management in Alcohol and Drug Treatment" *Families in Society* 75 (2), 67-73.

Swadi, H. (1988) "Drug and Substance Abuse among 3,333 London adolescents" *British Journal of Addiction* 83, 935-42.

Taylor, A. (1981) *Alcohol – Reducing the Harm*. London. Office of Health Economics.

Taylor, P. (1985) "Summary of the Results of Humberside Probation Client Caseload Survey" in Backhouse, M., Gurevitch, I. & Silver, S. (eds.) *Problem Drinkers and the Statutory Services*. Hull. Humberside Probation Service.

Tether, P. & Robinson, D. (1986) *Preventing Alcohol Problems: A Guide to Local Action*. London. Tavistock.

Thom, B. & Green, A. (1996) "Gender divisions and drinking problems" in Harrison, L. (eds.) *Alcohol Problems in the Community*. London. Routledge.

Thomas, T. & Sillen S. (1972) *Racism & Psychiatry*. Secaucus. Citadel Press.

Thompson N. (1993) *Anti Discriminatory Practice*. London & Basingstoke. Macmillan.

Thorley, A. (1982) "Medical Responses to Problem Drinking" *Medicine* 35. 1816-22.

Thorley, A. (1985) "The Limitations of the alcohol dependence syndrome in multi-disciplinary service development" in Heather, N., Robertson, I & Davis, P. (eds) *The Misuse of Alcohol: Crucial Issues in Dependence Treatment and Prevention*. London. Croom Helm.

Thurman, C. (1981) *The structure and role of the alcohol drinks industry*. Unpublished paper. London. Brewers Society.

Townsend, P. (1986) "Ageism & Social Policy" in Phillipson, C & Walker, A. (eds). *Ageing & Social Policy. A Critical Assessment.* Aldershot. Gower.

Treadway, D. (1989) *Before it's too late: Working with adolescent substance abuse in the family.* New York. Morton.

Triseliotis, J. (1986) "Transcultural Social Work" in Cox J. (ed) *Transcultural Psychiatry*. London. Croom Helm.

Trower, B., Bryant, B. & Argyle, H. (1978) *Social Skills and Mental Health* . London. Methuen.

Truax, C. & Carkhuff, R. (1967) *Towards Effective Counselling and Psychotherapy*. Chicago. Aldine Press.

Tuck, M. (1989) *Drinking and Disorder: A Study of Non Metropolitan Violence*. London. HMSO.

U S Department of Health Education & Welfare (1971) *First Special Report to the U. S Congress on Alcohol & Health from the Secretary of Health Education & Welfare*. Washington. U.S. Government Printing Office.

Valle. S (1981) "Interpersonal Functioning of Alcoholism Counsellors & Treatment Counselling". *Journal of Studies on Alcohol* 42.783-90.

Vaughan. P & Badger D. (1995) *Working with the Mentally Disordered Offender in the Community*. London. Chapman & Hall.

Velleman, R. *Counselling for Alcohol Problems*. London. Sage.

Voakes. R & Fowler. Q (1986) *Sentencing, Race & Social Enquiry Reports*. Wakefield. West Yorkshire Probation Service Service.

Vogler, R., Compton, J., & Weissboch, T. (1976) "The referral problem in the field of alcohol use" *Journal of Community Psychology* 4. 357-61.

Walker, F., Baker, O. & Bennett, M. (1996) "Facts That Really Matter" Community Care 25-31 Jan. 2-3.

Waterson, J. (1996) "Services for Women : The way forward" in Harrison, L. (ed.) *Alcohol Problems in the Community*. London. Routledge.

Watson, C., Brown, K., Tilleskjor, C., Jacobs, L. & Pucel, J. (1988) "The comparative recidivism rates of voluntary and coerced admission of male alcoholics" *Journal of Clinical Psychology* 44. 573-81.

Watts T & Wright. R. (eds) (1983) *Black Alcoholism:Toward a Comprehensive Understanding*. Springfield Ill: Charles.C. Thomas.

Wegscheider, S. (1981) *Another change: Hope and Health for the Alcoholic Family*. Palo Alto. Science & Behaviour Books.

Welte, J. & Miller, B. (1987) "Alcohol Use by Violent and Property Offenders" *Drug and Alcohol Abuse* 19. 313-24.

Wesson, J. (1992) "Alcohol problems and elderly people" *Alcoholism: the quarterly newsletter.*

Westermayer J (1984) "The role of ethnicity in substance abuse" *Advances in Alcohol & Substance Abuse* 4.1 9-19.

Whitehouse P (1986) "Race & The Criminal Justice System" in Coombe. V & Little. A (eds) *Race & Social Work* London. Tavistock.

Whitfield, D. (1993) *The funding of alcohol services post April 1993 - The impact of community care on residential alcohol services – implications for non-residential sector.* A briefing for non-residential alcohol services prepared for Alcohol Concern, SCODA. January.

Williams. F. (1989) *Social Policy: A Critical Introduction.* London. Polity.

Wilson, P. (1992) "Relapse Prevention: Conceptual and Methodological Issues" in Wilson, P. (ed) *Principles and Practice of Relapse Prevention.* New York. Guildford Press.

Winnicott, D. W. (1965) *The maturational process and the facilitating environment: Studies in the theory of emotional development.* New York. International Universities.

Woodhouse, P. (1987) "Factors associated with hypothermia in-patients admitted to a group of inner city hospitals" *Lancet* October, 1987. 1201-5.

Woods, J. & Mansfield, J. (1983) "Ethanol and disinhibition : Psychological and behavioural links" in Room, R. & Collins, G. (eds) *Alcohol and Disinhibition: Nature and Meaning of the Link.* Washington. NIAA Research Monograph 12, 4-23.

World Health Organisation (1951) *World Health Organisation Expert Committee on Mental Health.* Geneva. W.H.O.

Wright, F. & Whyley, C. (1994) *Accident prevention and risk taking by elderly people.* London. Age Concern.

Zimberg, S. (1974) "The elderly alcoholic" *Gerontologist* 14, 221-4.

Ziter. M (1987) "Culturally Sensitive Treatment of Black Alcoholic Families" in *Social Work* 32(2) 130-5.

Author Index

Subject Index

problem drinking: and alcohol education groups 184-190; and black communities 135-161; and community care 18-20, 41-68; and offenders 163-190; and probation 168-172; structural context of 11; and Thorley's model 5; and Saunders model 14; and young people 90-96, 102-104. Also see intervention

psychiatrists: 6, 8, 13, 33-35, 39, 61-62, 80, 103, 138-140, 150, 187

purchaser/provider: 51-59, 69-72, 117

'race': 11, 115, 133, 137-139, 147, 160

racial group: 137, 145, 158

racism: 11, 107, 118, 135-147, 153, 157-160

recreational use of alcohol: 96, 136

referrals: 41, 44, 52, 62, 70, 102, 155-156, 189

reinforcement: 22

relapse: and AA 34; and community care 47-54, 58; and dependency 7; and health care 54; intervention 83-84; and lapse 67; and offenders 173, 181-1184, 190; precursors of 22; prevention of 12, 70-73, 80, 84, 171; and social problems 42; and treatment 21, 51-52; and the social work provider 69-74; and young people 101-102

religion: 148, 152-153, 159

reports (for court): 167-169, 171

residential provision: 3-5, 13, 18, 29, 39, 42-46, 55-56, 61-63, 70-71, 121, 129

rewards: 96, 99, 176, 180

'ring fenced' funding: 44-45

risk: 9, 124, 127, 154, 179, 180-181

risky behaviour and situations: 94, 101, 113, 173, 179, 181-183, 186

role adequacy 69; legitimacy 69; support 69

schizophrenia: 140, 150

Scottish Council on Alcohol: 4

self esteem: 11, 14, 50, 75, 116, 122-123, 160

self help: 13, 24, 28-29, 39, 47, 52, 66, 178

sentences: 166, 168, 187-188, 190